OIL PRICES,
ENERGY SECURITY,
AND
IMPORT POLICY

OIL PRICES, ENERGY SECURITY, AND IMPORT POLICY

Douglas R. Bohi
W. David Montgomery

Published by Resources for the Future, Inc., Washington, D.C.
Distributed by The Johns Hopkins University Press, Baltimore and London

589423

Published by Resources for the Future, Inc., 1755 Massachusetts Avenue, NW, Washington, D.C. 20036

Distributed by The Johns Hopkins University Press, Baltimore, Maryland 21218/ The Johns Hopkins Press, Ltd., London

Library of Congress Cataloging in Publication Data

Bohi, Douglas R.
  Oil prices, energy security, and import policy.

  Bibliography: p.
  Includes index.
  1. Petroleum industry and trade—Government
policy—United States.   2. Energy policy—United States.
I. Montgomery, David, 1944–   II. Title.

HD9566.B6   1982   333.79'0973   82-15083
ISBN 0-8018-2821-X

RESOURCES FOR THE FUTURE, INC.
1755 Massachusetts Avenue, N.W., Washington, D.C. 20036

Resources for the Future is a nonprofit organization for research and education in the development, conservation, and use of natural resources, including the quality of the environment. It was established in 1952 with the cooperation of the Ford Foundation. Grants for research are accepted from government and private sources only on the condition that RFF shall be solely responsible for the conduct of the research and free to make its results available to the public. Most of the work of Resources for the Future is carried out by its resident staff; part is supported by grants to universities and other nonprofit organizations. Unless otherwise stated, interpretations and conclusions in RFF publications are those of the authors; the organization takes responsibility for the selection of significant subjects for study, the competence of the researchers, and their freedom of inquiry.

This book is a product of RFF's Center for Energy Policy Research, Milton Russell, director. It was edited by Ruth B. Haas and designed by Elsa Williams.

Contents

Foreword   *xi*

Preface   *xiii*

1   Introduction   *1*
   Purpose of this Study   3
   Overview   5

2   Import Demand and the World Price   *11*
   The Demand Component: The Conventional View   13
   The Demand Component: Another View   29
   Implementing the Premium: Other Considerations   37
   Conclusions   41

3   Indirect Effects of Higher Oil Prices   *43*
   Distribution of Income   44
   Terms of Trade   47
   Income Determination   49
   Conclusion   57

4   Private Markets and Disruption Risks   59

   Private Adjustments to Disruption Risks   60
   Private Adjustments and the Market for Imports   72
   *Private Adjustments, the Demand Component, and
      the Optimal Tariff   81*
   The Efficiency of Private Expectations   86
   Conclusions   89

5   Disruption Costs and the Premium   90

   Rationales for Intervention   91
   Disruption Costs and Tariff Policy   101
   Factors Affecting the Magnitude of the Tariff   108
   Conclusions   115

6   Petroleum Reserves and Oil Import Policy   117

   Relation Between Private and Public Inventories   118
   *Total Reserves and the Components of the Import
      Premium   125*
   Policy Implications   130

7   Policy Conclusion   134

   Appendix A: OILSIM: A Simple Oil
      Market Model   137

   Appendix B: Mathematical Analysis of
      Disruption Costs   156

   References   192

   Index   199

Figures

2-1   Derivation of net U.S. import demand and supply   15
2-2   Relationship between long-run and short-run demand   17
2-3   Import supply and the marginal social cost of imports   18
2-4   Gains and losses from a tariff   21
2-5   A backward-bending supply curve for aggregate world oil
          production   31
2-6   A tariff with backward-bending supply   33
2-7   Alternative tariff gains with backward-bending supply   36
2-8   Tariff gains with retaliation   38
2-9   Short-run versus long-run gains with a tariff   40

3-1   Income determination and economic growth   50

4-1   Short-run demands for oil at different prices   63
4-2   Comparison of rigid and flexible demands for oil   65
4-3   Change in short-run domestic oil supply because of the
          prospects for a disruption   69
4-4   Effect of price uncertainty on the scale of production   70
4-5   Private adjustments to price uncertainty and the demand
          for oil imports   74
4-6   Individual planning prices and the intersection of long-run
          and short-run market demand curves   75
4-7   Market equilibrium prices in normal and disrupted periods   77
4-8   Effect of private adjustments to disruption risks on the
          demand component of the premium   82
4-9   Effect of a tariff on the expected cost of oil imports   84

5-1   Difference between marginal cost and price with normal and
          disrupted supply curves   95
5-2   Comparing optimal tariffs under alternative assumptions   109

6-1   Costs of filling a strategic oil reserve in normal supply periods   122
6-2   Benefits of drawing down a strategic oil reserve in a disruption   123

A-1   The optimal macro externality tariff   143

B-1   The planning price relative to the normal and the disrupted price   160
B-2   Tradeoffs between static efficiency and flexibility   162
B-3   Constant, increasing, and decreasing flexibility in energy demand   164
B-4   Change in the marginal product of oil and in oil consumption   165
B-5   Increasing flexibility and the planning price   167
B-6a Relation between marginal cost curves when the optimal
          capital stock K^* is greater than that chosen when the
          price is certain to be $E(P)$ 168
B-6b Relation between marginal cost curves when the optimal
          capital stock K^* is less than that chosen when the price
          is certain to be $E(P)$ 168

Tables

2-1 Calculated Values of the Optimum Tariff for Alternative Supply and Demand Elasticities — 28

4-1 Effect of Private Adjustments on Market Equilibria with Alternative Disruption Probabilities — 80

4-2 Effect of Private Adjustments to Disruption Risks on the Demand Component of the Premium Using Various Disruption Risks — 86

5-1 Optimal Tariff Measures Under Alternative Conditions — 113

A-1 Variations in Input Values for Short-Run and Long-Run Demand Elasticities — 148

A-2 Variations in Input Values for Disruption Size — 151

A-3 Variations in Input Value for Normal Supply — 152

A-4 Variations in Input Value for Disrupted Supply Elasticity — 153

A-5 Variations in Input Value for Slope Ratio MSV2/SRD — 154

Foreword

Changes in oil prices and availability over the past decade have affected the economic well-being, international security, and political stability of consuming countries. Because these changes were initiated by exporters, the energy problem has come in the guise of an oil import problem and has tempted some to focus on oil import levels as the target for action.

This surely puts the matter wrong. Oil import levels are more properly the result of optimal energy policy rather than a measure of its success; the same levels of imports can be associated with greatly different degrees of welfare, depending upon how these levels are achieved. This does not mean that the quantity of oil imports is irrelevant, nor, of course, that policies may not work through changes in oil imports to achieve beneficial ends. What it does mean is that the policy analyst must dig beneath the aggregate oil import number to examine whether the combination of private decisions and government policies that led to it can be improved.

This book takes the interaction between the domestic economy and the international trade in oil as its starting point. Through use of a consistent microeconomic framework, it examines the conditions under which energy and related policies may or may not improve the performance of the U.S. economy, during both normal periods and oil supply disruptions. The United States is likely to remain linked to international trade in oil for the foreseeable future and so long as it is, the analysis developed in this volume will be of policy importance.

The treatment in this book is distinguished by its attention to three discrete (but interacting) paths through which the conditions under which oil is imported may affect the overall performance of the economy. There are potential efficiency issues, to the extent that private agents cannot properly anticipate and act on changes in the price of oil; international wealth transfers, to the extent that import demand affects the price U.S. consumers must pay for imported oil; and macroeconomic consequences, to the extent that employment of other resources is affected by changes in the availability and price of oil.

The authors demonstrate that optimal U.S. policy depends on the behavior of the oil-exporting countries, which is poorly understood. Research addressing this issue is now underway at the Brookings Institution under a coordinated Brookings–RFF research program designed to advance understanding of the determinants of world oil supply and of how oil importers might improve their overall well-being in an era of high and fluctuating oil prices. This work has been facilitated by funds from the Department of Energy.

Oil Prices, Energy Security, and Import Policy serves to unify and provide solid analytical foundations for a growing literature on both the "oil import premium" and its use as a guide to energy policy. It should also serve as an introduction, for students of economics and public policy, to methods of applied microeconomic theory and as an illustration of how a public policy problem can be formulated in concrete terms and yield policy recommendations.

August 1982   Milton Russell

                                                     Director, Center for
                                                     Energy Policy Research

Preface

This book applies the basic principles of microeconomic theory to the central problem of energy policy: How can the nation respond to the high and uncertain price of oil? The analytical tools chosen are the simplest that can provide a comprehensive characterization of the nature of the problem, the reasons for government intervention, and the types of policy instruments that are appropriate to dealing with the problem. In bare outline, the book formulates the energy policy problem as one of maximizing welfare under conditions of price uncertainty. Two analytical constructs are necessary: in order to represent the influence of the United States on the world supply of oil, we posit a relationship between the level of U.S. imports and the world oil price and examine the difference between the price of imports and their marginal cost. In order to represent price uncertainty, we formulate an elementary two-stage dynamic programming problem in which some irreversible decisions must be made before the price of oil is known. Taken together, these two models make it possible to examine why private market outcomes will fail to achieve an economic optimum, and how government intervention can achieve an optimum.

More advanced analytical techniques, such as, for example, using game theory to explore interactions in the world oil market or dynamic models of exhaustible resources to characterize oil production, would provide additional insights, but are not necessary to formulate the central policy problem.

Analysis of the energy policy problem also requires an integration of macroeconomic and microeconomic perspectives, particularly in dealing with uncertainty in the price of oil. Building on the basic microeconomic framework, we develop a conceptually simple approach to analyzing the macroeconomic costs of price uncertainty and their implications for government intervention in energy markets.

The research for this study was conducted as part of two ongoing projects at Resources for the Future. Primary funding was provided under a contract from Brookhaven National Laboratory to study the appropriate long-run premium on domestic over imported oil. The authors would like to thank Jerome Lamontagne at Brookhaven for his assistance with this project. Additional funding, provided by the Office of Policy Planning and Analysis, U.S. Department of Energy, through a contract with the Brookings Institution and Resources for the Future, supported complementary research on the problem of oil import insecurity. Thanks are due to Michael Barron, Jerry Blankenship, Lucian Pugliaresi, and Nicolai Timenes, Jr. for their assistance on this research.

The intellectual credits that should be acknowledged include practically all authors who have contributed to this topic, including in particular the works of Michael Barron, Jerry Blankenship, William Hogan, Knut Mork, James Plummer, and James Sweeney. We are especially grateful to Robert Halvorsen, Alan Krupnick, Knut Mork, and Milton Russell for their thorough comments on the entire manuscript; to Harry Broadman and Michael Toman for their helpful suggestions at various stages; and to George Eads and James Quirk for their comments on an early draft of the study.

James Bresler provided valuable assistance by writing the computer program for the simulation model and the description of the program provided in appendix A. Caroline Bouhdili wrote portions of appendix B, checked the manuscript for errors, provided finished drawings for the figures, and generally organized the process for bringing rough drafts to their final stage. Anne Farr and Oya Aksoy typed early drafts of the manuscript, while Rose Mangoba inherited this task in the final stages. Last, but certainly not least, we are grateful to Ruth Haas for her usual care and skill in editing the manuscript.

August 1982   D.R.B.
                                               W.D.M.

OIL PRICES,
ENERGY SECURITY,
AND
IMPORT POLICY

1

Introduction

Oil import controls have been an object of U.S. government policy for over five decades. The first taxes on imported oil were levied in 1932, establishing a tariff structure for crude oil and products that continues to this day.[1] The most stringent restrictions came in 1959 with the Mandatory Oil Import Control Program, which imposed quota allocations that limited the volume of imports to a fraction of domestic production.[2] The quota program is significant in the history of oil import controls because it was implemented specifically for national security reasons. In this case, with cheaper foreign oil threatening to displace more expensive domestic oil, the viability of the domestic petroleum industry was at stake.

Faced with the realities accompanying price controls starting in 1971—namely, declining domestic oil production and rising consumption—the Nixon administration ended the quota program in April 1973 and allowed unrestricted foreign access to U.S. markets. With the Arab oil embargo in October 1973, and the quadrupling of oil prices by January 1974, the Nixon administration adopted the short-lived strategy of energy independence. While Project Independence, as it was called, slipped into obscurity in the Ford administration, and

---

[1] The duties were established as part of the Internal Revenue Act of 1932. See Bohi and Russell (1978, chapter 6), for a history of oil import taxes.

[2] See Bohi and Russell (1978, chapter 3), for details.

1

into history in the Carter years, a reduction in oil imports nevertheless remained the cornerstone of U.S. energy policy.

During the Carter administration, the analysis of import policy reached a new level of economic sophistication. Unlike the arguments supporting the quota program initiated during the Eisenhower years, which were more on the order of a series of assertions, the analysis of import policy under Carter focused on imperfections in a market economy as a rationale for government action. Conditions in both domestic and world oil markets changed considerably over twenty years, necessitating a more enlightened approach to import policy. The United States no longer enjoyed excess production capacity, domestic prices were driven by world supply conditions, and the risk of oil supply disruptions, though always present in import policy debates, had a sense of urgency attached to it.

The rationales for government intervention were embodied in the concept of an "oil import premium," which, at its simplest, refers to the difference between the cost of imported oil to individuals and to the country as a whole. The discrepancy between the cost to the economy (sometimes referred to as social cost) and to individuals implies that consumption and production decisions will not be based on the true cost (or value) of oil.[3] In short, individuals in the United States will consume more and produce less oil at the market price than is collectively appropriate.

At the most general level, this suggests that there should be some combination of a tax on oil consumption and a subsidy to domestic oil production. Because a tariff on imported oil serves both ends simultaneously, the premium is frequently (though erroneously) interpreted as synonymous with an "optimal" tariff. Alternatively, the premium may be used as a measure of the net benefits of reducing oil imports. If imports are at the level determined by the free play of market forces, elimination of a barrel of imports reduces private costs and benefits by an amount equal to the price of that barrel, but reduces social costs by an additional amount that is equal to the premium. Viewed this way, the premium provides a guide for judging the value of import-reducing programs other than direct taxes and subsidies, such as energy research and development or energy conservation programs.

[3] The term social is used in this book to refer to the United States rather than global society.

A single concept that can be applied so broadly to all aspects of energy policy is very appealing. In 1980, the premium was proposed as the standard of evaluation for all federal energy programs when the secretary of energy issued policy guidelines stating that "a single measure of the benefits of reducing imports should be applied consistently over all programs. The oil import premium is a measure of the benefit, over and above the world oil price, of reducing oil imports."[4] All that was required was to calculate a number for the premium, and to this end the secretary stated that "over the next few months, the Department should settle on an appropriate range to be used for planning purposes."[5]

Considering the immediate policy relevance of the premium, it is understandable that research focused on empirical measures of its size. The task proved to be more difficult than many expected. At least sixteen separate estimates of the premium and its components became available in 1980 and 1981, but they did not resolve the issue.[6] The estimates ranged from near zero to well over $100 per barrel, depending on assumptions and methodology. The absence of a consistent analytical framework, moreover, made it impossible to resolve the differences and to evaluate alternative conclusions. Consequently, the estimates were of little help in determining how far the government should go in promoting conservation or domestic energy production and in fact reduced confidence in the premium as a guide to policy.

Purpose of this Study

The oil import premium is an important concept in that it provides the rationale for government intervention in the private sector. Although it is applied here to oil and energy, the logical arguments that underlie a premium on oil could be extended to other areas of public concern. Thus, understanding and measuring a premium for oil has broader implications than energy policy alone. If the premium is to guide government intervention that alters or supplements private actions,

[4] U.S. Department of Energy (1980), p. 15.
[5] Ibid.
[6] A survey of premium estimates may be found in Broadman (1981).

the instruments of intervention must be designed to address the reasons a premium exists. As we shall see, these derive from several diverse economic phenomena, indicating that no single instrument should be expected to adequately address separate objectives.[7]

In order to better understand what the premium means and how large it might be, this study develops a conceptual framework that enables us to bring together the separate arguments for government intervention, evaluate their determinants, show how they are interrelated, and assess the proper instruments for intervention. The study is conceptual rather than empirical and is developed from the conventional tenets of the theory of the firm and consumer choice. Thus, its objective is to draw qualitative rather than quantitative conclusions about energy policy. Nevertheless, this limited objective is sufficiently fruitful to allow specific conclusions about the wisdom of various policy recommendations, the importance of the premium, and the reliability of estimates of its size.

The focus of the analysis and the distinguishing feature of this approach is the behavior of the private sector in response to price uncertainty and government intervention. We assume that private agents behave in ways that are consistent with their best interests, as defined by market incentives, subject to constraints imposed by government. When private actions create additional public costs or benefits, or if there are imperfections in the market, private incentives are not consistent with the best interests of the U.S. economy as a whole. As a result, there is a rationale for government to correct the imperfection or to incorporate public benefits and costs into private decisions. However, when the government intervenes in the market, private behavior changes along with the conditions that warranted action in the first place. The appropriate amount of intervention, therefore, should always take into account the response of the private sector to the intervention itself.

This study concentrates on the policy problems associated with international trade in oil. Attention naturally focuses on import policy—in particular the import tariff—yet oil inventories, conservation, and supply enhancement each play a separate role in dealing with specific problems. Instruments other than a tariff may be required to achieve a proper mix of outcomes.

[7] Similar reflections are found in Dorfman (1981).

Overview

The United States derives large benefits from oil imports, otherwise Americans would not pay great sums to foreign oil producers. This obvious fact deserves to be emphasized at the outset before it becomes obscured by repeated references to the costs of oil imports. Imports enable Americans to consume more energy, and more goods and services produced with energy, than is possible with autarky. In spite of the rising price of oil, imports cannot be replaced from domestic sources of oil at the same cost. The price of oil products, the prices of substitutes for oil, and the prices of commodities produced by energy are less than they would be without oil imports. In other words, it would be unwise to pursue a policy of eliminating all imported oil: the benefits of imported oil are greater than the costs.

At the same time, it may be beneficial to *reduce* the quantity of imports. The distinction between total benefits and costs of imports, and marginal benefits and costs, is crucial in understanding the premium. While total benefits of imports may exceed total costs, the benefit derived from the last barrel imported (i.e., the marginal benefit) may be lower than the cost of the last barrel (i.e., the marginal cost). Net benefits may be increased, therefore, by eliminating the last barrel imported.

The premium is a marginal concept that applies only to the last increment of oil imported. It is meaningful to refer to a measure of the premium on oil imports only in a specific context: with reference to the initial volume of imports, the size of the incremental change, and the individual country or group of countries under consideration. Moreover, the premium may be defined differently depending on the objective of the analysis. Throughout this study we shall refer to the import premium as the discrepancy at the margin between the cost of imports to individuals and to the U.S. economy, measured at the level of imports that maximizes net benefits to the United States.[8]

The premium on oil imports derives from two broad sources: the effect of import demand on the world price of oil and the costs that arise from a disruption of imports. For convenience, these two sources will be referred to as the "demand component" and the "disruption

---

[8] We assume no cooperation on the part of other importing countries, nor that their import policies respond to a change in U.S. import policy or to a change in world supply prices.

component" of the premium.[9] Within each component, moreover, we distinguish between direct and indirect elements; the direct elements refer to events that occur within the market for oil, while the indirect elements are events that occur outside the market for oil. This distinction usually means that the direct cost of oil imports comes from the wealth transferred abroad to pay for them, while the indirect cost comes from macroeconomic dislocations in the domestic economy because of higher oil prices. We briefly discuss each component below while describing the structure of arguments that flow through the following chapters.

The Demand Component

The direct and indirect demand components of the premium, discussed in chapters 2 and 3 respectively, are determined by the long-run relationship between the size of the demand for imported oil and the world price of oil. Both chapters ignore for the moment the dislocations and adjustments caused by short-term oil supply disruptions.

The argument for a premium supposes that there is a feedback relationship from import demand to the world price that creates an opportunity for U.S. consumers as a group to benefit from reducing imports below the market-determined level. When an increase in import demand causes an increase in the world price, the cost of that increment to the U.S. economy will exceed the market price because the total cost of imports will rise faster than the price. Individual decisions to purchase imports are of course affected by the higher price, but not by the fact that others must also pay a higher price. The higher price paid by other consumers is a cost of individual actions that is borne collectively, but is not incorporated in individual import decisions.

For the U.S. economy, the cost of the last increment of imports is its effect on total import costs. A numerical example will illustrate the difference between marginal cost and the price. Suppose the United States imports 5 million barrels per day at $30 per barrel for a total daily cost of $150 million. If an increase in imports of 1 million barrels per day causes the price to rise to $31, the private cost of the last million barrels is $31 per barrel, but the marginal cost is $36 per

---

[9] The demand component is also referred to in the literature as the "price effect," "monopsony wedge," "buying power wedge," or "optimum tariff." The disruption component has generated a less confusing array of nomenclature, but has been variously interpreted to include a confusing array of cost elements.

barrel. The higher marginal cost is due to the increase in the total import bill from $150 million to $186 million per day, a change of $36 million, which amounts to $36 per barrel for each of the last million barrels of imports.

The difference between marginal cost and price, or $5 per barrel in this example, is frequently referred to as one component of the premium on oil imports. A restriction on oil imports will be beneficial to the economy because payments to foreign suppliers will be reduced by more than the value of the oil to private consumers. Occasionally it is argued that the premium derived in this fashion is equivalent to a tariff on imports needed to equate marginal cost and price. However, as demonstrated in chapter 2, a somewhat smaller tariff is sufficient because a tariff also reduces the discrepancy between marginal cost and price.

The example indicates that the responsiveness of the world price to a change in import demand is crucial in calculating the magnitude of the demand component. The degree of price responsiveness is determined, in turn, by the behavior of U.S. and world oil supply and demand. These relationships are discussed in chapter 2, along with their implications for import policy. The chapter concludes that the specification of supply behavior is the single most important element that determines the demand component and, consequently, the wisdom of a restrictive import policy.

In addition to the direct cost of wealth transfers abroad (i.e., the direct demand component), there are potential secondary repercussions of price increases caused by changes in exchange rates, capital formation, income distribution, and productivity. Chapter 3 explores each of these arguments as possible components of the import premium. The chapter concludes that in each case there are offsetting considerations that moderate the importance of secondary repercussions on income and that, furthermore, the chain of reasoning is too weak to provide sufficient justification for adding another element to the premium. Equally important, the chapter demonstrates that a tariff implemented to reduce these indirect macroeconomic costs may instead aggravate them.

It is important to interject at this point that the benefits to the United States just discussed are achieved at the expense of the oil-exporting countries. Import restrictions can enrich the United States (and similarly benefit other oil-importing countries) at the expense of oil exporters, but nothing is implied by this result about the efficiency of the world economy. The ability to manipulate the market price through buying power is not, by itself, an adequate justification for limiting imports. It is a necessary but not sufficient condition for government intervention. History makes it clear that when countries attempt to take advantage of their trading partners by exercising monopsony power, the result may be a tariff war that would make all participants worse off by restricting international commerce. Thus, if buying power is to provide a rationale for intervention, it requires additional justification that makes oil a special case.

There are three reasons why oil is a special case. The first and most obvious is that the supply of oil is not determined by conventional market forces but is already controlled to some extent by exporters for their own self-interest. The exercise of monopsony power is justified as a form of retaliation to reduce monopoly rents. Second, the exercise of monopsony power is considered beneficial rather than harmful to other oil-importing countries because their energy costs are reduced as well. A restrictive trade policy will not cause a chain reaction among other trading partners of the United States.

Finally, and probably most important, there is the economic vulnerability argument. World oil supply is unstable and governments have an obligation to protect their economies from the destabilizing effects of changes in world oil prices. In short, the importance of oil in an industrial economy as well as in world trade, and the peculiar characteristics of world supply, make oil a unique commodity that justifies deviations from conventional rules governing trade policy. The last argument suggests that the rationale for the demand component of the premium cannot be separated from the disruption component. It is also true, as chapter 4 demonstrates, that the measurement of the demand component cannot be separated from the effects of supply disruption.

The Disruption Component

The discussion of the disruption component of the premium begins in chapter 4 with the response of private agents to the risks of supply disruptions. The theme is that disruption risks do not alone justify government intervention because the private sector will be motivated to prepare for a disruption, and arguments for intervention depend on deficiencies in the private sector.

A disruption in world oil supplies imposes three different kinds of economic costs: (1) an increase in the wealth transferred abroad because imports become more expensive; (2) a reduction in domestic production of goods and services as a consequence of lower oil consumption; and (3) a reduction in total domestic output because nonoil markets cannot adjust efficiently to the higher price of oil. The first two categories of costs are borne directly by consumers of oil and oil products during the time a disruption occurs. Whether they contribute to an import premium depends on whether the price of oil in a disruption adequately reflects these costs, and on whether this price is fully incorporated in planning decisions in advance of a disruption. Costs in the third category are not internalized in private decisions, but whether they add to the import premium depends on their relationship to the quantity of imports.

For the costs borne by private agents, investment in capital stocks and inventories will be affected by the prospects for a disruption. Planning decisions will be based on the anticipated probability and size of a disruption, and on the corresponding expected price of oil. These expectations will reduce the demand for imports and increase the responsiveness of import demand to changes in the price of oil. These outcomes are the combined result of the higher expected cost of oil due to disruption risks and the greater variance in oil prices across normal and disrupted supply periods.

Two major conclusions follow from the analysis of private adjustments to disruption risks. First, the size of the demand component calculated under the assumption of no disruption risks, or, alternatively, under the assumption that the private sector is completely myopic about the prospects for disruptions, is too large. Private sector adjustments to disruption risks will reduce the demand component of the premium and the size of the corresponding import tariff. Second, private adjustments will also reduce the potential impact of a disruption and, therefore, the necessity for government intervention to prepare the economy for a crisis. The disruption component of the premium, like the demand component, is reduced by actions taken by the private sector. Thus, estimation of the import premium depends heavily on private sector adjustments to disruption risks. Moreover, the nature of these adjustments cannot be inferred from historical data that predate experience with disruptions, or in which insufficient time has passed to accurately measure private adjustments.

Chapter 5 focuses on two robust arguments for government intervention to prepare the economy for disruptions. One is the change in wealth transfer during a disruption, which is analogous to the demand component described in chapter 2 for normal supply periods. The second argument is based on the macroeconomic dislocations caused by a rapid increase in the price of oil. The first argument supports a restrictive import policy during disruptions, while the second favors a course of action that reduces the price shock on the economy. The tradeoff between wealth transfer gains and macroeconomic costs suggests that in normal supply periods the tariff should be increased above the level justified by the demand component alone, and in a disruption it should be reduced below the level justified by the demand component. Such a course of action retains long-run incentives without exacerbating the price shock of a disruption. However, macroeconomic costs are related to total domestic consumption rather than to imports alone, and are not addressed efficiently by a tariff that provides equal incentives to domestic conservation and production. Tailoring solutions more carefully to problems would suggest supplementing a tariff based on the demand component with an excise tax in normal periods, in order to encourage conservation investments, and providing separate incentives for additional flexibility in energy production.

A corollary of this analysis is that more than one policy instrument is required to address the different kinds of disruption costs. The obvious companion to an import tariff is a stockpile of petroleum to be used during a disruption. Chapter 6 investigates the relationships among petroleum reserves, import policy, and the import premium. The arguments for the existence of an oil import premium are identical to those that specify the need for, and size of, precautionary oil stocks. Consequently, the size of an optimal stockpile is jointly determined with an optimal oil import policy. Our analysis shows that additions to precautionary petroleum reserves, whether privately or publicly owned, increase the optimal tariff in normal supply periods and reduce the need for a tariff during disruptions. A stockpile policy is therefore complementary with an import tariff during normal supply conditions and a substitute for a tariff during disruptions.

Chapter 7 draws together our results in the form of a policy conclusion. Briefly, we conclude that an import tariff is warranted as an ongoing policy during normal supply periods, but we recommend a conservative approach that sets the tariff below the estimated demand component. Our conclusion is, moreover, consistent with continued public support for a Strategic Petroleum Reserve (SPR). We find the decision to build the SPR adds force to the argument for a tariff and that, conversely, a tariff would lower the opportunity cost of oil in the reserve. Although the issue is not explored in this book, it is expected that revenues from the tariff would finance the reserve.

2

Import Demand and the World Price

The first of two components of the oil import premium examined in this and the next chapter concerns the world price of oil in normal supply conditions. Even in a world free from the risk of a sudden interruption in the supply of oil, imports may cost the U.S. economy more than the existing market price. Payments for imports constitute a flow of wealth outside the U.S. economy, and this flow will increase with both the volume of imports and the per unit price. The effect of a reduction in imports on total U.S. payments for oil depends on whether the world oil price rises, falls, or stays the same as a result of a change in demand.

The United States is only one of a number of nations participating in the world oil market, albeit a very large participant, and other oil consumers and suppliers will be affected by a reduction in U.S. demand. In perfectly competitive markets, each participant simply chooses the preferred level of supply or imports on the basis of the prevailing price, and the price adjusts to make supply equal demand. It is normally thought that, other things being equal, a reduction in U.S. import demand would make supply exceed demand, and the price of oil would fall. As the price fell, other consuming nations would increase their imports, while oil producers who wished to maximize current profits would reduce their exports. The price decline would be halted when quantities demanded and supplied were brought back into equilibrium.

The benefits and costs of import reductions designed to lower the world price in a competitive market have been studied extensively. One way of achieving reductions is to place a tariff on imported oil and, in general, there is an optimal tariff whose value can be calculated on the basis of demand and supply elasticities. This tariff will lower imports to a level at which the benefits of reducing prices are in balance with the costs of reducing consumption or increasing supply.

However, it is possible that, even in a competitive market, a declining price would cause oil producers to increase output and a rising price would cause them to reduce output. This may occur if producers have objectives other than (or additional to) profit maximization. Depending on producer behavior, the effect of an import reduction policy on price is less certain and possibly destabilizing. It is conceivable that an unwisely chosen tariff could actually increase the world price.

If the structure of the world oil market is not competitive, the benefits of reducing imports become even less certain. There is no general theory that can be used to predict price levels in a noncompetitive market. Some departures from perfect competition can be modelled in a way that leads to a definite price prediction, but in other cases the price that will be established depends on perceptions of values, tactics, and strategies. The outcome can best be described as depending on the relative "bargaining power" of participants. A classic result in this type of market structure is that a tariff imposed by an importing nation can cause exporters to retaliate. Retaliation, for retribution or strategic advantage, could take the form of a reduction in supply greater than the reduction in U.S. imports. Retaliation could lead to higher world oil prices after the United States initiated import-reducing measures, and would make the United States and the retaliating exporter worse off than they were in the status quo ante.

The motivations of oil-exporting countries are not clearly understood nor is the degree to which world oil markets approach the competitive norm. Hence caution is in order in interpreting the costs and benefits of tariffs designed to reduce world oil prices. The dependence of the world oil price on the level of U.S. demand creates a true social cost different from the private cost of imports. A reduction in imports may produce a gain in economic welfare, but the gain depends on favorable conditions in the oil market. Moreover, if the threat of strategic retaliation is real, other less visible means of reducing imports may be preferable to a tariff, even though some potential benefits are sacrificed.

This chapter expands on the analytical foundations of this characterization of the costs and benefits of import reduction. Using supply and demand relationships, we wish to show how alternative conditions can lead to diverse conclusions about the size of the import premium and the appropriate policy prescription. The possibility of supply disruptions is ignored in this chapter, except in the context of retaliation to an import-limiting policy.

The Demand Component: The Conventional View

The argument that the United States exerts monopsony power over the world price of oil depends on a systematic relationship between the price of oil and world supply. This means, in short, that the notion of a supply curve for world oil is real and believable. However, the validity of this view cannot be verified by observed behavior. The market has experienced fundamental changes in recent years and competing hypotheses that the market is competitive or dominated by a cartel are not always consistent with actual events.

This section develops the standard argument for a premium based on monopsony power, using the conventional view of supply that the rate of output is a positive (or at least nonnegative) function of price. A later section compares this argument with another plausible and popular view—that the supply curve is backward bending, and quantity may fall when the price rises. These two views can yield widely contrasting conclusions about the premium. Two additional problems of assessing the premium, retaliation and domestic adjustment costs, are addressed in subsequent sections.

Import Supply and Demand

The use of supply and demand relationships requires some elaboration. The world oil market is neither competitive nor monopolistic, which means that the two well-defined market structures of economic analysis do not strictly apply. A supply curve is well defined only in a competitive market, but events in the oil market after 1970 make this assumption seem unrealistic. On the other hand, the view that producers operate as a profit-maximizing monopoly is not supported by past pricing and output behavior. The major production cutbacks (e.g., the 1973–74 embargo and the Iran-Iraq war) were based on non-market reasons and the price increase following the Iranian revolution was demand-induced. In addition, the decisions to reduce production often follow rather than precede price increases and they usually have been determined individually by countries, not collectively.[1]

It is also unwise to assume that oil producers individually or collectively seek to maximize the stream of oil revenues. As long as worldwide demand is inelastic in some longer term sense, as it appears to be, producers can increase total revenues by raising prices. Instead of exploiting a joint maximum, countries seem to be following their individual self-interests. Some countries consistently produce to capacity, others below capacity, and some limit the expansion of capacity. These differences among countries may be explained in part by variations in their ability to absorb revenues in the domestic economy and the rate at which they choose to do so. They are also affected by noneconomic factors, including religious, political, social, and security considerations.[2]

Once it is conceded that oil supply behavior falls within the extremes of competition and monopoly, and that production objectives are not characterized by a maximization of discounted revenues alone, what is left is a vague area of possible market structures and diverse production motives. Various game theory models have been developed and applied to the world oil market, but none have been especially successful in predicting behavior. These techniques are not obviously superior to the simpler supply and demand constructs.

The notion of a well-defined supply relationship is further complicated because oil is an exhaustible resource. The unique relationship between the price of oil and the rate of output is oversimplified even in a competitive environment.[3] The act of producing oil today depletes existing reserves, raises replacement costs, and increases the opportunity cost of selling oil in the future. Because of the effect of depletion, production costs are therefore related to past as well as to current production, and output decisions are related to current and expected prices. The relationship between price and output becomes quite complex even in the simplest production model. The price of oil must rise continuously in order to maintain a constant level of output, and at an even faster rate to encourage increases in output. This

[1] In 1982 OPEC took unprecedented action by agreeing on a set of production ceilings to arrest the decline in nominal prices. This is a necessary step that would presage true cartel behavior.
[2] See Bohi and Russell (1975), especially chapter 3.
[3] See Bohi and Toman (1982).

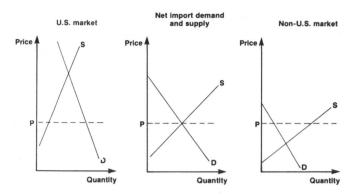

Figure 2-1. Derivation of net U.S. import demand and supply.

relationship is based on factors that are inherently unknown (e.g., the total stock of oil resources available in the earth and a profile of the costs of finding and exploiting each increment of the stock), and consequently cannot be specified in a well-defined manner.

These conceptual and institutional difficulties in specifying supply behavior, and the empirical problems of testing alternative hypotheses, mean in practice that there is no objective way of choosing among alternative plausible views. We take the position throughout most of the analysis in this study that the supply of oil imports available to the United States is a positive function of the world price. The conclusions that obtain from this conventional view of supply are, in this and later chapters, compared with the alternative view that the supply curve is backward bending. We believe these two alternatives effectively exhaust the plausible options for a systematic long-run relationship of price to supply, if indeed one exists at all.[4]

Our analysis is conducted primarily in terms of net U.S. demand for imports and net supply of imports from the rest of the world. The derivation of these net demand and supply curves is shown in figure 2-1, where the left panel illustrates the U.S. market and the right panel illustrates the non-U.S. market. The difference between U.S. demand and supply produces the net demand curve in the middle panel, and the difference between non-U.S. supply and non-U.S. demand yields the net supply curve. The world price is in equilibrium at P in the figure because the gap between domestic oil supply and demand (on the left) equals the gap between non-U.S. supply and demand (on the right). The equilibrium is illustrated in the middle

[4] Another option, that supply is downward sloping everywhere, can be ruled out as implausible.

panel by the intersection of import demand and net import supply for the United States. While this study focuses on the middle panel, it is useful to keep in mind the underlying functional relationships.

Most important, it may be proved that import supply to the United States is more elastic than world supply, and import demand by the United States is more elastic than total U.S. demand.[5] Import supply is more elastic because it reflects both the response of world production to an increase in the price and the diversion of imports away from other countries. Import demand is more elastic because an increase in the price simultaneously reduces consumption and increases production in the United States.

The curves in the figure refer to long-run supply and demand relationships and are intended to illustrate normal conditions without the threat of a disruption. When the risk of a disruption is introduced, as in chapter 4, the context shifts to the distinction between long-run supply and demand during normal periods and the short-run supply and demand that will prevail during a disruption. It is useful here to note briefly the connection between the short-run and long-run relationships.

The long-run relationships reflect changes in oil consumption and production when sufficient time has passed to vary the capital stock through changes in capital equipment, buildings, household durables, and cars that require energy for use. The capital stock can be made smaller or larger, and it can be made more energy-efficient. In the short run, in contrast, the capital stock cannot be changed, in which case variations in energy consumption are limited to variations in the rate of utilization of the capital stock. Because of this difference, short-run demand is considerably less elastic than long-run demand.

Long-run supply assumes analogously that existing reserves of oil can be exploited and brought to market by making additional investments in drilling, refining, and distribution. Changes in short-run supply are limited to more or less intensive use of existing production facilities. Again, short-run supply is less elastic than long-run supply because of the additional flexibility that investment allows.

The long-run relationships, moreover, may be derived from a series of short-run relationships, where each short-run curve is associated with a specific capital stock. The long-run demand curve represents a locus of "optimal" short-run demands, where each short-run demand

---

[5] The second statement can be proved using equation (2-3), while the first statement follows analogously.

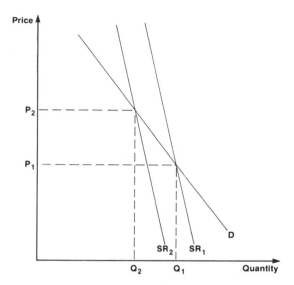

Figure 2-2.   Relationship between long-run
and short-run demand.

curve corresponds to an optimal capital stock associated with a
specific price of oil. Figure 2-2 illustrates this connection, where
SR_1 is the short-run demand that corresponds to the optimal capital
stock when the price of oil is P_1. The optimal rate of utilizing the
capital stock at P_1 is indicated by the rate of oil consumption given
by Q_1. The point on the short-run demand given by (P_1,Q_1) is therefore a point on the long-run demand curve. At the higher oil price
P_2, the optimal capital stock is given by short-run demand SR_2, and
the optimal utilization rate occurs at the point given by (P_2,Q_2). The
locus of all such points on successive short-run demand curves defines
the long-run demand curve D. Long-run demand, in short, intersects
each optimal short-run demand curve at a point corresponding to the
optimal rate of utilization of the capital stock.

Marginal Cost of Imported Oil

We use the (net) oil supply curve to illustrate the distinction between
the marginal social cost and the marginal private cost of imported oil.
The curve S in figure 2-3 represents the supply of foreign oil available to the United States at various prices. Movement along the curve
shows a direct (positive) relationship between price and quantity

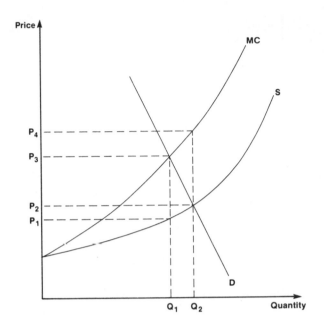

Figure 2-3.   Import supply and the marginal
social cost of imports.

supplied. The S curve also represents the marginal private cost of oil
by indicating the additional price individuals must pay for an additional unit of imports (and the average cost of oil to the country as
a whole). The per unit price is P_1 for volume Q_1 and P_2 for the higher
volume Q_2, and P_2 is the marginal private cost of oil at Q_2. The
marginal social cost of oil is higher than P_2 because the increase in
imports drives up the cost of Q_1. The marginal cost of oil to the
country is measured by the change in total cost of oil resulting from
the move from Q_1 to Q_2, which increases from P_1Q_1 to P_2Q_2, divided
by the change in imports $Q_2 - Q_1$. From inspection of these two
rectangles in figure 2-3, it is evident that the change in total cost
exceeds P_2.

More precisely, if the supply curve is represented by the function
$P(Q)$, the total cost of oil at each price and quantity is $P(Q) \cdot Q$, and
the marginal cost of imports is

$$MC = \frac{d[P(Q) \cdot Q]}{dQ} = P(Q) + Q\,\frac{dP(Q)}{dQ}$$

Notice that the marginal cost of oil exceeds its supply price by the second term in the equation. This term is the product of the slope of the supply curve for oil and the amount of imports. It is this term, and in particular the slope of the supply curve, that embodies the essence of the argument that the marginal social cost of oil imports exceeds the marginal private cost. As long as the slope is positive—indicating that price is positively related to quantity—the marginal cost is greater than the price. If the slope is zero because the price is unaffected by a change in imports, there is no discrepancy between the two; and if the slope is infinite because production is fixed, marginal cost is also infinite. Thus, the conventional view that supply is upward sloping, as shown in figure 2-3, corresponds to the view that the marginal cost of imports is always above the supply price for imported oil.

The equation indicates further that marginal cost varies directly with the quantity of imports. A larger quantity means a larger marginal cost of imports, and vice versa, given a fixed slope. It is also reasonable to believe that the slope of the import supply curve increases with the quantity of imports, because exporters' desires for additional earnings will decline and because other importers' desires to maintain their share of supply will increase. As a consequence, the marginal cost of U.S. imports will be larger, and the spread between marginal cost and the price will widen as the volume of imports grows. This line of reasoning argues strongly in favor of a reduction in imports to lower the marginal cost of imports to society and to reduce the discrepancy with the price.

The competitive equilibrium illustrated in figure 2-3 is given by the intersection of import supply and demand at quantity Q_2 and price P_2. At this quantity of imports, the marginal cost of oil is P_4. The difference between P_4 and P_2 is sometimes regarded as a measure of the import premium. This view is incorrect if the premium is interpreted as the adjustment in the domestic price that will equate private and social costs, that is, if the premium is regarded as the correct tariff on imports.

The discrepancy between social and private costs can be corrected by raising the price to domestic consumers to P_3, where the marginal social cost of imported oil equals the price of oil to consumers. Note that the amount by which the price should be increased (the distance from P_2 to P_3), is less than the difference between the marginal social cost of imports and the price (the distance from P_2 to P_4). That is, if the premium is interpreted as a measure of the charge to be added to the price of imported oil, it cannot be measured by the difference between social and private costs before the charge is added, but afterward. The higher price will reduce quantity demanded and lower the import price to P_1 in figure 2-3. These changes should be included in any determination of the appropriate domestic price of oil.

A tariff of an amount equal to the distance from P_1 to P_3 is the optimal method of equating the domestic price and the marginal cost of imports.[6] A tariff will be more efficient than any other combination of policies that achieves the same import reduction but which fails to equate the marginal cost of oil consumption or oil production in all transactions throughout the economy. The level of imports that a tariff will bring about depends on individual private comparisons between the costs and benefits of specific actions that will reduce oil consumption or increase oil production. A homeowner may find that the savings from maintaining a lower indoor temperature in winter will outweigh the resulting discomfort, or may choose to invest in insulation. A factory may invest in more efficient machinery. An oil producer may work over a well and increase its production rate. A wildcat explorer may turn attention to a new field. The higher price of oil caused by the tariff will encourage obscure and unexpected actions as well as commonplace and noticeable ones. Other measures—gasoline taxes, conservation incentives, subsidies to oil production, etc.—are not as effective and efficient as a tariff because they are not as broadly based and uniform.

The Optimum Tariff

The preceding analysis of marginal costs of imports focuses on the gain that may be achieved with a tariff without explicitly recognizing the losses that also occur. The gains from a tariff for the United States derive from a decline in the world price of oil, while the losses from a tariff derive from an increase in the domestic price (world price plus tariff). A tariff is desirable only when the balance of the two is a net gain. This section explores the factors that determine the gains and losses, and introduces the notion of an optimum tariff. The optimum tariff is of a magnitude that maximizes the net gain; it will be shown that the optimum tariff also equates marginal social cost and the landed price of imports.

[6] This assertion follows from work in the theory of second-best, such as Bhagwati and Ramaswami (1963).

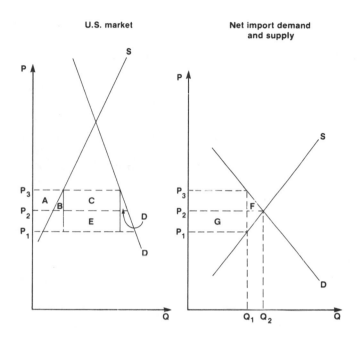

Figure 2-4. Gains and losses from a tariff.

We continue with the conventional supply case, using figure 2-4 for illustration (which reproduces the left and middle panels of figure 2-1). The world oil market is initially in balance at price P_2, with U.S. imports equal to Q_2. A tariff imposed by the United States will reduce domestic consumption and increase domestic supply (perhaps only slightly), causing a reduction in the quantity of imports. The reduction in imports will, in turn, depress the world price according to the supply function in order to maintain balance in the world market. A tariff in the amount $P_3 - P_1$ will thus raise the U.S. price from P_2 to P_3 and lower the world price from P_2 to P_1. Imports fall to Q_1 (right side), which is equal to the difference between domestic demand and supply at price P_3 (on the left side).

The direct impact of the tariff on the United States is reflected in the areas denoted by the letters A through E. The cost of the tariff to U.S. consumers, caused by raising the domestic price of oil, is measured by the area $A + B + C + D$. The increase in the price reduces oil consumption and imposes costs on consumers in the form of conservation and the value of forgone uses. This cost is captured by area D, which is the difference between the value that consumers place on the forgone quantity of oil and the amount that would have been spent on that quantity at the pretariff price.[7]

Increased expenditures on remaining oil consumption are given by the area $A + B + C$. Of this area, $A + B$ is a transfer to the domestic petroleum industry. The transfer encourages additional domestic oil production activity, though at an additional cost represented by the area B; that is, B is the resource cost of additional domestic production in excess of the cost of the same quantity of imports at the pretariff price. Area A represents a windfall gain to domestic oil producers (although part of the gain will transfer to the government because of taxes). Area C is a direct transfer from consumers to the government to pay for the import tariff.

Notice that of the total additional cost to consumers given by $A + B + C + D$, the amount $A + C$ is a transfer among residents of the United States and the amount $B + D$ is lost in added costs of domestic production and in the value of forgone uses of oil. In calculations of the optimum tariff in this study, the income transfers among U.S. residents are not treated as net costs to the nation as a whole, only the "deadweight loss" given by area $B + D$. This procedure assumes that the impact of a change in the distribution of income on the economy is neutral, and that questions of equity in the distribution of the burden of the tariff can be ignored. Both assumptions are explored further in chapter 3.

The gain from the tariff to the United States (at the expense of the oil-exporting countries) is given by area E which measures the savings in the total cost of imports, compared to the pretariff world price, because the reduction in imports drives down the world price. Area E is therefore a transfer of income from oil exporters to the United States which accrues to the government as tariff revenues. Of total tariff revenues, given by $C + E$, U.S. consumers pay the

---

[7] There is a considerable literature on how deadweight losses from taxes should be measured. At best, the area under a market demand curve is an approximation to the correct measure, which involves a construction known as the "compensated demand curve." Although consumer's surplus $(A + B + C + D)$ can be approximated accurately (Willig, 1976), the estimate of deadweight loss D can involve large errors when a market demand curve is used (Hausman, 1981). Moreover, a complete accounting would include changes in the prices of other goods due to the tariff and resulting deadweight losses or gains from changes in consumption of those goods (Newbery and Stiglitz, 1982, pp. 113–115). Nevertheless, the simple diagram we use serves to identify the nature of the costs and benefits of a tariff. The marginal conditions for the size of an optimal tariff developed below are not sensitive to these biases in measuring inframarginal costs.

amount C while oil exporters pay the amount E. There is also the possibility of indirect gains to the United States that are not reflected in area E, but this topic is deferred to chapter 3, along with the discussion of indirect costs.

Because area E is a transfer from oil exporters to the United States, the benefit to the United States and other oil-importing countries is not a net gain for the world as a whole.[8] Our focus on the costs and benefits of a tariff to the United States, rather than to the world, leads to an asymmetry in the way transfers among residents of the United States are evaluated relative to transfers among residents of the world. Ignoring the harm imposed on other countries is not, as discussed in chapter 1, generally acceptable commercial policy and requires special justification because of conditions peculiar to oil trade.

The net (direct) gain of the tariff is given by the quantity $[E - (B + D)]$, the difference between (direct) gains and losses. The optimum tariff, in this narrow sense, is defined as that import duty which will maximize the net gain. The optimum tariff is also represented in the right side of figure 2-4 by the difference between area G and area F. This follows because $G = E$ and $F = B + D$.[9] Thus, the optimum tariff can be analyzed using the right side of figure 2-4 for direct comparison with the marginal cost of imports discussed in figure 2-3.

It is instructive to consider how alternative supply and demand elasticities affect the size of the optimum tariff and the amount of the domestic price change. First, it is noted that the more elastic the supply of oil imports to the United States, the smaller the optimum tariff. In the limiting case, with infinitely elastic supply, the world price does not decline with the tariff (the area of G is zero), the domestic price rises by the amount of the tariff, and the tariff imposes only costs. The optimum tariff is zero in this case. (We are deferring until later the introduction of disruption risks and the argument that these risks provide an additional reason for a tariff.)

Second, the incidence of a tariff depends on the relative size of import demand and supply elasticities. If e_d is the absolute value of the import demand curve elasticity over the range under consideration,

---

[8] The net effect of the income transfer on world welfare requires a comparison of the welfare lost by oil exporters with the welfare gained by oil importers.

[9] Both G and E measure the change in world price times the quantity of U.S. imports, and are therefore identical, while $F = B + D$ because import demand is the difference between domestic demand and supply.

and e_s is the corresponding elasticity of import supply, it can be shown that a tariff of amount t will raise the domestic price by[10]

$$\frac{t}{e_d/e_s + 1} \tag{2-1}$$

and will lower the world price by

$$\frac{t}{e_s/e_d + 1} \tag{2-2}$$

Thus, the smaller e_d, or the larger e_s, the larger the increase in the domestic price and the smaller the decrease in the world price. Put another way, the potential gain from a tariff will decrease (increase) as elasticity of demand for imports decreases (increases) and as the elasticity of supply of imports increases (decreases).

Third, it is evident from figure 2-4 that the gain from an optimum tariff also depends on the magnitudes of the volume of imports, domestic production, and domestic consumption. As the volume of imports declines from the free-trade quantity Q_1, the areas represented by F and G will both increase, but eventually the area given by G will decline. That is, as the size of the tariff is increased, the net gain will increase at first, reach a maximum at the optimum tariff, and then decrease. The potential gain at the optimum will depend on the volume of post-tariff imports and, therefore, also on the volume of free-trade imports.[11]

The relation between the tariff and the quantity of imports may be connected with the size of the elasticity of demand for imports. We have noted that, given the supply elasticity, the tariff will increase the domestic price proportionately more the smaller the elasticity of demand for imports. The import demand elasticity, in turn, may be expressed as[12]

$$e_d = \frac{Q_d}{Q_m} n_d + \frac{Q_s}{Q_m} n_s \tag{2-3}$$

[10] See Kreinin (1971, pp. 430–431), for derivation.
[11] Since, use figure 2-4, $Q_1 = Q_2 - \Delta Q$, where Q_1 is tariff-restricted imports, Q_2 is free-trade imports, and ΔQ is the difference.
[12] Kreinin (1971, p. 428) gives a derivation.

where n_d and n_s are the elasticities of domestic demand (in absolute value) and supply, respectively; Q_d and Q_s are quantities of domestic consumption and production, respectively; and Q_m is the volume of imports. From this expression it is observed that elasticity of import demand will decline with smaller domestic elasticities and with a larger share of imports in domestic consumption. Thus, other things remaining unchanged, the larger the share of imports in consumption, the more a tariff increases the domestic price, and the greater the cost of a tariff.

Calculating the Optimum Tariff: An Illustration

In this section we derive an expression for the optimum tariff in the simple case of linear import supply and demand functions. This is done to show (a) how the optimum tariff depends on the position and slopes of the functions, (b) that the optimum tariff equates social and private costs of oil imports at the margin, and (c) how the tariff varies under different elasticity assumptions.

Import supply and demand are given by

$$P_s = a + bQ_s \tag{2-4}$$

$$P_d = c + dQ_d \tag{2-5}$$

where a, b, and c are positive (with $c > a$) and d is negative. Starting from the initial equilibrium of supply and demand at price P^E and quantity Q^E, we wish to find the quantity of imports where the difference between gains and losses from a tariff are maximized; that is, where the expression

$$L = Q(P^E - a - bQ) - 1/2(Q^E - Q)(c + dQ - P^E)$$

is maximized.[13] The necessary condition for a maximum is[14]

$$Q = \frac{a - c}{d - 2b} \tag{2-6}$$

[13] For comparison with figure 2-4, the tariff that maximizes L also maximizes the difference between areas G and F. Note that P^E and Q^E are equivalent to P_2 and Q_2, respectively, and the first term in the expression for L is equivalent to G and the second term is equivalent to F.

[14] The second-order condition for a maximum is satisfied as long as d is negative.

The same solution occurs when the marginal social cost of imports equals the demand price (marginal private cost). Using (2-4), the total cost of imports is

$$P_sQ_s = aQ_s + bQ_s^2$$

and marginal social cost is given by

$$\frac{d(P_sQ_s)}{dQ_s} = a + 2bQ_s$$

Setting the marginal social cost equal to price in (2-5), the equilibrium quantity of imports is

$$a + 2bQ = c + dQ$$

or

$$Q = \frac{a - c}{d - 2b}$$

which is the same as (2-6). Thus, the optimum tariff equates the marginal cost and benefit of imports to the country.

The optimum tariff is given by the difference between the demand price and supply price at Q, or

$$t = P_d - P_s = \frac{b(a - c)}{d - 2b} \tag{2-7}$$

which is derived by subtracting (2-4) from (2-5) and substituting (2-6). Moreover, from (2-7) we have

$$\frac{\partial t}{\partial b} > 0 \text{ if } d < 0 \tag{2-8}$$

$$\frac{\partial t}{\partial d} > 0 \text{ if } c > a \tag{2-9}$$

$$\frac{\partial t}{\partial a} < 0 \tag{2-10}$$

$$\frac{\partial t}{\partial c} > 0 \tag{2-11}$$

That is, the optimum tariff will be larger: (1) the steeper the slope of the supply schedule; (2) the flatter the slope of the import demand schedule (remembering that d is less than 0); and (3) the larger the quantity of imports (i.e., with an increase in either import demand or import supply).

The optimum tariff can be expressed in terms of elasticities by substituting for c and a in equation (2-7), using (2-4) and (2-5), and remembering that the supply elasticity is $e_s = P_s/bQ_s$ and the demand elasticity is $e_d = P_d/dQ_d$. The result can be written as[15]

$$t = \frac{b}{2b - d} \left[b(1 - e_s) - d(1 - e_d) \right] Q \qquad (2\text{-}12)$$

All of the terms on the right-hand side are positive except $b(1 - e_s)$ when e_s is greater than 1. Again, we conclude that the optimum tariff will be larger (up to a point) the smaller the elasticity of supply, the larger the elasticity of demand, or the larger the level of imports.

The terms in expression (2-12) are interrelated, however, indicating a tradeoff which limits the size of the tariff. The elasticity of supply, e_s, cannot decrease without an increase in b or Q (relative to P_s), and e_d cannot increase without a reduction (in absolute value) in d or Q (relative to P_d). Thus, as noted above, t will increase with higher values of b and lower (absolute) values of d, but eventually Q will decline enough to limit the size of t.

Table 2-1 provides a range of calculated values of the optimum tariff for alternative values of the supply and demand elasticities. As expected, the size of the optimum tariff increases as the elasticity of either import demand or import supply declines. Of particular interest in the table is the relatively greater sensitivity of the tariff to the supply elasticity compared with the demand elasticity. From the lowest to the highest demand elasticity, the tariff increases by less than 75 percent, regardless of the supply elasticity; whereas from the highest to lowest supply elasticity, the tariff increases from 5,600 to 7,500 percent, depending on the demand elasticity.

These figures illustrate the importance of the elasticity of supply in calculating the premium. Unfortunately, our understanding of supply behavior is more uncertain than that of demand. Empirical

---

[15] Alternatively, $t = P_s/e_s$, indicating that the tariff can be expressed in terms of the supply price and supply elasticity alone.

Table 2-1. Calculated Values of the Optimum Tariff for Alternative Supply and Demand Elasticities

($/bbl)

Net oil supply elasticity	Import demand elasticity						
	−10	−5	−1	−0.5	−0.4	−0.2	−0.1
10	2.33	2.63	3.21	3.34	3.37	3.43	3.47
8	2.81	3.16	3.94	4.13	4.18	4.27	4.32
6	3.59	4.01	5.10	5.42	5.49	5.65	5.74
4	5.10	5.63	7.29	7.88	8.02	8.35	8.54
2	9.55	10.21	13.13	14.58	15.00	16.04	16.70
1	18.33	19.09	23.33	26.25	27.22	30.00	32.08
0.5	35.85	36.67	42.00	46.67	48.46	54.44	60.00
0.1	175.87	176.73	183.33	190.91	194.44	210.00	233.00

studies on U.S. demand for oil products, even allowing for considerable uncertainties, suggest a long-run elasticity somewhere in the range of −0.2 to −1.0.[16] Referring to table 2-1, it is noted that the choice of a specific demand elasticity within this range is not important to the size of the tariff. In contrast, the "correct" tariff can vary from $3 to $200 per barrel, depending on the assumed supply elasticity.

Assuming that oil supply curves are upward-sloping and oil demand curves are downward-sloping, something more specific can be said about the elasticity of import supply for the United States.[17] Recall from figure 2-1 that U.S. import supply is the difference between foreign supply and foreign demand. Thus, the elasticity of U.S. import supply may be written as

$$e_s = \frac{M + M_f}{M} e_w + \frac{M_f}{M} e_f$$

where M is the quantity of U.S. imports, M_f is the quantity of non-U.S. imports, e_w is the elasticity of supply from oil-exporting countries into the world market, and $-e_f$ is the elasticity of non-U.S. import demand. In 1980, U.S. imports averaged about 6 million barrels per

[16] See Bohi (1981, chapter 5).
[17] We are grateful to Knut Mork for this argument.

day and non-U.S. 18 million barrels per day. Assuming the U.S. share of trade remains unchanged, then $M_f = 3M$ and

$$e_s = 4e_w + 3e_f$$

Note that oil exports can be completely unresponsive to a change in price ($e_w = 0$) and the supply of imports into the United States will have an elasticity approximately three times the aggregate elasticity of other importing countries. To be more specific, suppose that non-U.S. import demand has a long-run elasticity of -0.5. Then U.S. import supply will have an elasticity in the range of 1 to 2. This calculation, together with the likelihood that export supply will exhibit some price responsiveness, lead us to believe that U.S. import supply is somewhere in the area of two or larger. Referring to table 2-1, it follows that the long-run optimum tariff is likely to be less than $10 per barrel.

The Demand Component: Another View

Our uncertainty about supply behavior is not restricted merely to the choice of a price elasticity for an upward-sloping function. Indeed, it is also possible that the supply is not upward-sloping in the relevant range, as the argument above assumes. Some observers contend that supply is more appropriately characterized as a backward-sloping function, indicating that quantity declines as the price rises over some range of the curve.[18] Because this view is both popular and on occasion consistent with events in the oil market, this section re-examines the demand component and the optimum tariff under the assumption that the supply of imports to the United States is backward bending.

The question of the shape of the import supply curve arises throughout this study, and we repeat the uncertainty associated with a specific assumption. Nevertheless, as the emphasis conveyed in our analysis suggests, we favor the position that the U.S. import supply is upward-sloping. Our position hinges less on the shape of supply from oil-exporting countries, where the major source of doubt arises, than on the relative importance of non-U.S. import demand and the certainty that the quantity demanded declines as the world price rises.

[18] This view is expressed in Adelman (1980).

Backward-Bending World Supply

The world oil supply can bend backward in a competitive market when some (major) producing countries have limited absorptive capacity, a reluctance to absorb excess revenues through increased consumption, and where oil revenues are a large proportion of GNP.[19] The supply curve becomes increasingly inelastic at higher prices, reflecting reluctance to increase oil production because rising revenues cannot be absorbed in the economy. Eventually a point is reached where a higher price does not induce additional output because the additional revenues which can be earned are valued less at the margin than oil left in the ground. As this point is reached by a larger number of producers, representing a larger proportion of total output, total output approaches a maximum. Still higher prices will further reduce the incentive to maintain production because revenues will continue to grow even with fixed output. The incentive is to reduce output at higher prices, causing the supply curve to bend backward. This is illustrated in figure 2-5 at world prices above P_2.

Figure 2-5 shows the supply curve passing through another point of inflection after P_3. This shape implies that the motive to reduce output will eventually slow down at higher prices, for otherwise total revenues would eventually begin to decline. The inflection point is required to avoid the implausible result of output and total revenues falling to zero. The curve may pass repeatedly through several points of inflection at prices above P_4, but figure 2-5 is sufficient to explore the possible outcomes.

The main consequence of a backward-bending supply curve is the possibility of multiple-equilibrium points on the same curve, some of which are unstable and others of which are stable. The possibility of multiple equilibrium is also consistent with a fairly inelastic demand curve, such as D_2, since a more elastic demand will tend to cross supply at fewer points.[20] Points such as P_3 represent unstable equilibria because a disturbance which causes a slight deviation away from

[19] Similar conditions have been suggested in connection with the supply of other factors of production. The most common is labor supply, where the income effect of rising wages becomes stronger than the substitution effect when valuing leisure time versus work time. The same idea has been applied to the supply of savings, where a rise in the interest rate may eventually produce a reduction in the quantity of savings.

[20] Unless the negative portion of supply also has a flatter slope. But this possibility, like an elastic demand curve, is not very realistic.

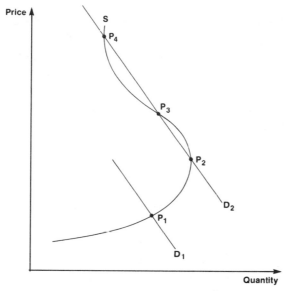

Figure 2-5. A backward-bending supply curve for aggregate world oil production.

P_3 will produce a further movement away from that position. At P_3 supply and demand are in balance (i.e., in equilibrium), but at a slightly higher price demand exceeds supply and at a slightly lower price supply exceeds demand. Thus, a higher price produces excess demand, which forces the price even higher, while a lower price produces excess supply, which depresses the price even further. Points such as P_2 and P_4 (and, of course, P_1) are stable equilibria; a slight deviation away from the equilibrium point will produce forces which lead to a return to the same point.

Several implications follow from this view of supply, some of which are consistent with actual supply behavior in recent years. Demand can increase over a range, such as between D_1 and D_2, where price and output both increase. This range may characterize events in the world oil market before 1973. After 1973, demand may have reached the position indicated by D_2, where price increases have been accompanied by output reductions. However, it is important to recognize that the reductions may be explained by individual self-interest rather than the collective decisions of a cartel. Furthermore, the possibility of unstable equilibria can explain how minor disturbances in supply or demand can lead to dramatic increases in the price.

More important, a backward-bending supply curve can produce perverse changes in the price. A minor decrease in world demand starting from equilibrium point P_3 could drive the price up to P_4, while a minor increase in demand could drive the price down to P_2. This will occur if oil exporters adjust the quantity supplied to clear the market: a reduction in demand causes excess supply, which in turn leads to a larger reduction in exports and a higher world price. It is possible, therefore, for a demand reduction to be followed by a price increase, and vice versa.

Another important implication follows from the reason for the backward-bending shape of the supply curve. Because the shape is a result of the declining (or negative) marginal returns from oil revenues, it can be altered with improvements in the return to investment. This will happen if there is an increase in absorptive capacity among exporting countries or an increase in expected returns from investment in international capital markets. The first may occur because of increasing returns to domestic investment in existing oil-producing countries with limited absorptive capacity or, more likely, because of the entry of new producing countries in the aggregate supply picture. Efforts that encourage the proliferation of new sources of supply will therefore not only reduce the current price, but will also reduce the potential variability of the price by changing the character of the aggregate supply relationship.

An increase in expected returns in international capital markets, the second source of a potential change in the shape of the supply curve, works as a substitute for domestic investment of oil revenues. An increase in expected returns means, primarily, a reduction in the risk of investing in foreign assets, not an increase in nominal rates of return. This view recognizes the imperfections of capital markets that result from a combination of domestic attitudes toward, and official sanctions on, foreign ownership of financial and tangible assets. Because the United States is the world's leading financial center and the major force behind international financial developments, actions to facilitate the investment of oil revenues will open a vast array of opportunities to the oil-exporting countries. This possibility has been developed in detail in Bohi and Russell (1975), together with an illustration of the effect on social discount rates and on world supply prospects. In short, expanding investment alternatives will act to reduce both the upward trend of future oil prices and short-run instability around the price path.

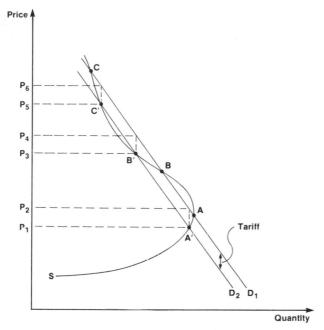

Figure 2-6.   A tariff with backward-bending
supply.

The Optimum Tariff with Backward-Bending U.S. Import Supply

Assuming world supply is backward bending, the supply of imports
facing the United States will exhibit the same characteristic under
appropriate assumptions about non-U.S. import demand. Figure 2-5
is used to illustrate this situation for U.S. import supply and demand.
In this analysis it is convenient to show the effect of an import tariff
as a leftward shift in import demand, where the vertical distance to
the new curve measures the amount of the tariff.[21] Referring to
figure 2-6, the distance between D_1 and D_2 is the tariff, and for each
world price (e.g., P_1), the landed price in the United States is higher
by the amount of this tariff (e.g., P_2).[22] That is, the relationship

[21] It is not possible to analyze the tariff in terms of the marginal cost of
imports because marginal costs are not single-valued. Corresponding to each
possible quantity of imports there are two (or more) marginal costs, one on the
upward-sloping portion of the curve and one (possibly undefined) on the
backward-sloping portion.

[22] The parallel shift in demand as drawn in figure 2-6 reflects a fixed per unit
tariff. An *ad valorem* tariff would show the distance between D_1 and D_2
widening as the price increased.

between import demand and post-tariff landed prices is given by D_1, while the corresponding relationship between import demand and world prices is given by D_2.

With the demand and supply situation pictured in figure 2-6, a tariff can yield at least three distinct outcomes, each corresponding to each of three initial equilibrium points denoted by A, B, and C.[23] If the initial equilibrium is at point A, the effect of the tariff is the same as that described above. Equilibrium is established at point A', with the world price declining to P_1 and the U.S. price rising to P_2. The United States will benefit from the tariff if the reduction in the world price offsets the losses caused by a higher domestic price of oil. A net loss can occur if the tariff is set too high.

In contrast, if the initial equilibrium is at an unstable position such as point B, the same tariff will cause the world price to rise toward B' (or possibly even higher, to point C', the next stable equilibrium). The new domestic price, including the tariff, will be at P_4 (or, possibly as high as P_6). Clearly, the United States is made worse off by a tariff if the world price rises: when both the world oil price and the domestic oil price rise, there are no international gains to offset domestic losses.

The third possibility is an initial equilibrium at a point such as C, where the application of a tariff reduces the world price by more than the amount of the tariff. The world price falls to P_5 and the U.S. price falls to P_6 even with the tariff included. The United States is unambiguously better off because U.S. consumers pay lower oil prices and the decline in the world oil price represents an even larger reduction in total expenditures on oil imports.

The conclusion that follows from the backward-bending supply case is that the United States can end up better off or worse off by imposing an import tariff, depending on the nature of the initial equilibrium position and the amount of the tariff. If the initial equilibrium is stable, the United States can be better off in some conditions with almost any tariff, but can be worse off in others if the tariff is set too large. If the initial equilibrium is unstable, the United States will be worse off with any size tariff. Perhaps the most important point that obtains from this analysis is that policy makers could be quite surprised by the results of a tariff. The surprise would be welcome if the world price declined by more than the tariff, but this would not be the case if the world price increased with a tariff. The latter

[23] The number of distinct outcomes corresponds to the number of points of inflection on the supply curve.

possibility cannot be ruled out if major oil exporters maintain revenue targets as implied in the backward-bending supply schedule.

The question we turn to next is the size of the optimum tariff with a backward-bending supply. The answer depends again on the initial equilibrium position. If it is at point A, the optimum tariff is calculated as in the conventional supply case. If it is at point B, the optimum tariff is negative (i.e., imports should be subsidized). If the initial equilibrium is at point C, the optimum tariff may be calculated in the narrow sense defined above, but complications ignored in this definition become too important to leave aside. These complications include income redistribution, disruption risk, and supplier retaliation. The problem of retaliation to a tariff is deferred to the next section.

The possible conflict between the magnitude of the gains from a tariff and the distribution of these gains illustrates at the same time the possible conflict between the objective of driving down the world price and reducing the quantity of imports subject to a disruption (see figure 2-7). Two alternative tariffs of different magnitudes are compared. The first tariff, of the amount $P_2 - P_3$, achieves a gain to domestic consumers of the amount measured by the trapezoid P_1CEP_2 and an additional wealth transfer (accruing to the government in tariff receipts) given by the rectangle P_2EGP_3. The total gain from the tariff is equal to the sum of these two areas.

The second tariff, of the amount $P_2 - P_4$, results in the same quantity of imports and the same reduction in the domestic price (to P_2) as the first tariff. The gain to domestic consumers is the same, but the wealth transfer from abroad in the form of tariff revenues increases to P_2EHP_4. Thus, the second tariff achieves a larger net benefit to the United States than the first, and on the basis of net benefit alone the second tariff would be regarded as superior to any smaller tariff.

The tradeoff between the gain to consumers and the size of government revenues, a typical characteristic of a tariff, is readily apparent. Notice that any tariff of a magnitude between the first two will achieve larger gains to consumers and tariff revenues smaller than the maximum. Compared with the optimum tariff, an intermediate tariff increases the gains to consumers and reduces tariff revenues. A welfare comparison requires additional knowledge of government fiscal policy and of how oil price changes affect aggregate consumer welfare.

The tradeoff between the objective of driving down the world price and preparing for a disruption has two dimensions. First, because the domestic price declines rather than increases with a tariff, the quantity

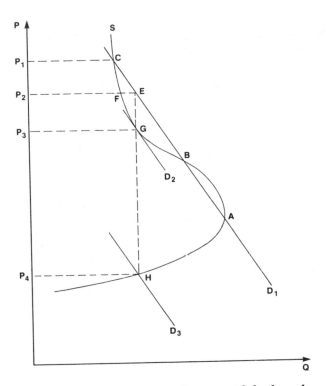

Figure 2-7.   Alternative tariff gains with backward-
bending supply.

of imports rises rather than falls. The larger volume of imports may
be detrimental to the security objective of a tariff. Second, the decline
in the domestic price of oil encourages additional use of oil in the
economy, and makes the economy increasingly sensitive to future
price shocks. We return to these and other questions of the consistency between a tariff and the separate components of the import
premium in chapter 5.

To conclude this section, the optimum tariff may be large, small,
or negative, depending on the specification of supply behavior and
the nature of the equilibrium condition. As noted before, knowledge
of supply behavior is not precise enough to allow a distinction among
these alternative situations. The uncertainty problem is even worse
than we have indicated so far. The analysis of tariff gains assumes
that exporters will not retaliate and that consumers will adjust
efficiently to the higher landed cost of oil imports. Both assumptions
are doubtful. Their consequences are explored in the next two sections.

Implementing the Premium: Other Considerations

Exporter Retaliation

A tariff imposed to drive down the world price of oil is, as we have discussed, a begger-thy-neighbor policy that is not recommended as a general approach to trade relations. The arguments for departing from the general rule of free trade and treating oil as a special case were given in chapter 1 and need not be repeated here. It is emphasized that an oil import tariff will tend to benefit all U.S. trading partners except the oil-exporting countries, and need not engender a return to a past era of unenlightened trade relations. That a tariff may cause a reaction in the oil-exporting countries is a possibility that cannot be discounted, however.

The oil-exporting countries, and in particular OPEC, are not presently maximizing their earnings by operating as a unified monopoly. We argued earlier that this conclusion is evident because of the pattern of pricing and output changes and because world demand appears to be in the inelastic range (that is, an elasticity less than unity). There is, in other words, the potential for exporters to take advantage of unexploited monopoly power, and the import tariff may provide the catalyst for collective action. In this case, the exporters will act to recapture earnings lost to an import tariff.

The second and less likely possibility for exporter retaliation is to discipline the market, even though retaliation may reduce export earnings. Exporters may not be able to recapture lost earnings, but they can act to reduce the benefits of an import duty by restricting the volume of oil trade. In effect, both sides are made worse off by interfering with trade, but exporters would take action to make importers reconsider the wisdom of using import duties.

To illustrate the impact of retaliation on tariff gains, we consider first the conventional case of upward-sloping supply (see figure 2-8). The pretariff equilibrium price is at point E, the intersection of supply and demand, and the optimum U.S. tariff is given by the difference between P_2 and P_1. The reduction in the world price to P_1, and the tariff revenues accruing to the U.S. government, provide the impetus to exporters to retaliate by restricting output. Suppose the restrictions take the form of an export tax, and suppose for simplicity that the export tax is set equal to the import tariff. This is reflected in the figure by the shift in supply from S_1 to S_2. The final outcome depends on what happens to the import tariff. If it is removed, the world and

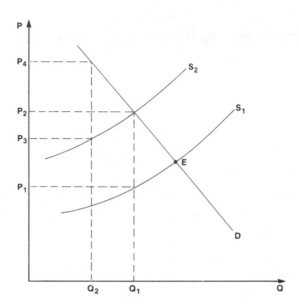

Figure 2-8.   Tariff gains with retaliation.

U.S. prices settle at P_2 and the United States is worse off compared with the pretariff situation. If the tariff is left in place, the world price will settle at P_3 and the U.S. landed price will rise to P_4.

The combination of tariff and export taxes will make the United States unambiguously worse off if the new world price is above the pretariff level.[24] The combined reduction in imports and increases in both world and domestic prices adds up to a net loss for the U.S. economy. If the new world price ends up below the pretariff level, the United States can be better off or worse off, depending on the appropriateness of the size of the tariff in the new situation. In general, the size of the tariff will no longer be correct: if it is too large, the United States will be worse off and if it is too small, the United States will be better off compared with the pretariff situation. Whether the tariff is now excessive depends on supply and demand behavior and whether the duties are fixed per unit or *ad valorem*. For example, if the supply and demand schedules are linear and the duties are *ad valorem*, the tariff will not be excessive.[25]

[24] Whether P_3 will be above or below the pretariff price depends on the relative elasticities of supply and demand, and the relative size of the import and export taxes.

[25] This conclusion follows from equations (2-8) and (2-10).

We conclude that retaliation on the part of exporters, by collectively raising export prices, can eliminate all or part of the gains that may be expected from a tariff, and can very well leave the United States worse off compared with a noninterventionist policy. The possibility that the United States will end up worse off increases with the size of the import duty (and if the duty is specific). This argues for a more conservative *ad valorem* tariff. The same conclusion follows from consideration of the likelihood of exporter retaliation. Other things considered, it is reasonable to expect the probability of retaliation to increase with the size of the tariff.

Exporters will also key their reaction to the effectiveness of a tariff in reducing the world price. This is to be expected because the gains to the importer and the losses to the exporter are determined by the responsiveness of the world price to a change in import demand. In short, the greater the expected benefits of a tariff, the more likely it is that exporters will act to recapture those benefits.

The extreme case where this may occur is given by the backward-bending supply schedule, where the introduction of a tariff reduces the world price by more than the size of the duty (point C in figure 2 6). Just as the tariff causes a sharp reduction in the world price in this market regime, the addition of an export tax will cause a sharp increase. The United States may again end up in a worse position, particularly if the tariff is set at a level to maximize the losses of exporters (i.e., the optimum tariff).

To conclude this section, the prospect of retaliation significantly alters the desirability of a tariff. Before this factor entered the picture, the principal question was determining the appropriate magnitude of a tariff to maximize the gains to the United States. With the possibility of retaliation, however, the question is reduced to whether a tariff is a good idea at all.

Costs of Adjusting to a Tariff

A thorny question ignored so far is how efficiently the domestic market adjusts to a tariff. The supply and demand curves used in the analysis reflect long-run equilibrium positions which assume that the market adjusts efficiently in a move from one point on the schedule to another. It is possible that the adjustment from a pretariff to a post-tariff equilibrium will involve transitory costs that are unacceptably high. The period of adjustment to a tariff can be quite long, and

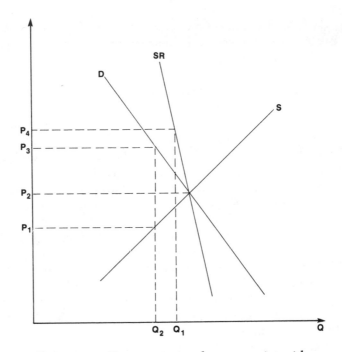

Figure 2-9.   Short-run versus long-run gains with a
tariff.

during this period prices and quantities could deviate substantially
from both the initial and the final equilibrium positions. The
adjustment costs will depend on the magnitude of the tariff and how
quickly it is phased in. If the tariff is large and is phased in rapidly,
the effect on domestic markets will approximate that of an oil supply
disruption. Consequently, the path of adjustment to a tariff can be
as important as the final equilibrium position in establishing the
wisdom of a tariff policy.

The problem is illustrated in a simple way in figure 2-9. Starting
with an initial free trade equilibrium at price P_2, suppose the economy
is in equilibrium with respect to this oil price. As explained earlier,
this means that capital stocks have adjusted according to short-run
demand SR, which intersects long-run demand D at the equilibrium
price. Also, SR is less elastic than D.[26] Suppose further that the
optimum tariff is given by the difference $P_3 - P_1$, as calculated

[26] It is also likely that the world supply response would be different in the
short run, although we ignore this complication in the figure.

according to the long-run schedule.[27] If the optimum tariff is imposed immediately, consumption will adjust initially according to SR rather than D. The domestic price will be higher (at P_4) and the quantity of imports larger (at Q_1) than the long-run equilibrium. Depending on the relative inelasticity of short-run compared with long-run demand, these deviations from long-run equilibrium could be substantial. Eventually the economy will adjust to the price change and move toward the final equilibrium position. In the meantime, the gains from the tariff will be smaller than anticipated and could be negative. It is emphasized that these adjustment costs are not included in the earlier representation of the long-run costs that determine the optimum tariff. Furthermore, as we shall discuss in chapter 5, an oil price shock has indirect macroeconomic costs because of inefficiencies in nonoil markets. A sudden and large tariff will cause adjustment problems in nonoil markets much like those caused by a supply disruption. When these costs are self-imposed on the economy because of import policy, they call into question the wisdom of that policy.

A fundamental question raised by the problem of adjustment costs is whether a series of oil price increases phased in gradually over time produces a smaller cumulative cost than a discrete jump of equal magnitude. Intuition suggests that the phased-in approach is less costly because nonoil markets would have more time to adjust. A macro simulation study by Jacobsen and Thurman (1981) comes to the same conclusion. However, the question requires additional study before an answer can be given. The process of adjustment in energy consumption over time to a price change is also poorly understood, in spite of numerous studies of energy demand that focus on short-run versus long-run responses.[28] The question raised here cannot be satisfactorily answered on the basis of available empirical evidence.

Conclusions

This chapter has presented the conventional argument for a tariff based on the demand component of the premium, and has described a number of complexities that tend to weaken the conventional argument. The crucial variable throughout this analysis is the nature of

[27] If calculated according to the short-run elasticity, the tariff would be too large.

[28] See Bohi (1981) for an analysis of the literature on energy demand.

supply behavior. Alternative views of supply behavior produce widely disparate conclusions about the wisdom of a tariff policy. The demand side of the argument is also affected by uncertainties, but less because of the specification of elasticities than because of the indirect costs of adjusting to a tariff.

In our view, the arguments presented in this chapter suggest moderation in the use of a tariff. The conventional view of import supply indicates an upper bound on the order of $10 per barrel. This argument is tempered by the potential for unfavorable surprises in both supply and demand behavior. Thus, a tariff of about $5 represents a reasonable adjustment of the potential for maximizing gains that recognizes retaliation and domestic adjustment costs.

3

Indirect Effects of
Higher Oil Prices

It is generally acknowledged that changes in oil prices affect economic welfare in ways that are not entirely reflected in transactions in the oil market. The pervasive importance of oil as a factor of production and in final consumption means that higher oil prices can potentially influence real income and its growth and distribution. Thus, to the extent that rising import demand pushes up the price of oil and indirectly produces adverse side effects on income, these economic costs are candidates for inclusion in the oil import premium.

This chapter explores the connections between import demand, the price of oil, and income determination to ascertain if the potential costs can be evaluated with sufficient confidence to be included in the import premium. Our conclusion is to the contrary: the connections are too weak and certain key long-term implications are too uncertain to justify their inclusion.

A second objective is to evaluate the usefulness of an oil import tariff as an instrument to deal with these indirect effects, assuming they are in fact significant enough to warrant intervention. Our conclusion is again to the contrary: a tariff may on balance exacerbate rather than ameliorate the long-run problems that may result from rising world oil prices. This conclusion is not particularly surprising in view of the fact that many of these indirect costs are determined by the domestic price of oil (sometimes relative to the world price), and that a tariff can be expected to drive up the domestic price at the same time that it reduces the world price. The conclusion, stated another way, is that even if rising import demand imposes indirect economic costs on society, direct limitations on imports will not succeed in reversing those costs.

The discussion is divided into three sections: the distribution of income, the terms of trade, and income determination. Each section addresses first the adverse implications of rising world oil prices and then the effectiveness of a tariff in ameliorating those conditions.

Distribution of Income

The analysis of the premium and tariff policy in chapter 2 indicated that a change in the price of oil involves transfers of income among residents of the United States. It was assumed that gains and losses within the same country were offsetting and produced no net change in economic welfare. Obviously, total welfare can be affected if the marginal value of income to losers is different from that of the gainers. In addition, a redistribution of income can affect the composition and level of aggregate expenditures, the savings rate, and possibly the rate of capital formation.

Potential Changes in Welfare

It must be conceded from the outset that one cannot make specific quantitative judgments about welfare changes associated with different income distributions. This involves comparisons of the marginal value of incomes at the individual level. At best, we can offer gross generalizations about different income groups and judge the effect of a price change in relation to these groups. For example, it may be assumed that a price change which transfers income from lower to higher income classes constitutes a reduction in aggregate social welfare.

An increase in the world price of oil, and a corresponding increase in the domestic price, will transfer income from American consumers of oil products as a group to American oil producers (including landowners, shareholders, etc.) as a group. This transfer may be assumed to constitute a shift in the distribution of income from lower to higher income groups. On this basis alone, the price change would constitute a reduction in aggregate economic welfare, and the reduction would be additional to the loss in real income resulting from the income transfer from the United States to the oil-exporting countries.

The practical problem of measuring the welfare loss raises additional considerations that further complicate the issue. One consideration follows directly from the source of the welfare change: that income losers buy a different volume and possibly a different array of goods than income gainers. The consequent change in the composition of aggregate demand can, in turn, affect the demand for oil and appropriate measurement of the areas under the demand curve discussed in chapter 2.[1] A related consideration is that an income redistribution may alter the aggregate rate of time preference and affect capital formation. The possibility that future income can thus be affected introduces an intertemporal complication (of uncertain consequences) in the measurement of the import premium.

Another consideration concerns that part of the income transfer that will be taxed away by the government in the form of income, profits, and oil taxes. This fraction of the income lost by consumers will be respent by the government in a variety of ways which may help to restore or further distort the original distribution of income. If the revenues are disbursed across the general population in the form of a tax reduction or rebate, they could partially reinstate the distribution of income to what it was before the tariff was imposed. Alternatively, if the revenues are tied to social welfare programs, they could be redistributed more to lower income groups; and if spent on energy-related investment programs, they could be redistributed more to higher income groups. Thus, the government could ameliorate or aggravate the distribution question.

The end result of these considerations is uncertain. The initial price increase may be regarded as adversely affecting welfare, but the change can be offset somewhat by government transfers. Adjustments in the composition and level of aggregate demand can occur, but there are no compelling reasons to believe that these adjustments will alter income or welfare, though they can affect the statistical measure of the oil demand curve. The net gain or loss to aggregate welfare is therefore uncertain, even assuming that the initial distributional effect of a price change is quantifiable. There is, in other words, no reasonable argument for a premium on imported oil.

---

[1] For an attempt to measure the welfare effect of a change in the price of oil that includes adjustments in the prices of other goods, see Jorgenson, Lau, and Stoker (1980).

The Effect of a Tariff

The same relationships can be retraced in the event that a tariff is used to restrict oil import demand. Assuming the tariff raises the domestic price of oil, possibly by less than the tariff rate, the distributional outcome described above for an increase in the world price holds, with one exception.[2] The exception is that the increased payments for imports accrue to the government as tariff revenues, along with any transfer from the oil-exporting countries. Thus, transfers through the government become a more important consideration in this case relative to a demand-induced increase in the world price.

The change in the distribution of income produced by a tariff will, as mentioned in the preceding section, alter the demand for oil and other goods and introduce complexities in the measurement of the optimal tariff. The tariff should be calculated on the basis of the demand curve that incorporates all tariff-induced changes in relative prices and the distribution of income. These changes are possibly more critical to the calculation of the tariff than to the measure of welfare because they imply a shift in the demand curve along the import supply function. Their importance, in other words, is a matter of the elasticity of import supply rather than import demand and, as shown in chapter 2, the former is the critical determinant of the optimum tariff.

The distributional consequences of a tariff suggest that other policy instruments should be considered if equity considerations are paramount. Fiscal programs, including direct cash payments, could be useful to avoid the distributional consequences of a tariff, assuming individual gainers and losers could be identified with sufficient precision. However, these programs are neither easy to construct nor costless to operate.

The distributional consequences of a tariff could be avoided by using alternative import reduction schemes. Identical targets for domestic production and conservation could be achieved through a combination of subsidies and taxes (or consumption regulations). The world price of oil would be reduced by the same extent as that achieved by a tariff without driving a wedge between the domestic and the world price. Consequently, the domestic income transfers (represented by areas *A* and *C* in figure 2-4) would not occur.[3]

---

[2] If the world price falls by more than the tariff, as in the backward-bending supply case, the distributional implications are reversed.

[3] Compensating adjustments in government expenditures and taxes should be considered as well.

Avoiding this distributional effect does involve a loss in efficiency, however. As argued earlier, the deadweight loss (measured by areas B and D in figure 2-4) will be larger with other policy options compared with a tariff. Hence, a judgment must be made about the relative importance of efficiency losses and adverse distributional consequences to determine a choice between a tariff and some other import reduction program. An alternative to a tariff may be the preferred method to reduce imports if the distributional consequences of a tariff are important enough and if their importance cannot be ameliorated through government transfers.

Terms of Trade

The analysis of the premium and tariff in chapter 2 also ignored the possibility of induced changes in the value or volume of nonoil imports and exports. The possibility that changes in the oil accounts may affect other sectors of the trade accounts should be considered in evaluating the import premium.

Potential Changes in Nonoil Accounts

A demand-induced increase in the world price will cause an increase in total expenditures on oil imports because of the inelasticity of import demand. A similar result occurs for all oil importers, assuming similar elasticities of import demand. This transfer of income from oil importers to oil exporters represents an increase in the supply of importers' currencies that must be matched by a corresponding increase in demand to maintain existing exchange rates among currencies. The increase in demand may be accomplished by additional sales of goods, services, and assets to the oil-exporting countries, or by an increase in current balances in the exporting countries.

It is unlikely that the importing countries all have the same elasticities of demand for oil imports or that the exporting countries will respend their earnings according to a pattern that will exactly match the increases in currency supplies. Some realignment of exchange rates is likely, both between oil-importing and oil-exporting countries and among oil-importing countries. It is uncertain how the United States will come out relative to the other importing countries and past experience does not suggest an answer.

It is clear that the United States (and other oil importers) must exchange more goods and assets per barrel of oil imports than was required before an increase in the price of oil. This is the terms-of-trade effect of the price increase, and it is measured in the oil market by the additional expenditures on imports. Unless currency values of other importers also change, there is no additional terms-of-trade effect to include in the demand component of the premium beyond that already accounted for in the oil market.

The added expenditures on oil may, on the other hand, overstate their true social cost. This is the case if the added payment for oil does not fully represent an additional opportunity cost to domestic residents; that is, if an additional dollar spent on oil does not constitute the loss of a dollar's worth of resources to domestic residents. There are reasons to believe that the opportunity cost may be smaller. First, accumulated dollar balances held by exporting countries may deteriorate in real value unless their investments properly hedge against inflation. If not, their earnings will command fewer resources when spent compared to the time when the original transaction took place. Second, some purchases in the United States may have a large rental component that does not reduce the amount of resources available to domestic residents.

Third, and perhaps most important, claims against U.S. resources represent an opportunity cost only when the domestic economy operates at full employment. When there is unemployment, the diversion of resources abroad does not mean an equivalent loss of goods and services available to domestic residents. On the contrary, the net result of larger exports to the oil-producing countries could stimulate U.S. export industries and the U.S. economy in general, contributing to a higher level of aggregate employment. In this respect, an increase in oil import demand could have beneficial side effects, while a reduction in oil import demand, by contributing to unemployment, could be detrimental.

To summarize the trade effect of a demand-induced increase in the world price of oil, the total cost to U.S. society is probably captured adequately by changes in expenditures in the oil market alone. We have indicated why the trade cost may be higher (if exchange rates with other industrial countries move against the United States) or lower (if exchange rates move in favor of the United States, or if oil expenditures overstate opportunity costs) because of secondary adjustments. These adjustments are likely to be small and to some extent offsetting, and on balance should not represent a measurable addition to the demand component of the premium.

The Effect of a Tariff

If an import tariff is imposed with the intention of reducing the balance of payments cost of oil imports, and the tariff succeeds in reducing the world price of oil, the benefit of the tariff will be captured adequately in oil accounts for the reasons given above. The wealth transfers from abroad sufficiently cover the gain in balance of payments. There is, however, an additional cost of the tariff that must be considered because of the induced increase in the domestic price of oil.

There is the possibility that U.S. export- and import-competing industries might be harmed by an oil import tariff. Assuming the United States is alone among her trading partners in establishing an oil tariff, the price of oil (and energy) will rise in the United States relative to the rest of the world, and the cost of energy in the production of export goods and import-competing goods will rise in the United States. The relative competitiveness of U.S. goods in both foreign and domestic markets will decline and the exchange value of the dollar will in general decline with respect to the rest of the world. The general decline in exchange rates represents an adverse change in the terms of trade that is not captured in the oil market. The resulting loss in the value of U.S. goods and services is a cost of the tariff that must be balanced against the gains achieved at the expense of oil-exporting countries.

The overall importance of a shift in energy competitiveness is not known. Specific sectors of the economy will of course feel a disproportionate share of the burden, particularly the energy-intensive industries such as petrochemicals, refining, and primary metals. Our qualitative conclusion is that a tariff will produce indirect costs previously unaccounted for in the determination of the optimum tariff and will dilute the benefits of the tariff.

Income Determination

The static analysis of the import premium and the tariff in chapter 2 does not allow for the possibility of induced changes in the capital stock that can produce a dynamic effect on the level or growth of economic activity. This section explores two such possibilities: one caused by changes in the rate of capital formation and the second caused by changes in factor productivity.

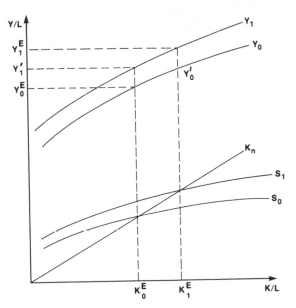

Figure 3-1. Income determination and economic growth.

Oil Prices and Capital Formation

The transfer of wealth abroad, generated by an increase in the world price of oil, is primarily responsible for a potential dynamic effect on income. An illustration of this potential requires a formal expression of the relationships between income and capital formation. We make use of a highly simplified neoclassical model of income determination (see figure 3-1).[4] In the model, capital (K) and other factors (L) produce a single good (Y) which constitutes aggregate income. The model focuses on the relationship between income and the rate of savings (S), and between the rate of savings and the rate of capital formation. The vertical axis of the diagram measures the amount of income and saving per unit of input L (for labor) and the horizontal axis measures the amount of capital per unit of L.

The production function Y relates the amount of income (per unit of L) to the size of K (per unit of L). Related to the amount of income is the savings ratio S, which gives the amount of savings per unit of

_____

[4] For a derivation and description of the model, see Johnson (1966).

L. Starting with a given capital stock, and assuming L grows at an annual rate of n percent, the line K_n shows the amount of new capital formation that must be added to maintain the stock of capital per unit of L at a constant ratio. Thus, K_n is a straight line through the origin with a slope determined by the size of n.

Equilibrium is achieved at Y_1^E with capital formation at K_1^E. This occurs because of the assumed dependence of capital formation on the supply of savings. The interest rate alters with savings to make *ex ante* investment equal to savings. Hence, if capital formation is less than K_1^E, savings is higher than the amount required to maintain the capital stock, interest rates will fall, and investment will increase. The opposite pressure on investment occurs when capital formation exceeds K_1^E.

Suppose that Y_1^E is the status quo before an increase in the price of oil. The initial effect of the price increase is to reduce domestic income by the amount of the wealth transfer required to pay for oil imports. This is represented in the figure by a drop in income to Y'_0 along the new income path Y_0. To repeat, this loss of income equals the additional wealth transfer measured by the marginal costs of oil imports in chapter 2.

In addition to this static decline in income, there is a further dynamic loss in income caused by the reduction in the savings rate to S_0. The economy is not in equilibrium at Y'_0 because the corresponding rate of savings (given along S_0) is less than the rate of capital formation (along K_n). Interest rates will therefore rise, discourage investment, and cause the rate of capital formation to decline toward K_0^E. The slower rate of capital formation, in turn, causes income to decline from Y'_0 to Y_0^E. This secondary reduction of income is the dynamic loss caused by the wealth transfer.

Saving rates and capital formation are, however, consequences of individual choices. A decrease in saving or investment simply means that decisions have been made to defer to the future some of the reduction in consumption necessitated by an oil price increase. These responses must be considered in estimating the long-run level of imports and value of the demand component, but they do not create an independent category of costs that could be reduced by import policy. If saving and consumption decisions are the product of individual utility maximization, the choice between consumption today and consumption tomorrow is no different in principle from a current choice between two consumption goods. In order to maximize utility, consumption will be arranged in such a way that no small change in consumption that is feasible given the budget constraint can increase (or decrease) utility. Therefore any change in consumption of other goods brought about by a small change in imports will have no effect on utility. Consequently, on the margin the dynamic effects of import policy do not constitute an additional cost or benefit.[5]

The Effect of a Tariff

The other side of the argument just described demonstrates that a tariff can completely reverse the dynamic cost of imported oil, as long as the tariff reduces the wealth transfer abroad (i.e., lowers the world price). To retrace the argument in reverse, suppose the initial equilibrium is given by Y_0^E and that the tariff increases domestic income to Y'_1 (along Y_1). The shift to the higher income path causes an increase in the rate of savings (along S_1), which causes capital formation to expand from K_0^E to K_1^E. Consequently, there is a dynamic expansion in income (from Y'_1 to Y_1^E). The tariff cannot completely restore income (to Y_0^E) because of the deadweight loss involved in the conservation and production measures that lower imports.

These dynamic considerations suggest additional complexities in the calculation of an optimal long-run tariff. By increasing future income, a tariff imposed in the present will also increase future oil import demand. But then, other things being equal, oil imports and the magnitude of the demand component will also be larger in the future. Estimating a premium requires a projection of how import demand will change over time as well as an estimate of how oil imports adjust in the present. These issues, to reiterate, have to do with methods of calculating an optimal tariff based on the demand component. In an economy growing over time, the demand curve for imports can be expected to shift outward, and a tariff calculated on the basis of current demand will be too low in the long run. If imposing a tariff increases the rate of growth, the degree of underestimation will increase.

[5] This is the celebrated "envelope theorem" used in appendix B to analyze optimal import levels and stockpiles under uncertainty.

Oil Prices and Factor Productivity

Because oil (or more generally, energy) is an important factor used in the production of other goods and services, changes in the price of oil can alter potential output by changing the efficient combination of inputs in production. An increase in the price of oil will encourage the substitution of other inputs for oil, and this may reduce overall factor productivity. In this section it is unnecessary to draw a distinction between a demand-induced increase in the world price and a tariff-induced increase in the domestic price. The two are indistinguishable in terms of input costs in domestic production. The policy implication is therefore obvious: while an increase in the cost of energy in production may affect economic growth adversely, there is no advantage to be gained from the use of a tariff and there is possibly an additional economic cost.

The simplest model to illustrate the productivity argument supposes an aggregate production function of the form

$$Q = F[E,C] = [aE^{(v-1)/v} + bC^{(v-1)/v}]^{v/(v-1)} \qquad (3\text{-}1)$$

where C is a composite of capital and labor and E is energy. The parameter v measures the constant elasticity of substitution between C and E: if $v = 0$, C and E can be used efficiently only in fixed proportions; if v is large, the two inputs can be substituted with little loss of output. The ratio of the constants a and b measures the relative importance of the two inputs in production.

The production function focuses on energy as an explicit factor of production and, for our purposes, the price of energy is regarded as synonymous with the price of oil. The aggregation of inputs other than energy into a composite factor of production is largely a matter of convenience and is not by itself a serious oversimplification. On the other hand, the concept of an aggregate production function, the meaningfulness of aggregates of inputs and outputs, and the resulting simplified characterization of the growth process are matters open to serious controversy.[6] In addition, the model is not amenable to testing hypotheses about technical progress, the central question of economic growth. Technical progress is essentially an unexplained residual in

[6] For a discussion of the controversies, and of alternative growth models, see Wan (1971).

the growth of total factor productivity that is reflected in trends over long periods of time. Consequently, applications of the model to test the empirical importance of rising energy prices depend upon a questionable symmetry between observed events during past periods of falling energy prices and expected events with rising energy prices.[7] Unfortunately, the established theory of economic growth provides no better alternative to explore the issues in question.

Accepting equation (3-1), assuming it possesses the required properties for differentiability, and assuming further that the economy responds to energy prices efficiently, the share of energy in gross output may be expressed by

$$s = a^v P^{(1-v)} \tag{3-2}$$

where P is the price of energy. Furthermore, the effect of a change in the price of energy on output is given by the elasticity

$$e = \frac{-s}{1-s} \tag{3-3}$$

Equation (3-3) indicates that the effect of an increase of P on aggregate output is more damaging the larger the size of s. From (3-2) we see that v is the crucial parameter that describes how s changes in response to a change in P: s gets bigger as P rises when v is less than 1, and s gets smaller as P rises when v is greater than 1. From this condition one can appreciate why empirical research has concentrated on the magnitude of v and, specifically, on whether it is less than or greater than unity. Continuous increases in the price of energy present no problems for future growth of the economy if the elasticity of substitution between energy and other inputs exceeds unity.

Before turning to the empirical literature, the influence of technological change should be introduced. This is achieved in the model merely by specifying parameters a and b as functions of time: $a(t)$ and $b(t)$. The ratio

$$H(t) = \left[\frac{a(t)}{b(t)} \right]^{(v-1)/v} \tag{3-4}$$

measures the relative importance of energy as an input over time: $H(t)$ will remain constant through time if $a(t)$ and $b(t)$ increase

---

[7] Examples are Solow (1978) and Hogan and Manne (1977).

proportionately, in which case technological change is said to be neutral; technology is said to be energy-saving if $H(t)$ falls over time. There is no hypothesis about technical change; it is a conclusion to be deduced from empirical observation under the assumption that alternative sources of growth can be identified.

The sources of growth are given in equation (3-5), which is a decomposition of equation (3-1) with a and b expressed as functions of time:[8]

$$g_Q = s(g_a + g_E) + (1 - s)(g_b + g_C) \qquad (3\text{-}5)$$

where g_i stands for the rate of growth of i ($i = Q, a, E, b, C$) and s is the share of energy defined in (3-2). This formulation states the intuitively obvious notion that a decline in the availability of energy can be offset by improvements in energy-augmenting technology, or by increases in the growth rates of labor and capital inputs and of technology to augment labor and capital. Because in practice the effect of the growth of inputs cannot be separated empirically from that of technology, interest focuses on the magnitude of s and how it changes when the price of energy rises. As before, if s increases with the price of energy (because v is less than 1), the economy becomes more vulnerable to rising energy prices. Increasingly scarce energy resources exert a more depressing effect on output and can be offset only with more rapid growth of other inputs. Again, the crucial parameter is the elasticity of substitution v, and whether it is greater than or smaller than unity.

The empirical information on v is inconclusive. The magnitude of v is inferred from trends in the share of energy in national income, assuming that returns to factors of production equal the value of their marginal product. If v is less than unity, we should expect the share of factors that are becoming relatively scarce to increase over time, and the share of factors that are relatively abundant to decline; if v is greater than unity, we should expect the share of scarce factors to decrease and abundant factors to increase over time.

Solow (1978) and Nordhaus and Tobin (1972) refer to Denison's (1962, 1974) measures of the share of land in national income and nonresidential business income, respectively, to conclude that the elasticity of substitution between resources (not just energy) and

[8] Relationships between growth rates of inputs and outputs in different models are described in Branson (1972, chapter 22).

labor and capital is greater than unity. Denison's series show the share of land declining over the period from 1929 to 1968. Given the increasing ratio of population to land, the conclusion follows that v is greater than unity, or that technical change has been resource-augmenting. The authors conclude that the prospects for economic growth are optimistic in spite of increasing resource scarcity.

One may argue with the optimistic conclusion on several grounds: (1) resource markets have become less competitive over the years, causing a deviation between returns and productivity; (2) the elasticity of substitution is not constant, but may be expected to decline as resources become scarcer; (3) the level of aggregation is too great to constitute a real test of substitution possibilities;[9] and (4) the historical relationship during periods when energy prices were falling may be unlike the future when energy prices are rising.

With respect to the last point, Denison (1979) has been unsuccessful in explaining the decline in U.S. productivity after 1973, the year energy prices began to rise dramatically. Denison investigates seventeen possible explanations of the slowdown, including rising energy prices, and concludes that "no single hypothesis seems to provide a probable explanation of the sharp change after 1973" (p. 145). As for the energy price hypothesis, Denison is unable to investigate the question directly because "a suitable time series for actual energy consumption by nonresidential business has not been compiled for either the historical or recent period" (p. 139).

The missing series has been compiled recently by Alterman (1982) at Resources for the Future. Alterman generated time series on energy consumed for intermediate use by nonresidential business, including fuel and nonfuel uses, and for components of the nonresidential business sector, for the period 1929 through 1977. Energy consumption per unit of total output declined over this period, with the exception of brief interruptions following World War II and during the late 1960s. After 1973, when energy prices rose, the downtrend continued. Consumption per unit of output in manufacturing follows the same general pattern as total nonresidential business, but with a more rapid decline after 1970.

The declining share of energy between 1929 and 1973 implies that the elasticity of substitution between energy and other factors of production is below unity, contrary to the conclusion based on Denison's series. During this period the price of energy declined con-

---

[9] Stiglitz (1979, p. 46) argues effectively that aggregate data will not yield the kind of information required to resolve the issue.

tinuously in real terms, and in relation to labor income, indicating that energy was a relatively abundant factor of production. Thus, before 1973, the declining share of energy is consistent with an elasticity of substitution less than unity. After 1973, the share of energy increased as the relative price of energy increased, indicating that the substitution elasticity remains less than unity when the price of energy increases. Of course, not too much can be made from this brief post-1973 period because there are compelling reasons to expect a substantial lag between rising energy prices and adjustments in the way energy is used in production.

Alterman's series, at least before 1973, indicates that rising energy prices will have a depressing effect on economic productivity, in contrast to earlier optimistic conclusions. The question is still open, and likely to remain open for several years, whether the apparent symmetry in the substitution relationship holds both for periods of falling and periods of rising energy prices. The history of technological change offers little guidance on this issue because there has been no historical test that parallels current conditions. The answer, at this stage, is therefore a matter of speculation.

For our purposes, the argument demonstrates another potential source of social costs of increasing import demand, but the evidence is not conclusive enough to warrant government intervention to control the price of energy. Furthermore, restrictions on import demand, which may temporarily halt the upward trend in world oil prices, will only speed up the trend in the domestic price. The fundamental question is whether to accept the price trend set by world supply and demand or speed up the transition in the domestic economy through import limitations. The correct decision depends again on perceived conditions of resource supply: whether recent trends in oil prices correctly reflect increasing scarcity or artificial constraints imposed by exporters. If the former, the United States will bear the economic costs of starting the transition too early, but may recoup some of those costs later when the rest of the world makes the transition. If the latter, the United States would be better off avoiding a premature transition to less oil consumption and seeking ways to lift the artificial constraints on production.

Conclusion

This chapter has sketched a number of ways oil price increases may adversely affect economic welfare that are not reflected directly in the market for oil. These indirect costs are sometimes thought to constitute additional arguments for a premium on imported oil. There is some substance to the arguments in connection with the distribution of income and the dynamic effect on income, but on further analysis they suggest additional complexities in estimating the demand component rather than an additional element of the premium. The terms-of-trade argument and the factor productivity argument, on the other hand, could go either way and the empirical evidence is inconclusive.

While the arguments for a premium are wanting, the corresponding arguments for limiting oil imports are even weaker. A tariff will tend to exacerbate trade and productivity costs, and can heighten the distributional problem unless the government transfers tax revenues appropriately. The potential dynamic income gain from a tariff is therefore negated by potential costs. In short, while there may be indirect economic costs of rising world oil prices, those costs should not be treated equivalently as rationales for restricting imports.

4

Private Markets
and Disruption Risks

The second of two broad components of the oil import premium, discussed in this and the next two chapters, concerns the economic costs of disruptions in normal oil supply conditions. This chapter explores how private markets may be expected to respond to disruption risks because this adjustment is central to the determination of the premium. In particular, we will show how private actions alter the demand as well as the disruption component of the premium.

Explicit recognition of private sector behavior is also required in order to evaluate the effect of government actions. Government policy will alter incentives for private actions and thus private behavior. While market behavior determines the oil import premium, government policy based on the premium will change market behavior as well as size of the premium. The net result of a policy intervention must be evaluated in light of these effects. The interactions between the public and private sectors provide the key to understanding how separate components of the import premium are related and how the total premium can be determined from its components.

The theme that runs through this chapter is that private agents will be motivated to guard against oil supply disruptions, and hence that disruption risks alone do not justify government actions to facilitate or complement private ones. Private actions that are effective in reducing the costs of a disruption require changes in the way oil is produced or consumed, and these changes have costs of their own. Each individual will strike a balance between the costs of preparing for a disruption, and the expected costs that are avoided. That balance, and the extent of private adjustments to disruption risks, will be heavily influenced by the difference between current and anticipated prices of oil. While private preparations are motivated by selfish goals, their effect is to lower the potential cost of a disruption and reduce the need for government action. Nevertheless, the nation's welfare may require a different balance than that determined by the private sector. A role for the government may be justified if there are disruption costs that are ignored in private decisions, or if individuals systematically underestimate the probability and severity of a disruption. These topics are deferred to the next chapter.

The argument in this chapter is as follows. First, we indicate how disruption risks alter private investment decisions by creating incentives to purchase capital stocks which use less oil or which permit greater substitution away from oil, and to invest in inventories of oil or oil-intensive goods for use during a disruption. The discussion then turns to how the aggregate of individual investment decisions affects the domestic market for oil, the demand for imports, and the price of oil. Based on this analysis, we show how private adjustments to disruption risks alter the demand component discussed in chapter 2 and reduce the need for government intervention to prepare the economy for disruptions. Readers interested in a rigorous treatment of the arguments in this chapter may refer to appendix B.

Private Adjustments to Disruption Risks

It is useful to begin by defining what we mean by a disruption in oil supplies. In general, we compare two possible states that characterize world oil supply conditions—normal and disrupted. A normal state reflects long-run supply conditions characterized by gradual price changes (possibly a long-run upward trend) and the disrupted state reflects short-term supply conditions characterized by a sudden jump in price. In a disruption the price of oil will be higher at all possible levels of imports compared with a normal state, but the quantity of imports may be expected to vary with the price. Once a disruption ends, the price is assumed to return to the long-run trend associated with normal supply conditions.[1] All references to prices throughout this discussion are in real terms.

[1] The price after a disruption need not fall to the level prevailing before the disruption. Nevertheless, even allowing for real price trends, our characterization of a disruption does not conform precisely to the pattern experienced in the 1970s.

We abstract from a number of complications that would appear in an exhaustive treatment. It is assumed that all decision makers are risk neutral and seek to maximize the expected value of profits (or consumer satisfaction). The probability of a disruption can be interpreted as the fraction of a time period the world will be in a disrupted state. The specific length of a disruption is also ignored by referring to disruptions as short-term phenomena (for example, several months) and to the period between disruptions as long (for example, a few years). We avoid discounting future values to the present by assuming that discount factors are already embodied in expected prices.

Consumers of oil products, including firms and households, can take actions in advance of a disruption that will reduce the burden of an expected price increase. Similarly, domestic producers of oil products (and substitutes) can take actions in advance of a disruption that will increase the potential gains from a price increase. This section describes the responses of individuals to price incentives without concern for how those prices are determined. The next section shows how individual behavior and market prices are jointly determined. Throughout this discussion we assume no government intervention is anticipated; the *ex ante* and *ex post* effects of intervention on private behavior and the import premium are discussed in chapter 5.

Consumer Responses to Disruption Risks

The cost of a sudden increase in the price of oil to consumers is determined by oil consumption requirements and consumers' ability to change them. These, in turn, are determined by the characteristics of the capital stock at the time of the increase. The capital stock is crucial because oil (indeed, energy in general) is not consumed for its own sake, but in conjunction with energy-using equipment to provide other goods and services. Household energy demand is determined by the type of housing, appliances, automobiles, and so on, and their respective energy requirements. Energy requirements for firms are determined by the type of product and the production process. Once each of these consumers chooses a capital stock, the ability to respond to an increase in the price of oil is limited: oil consumption can be reduced only by changing the use of the capital stock. Over the long term, consumers may change their capital stocks in response to a change in the price of oil, but this option usually cannot be exercised during a short-term disruption. Consequently, households are forced to suffer inconveniences, while firms are forced to cut back on the production rate for goods and services. A disruption therefore imposes costs on consumers in the form of lower income and welfare.

This burden may be reduced if individuals make investment decisions that take into account the prospect of a disruption. They could purchase capital goods that require less oil or that permit substitutions away from oil, and they could invest in precautionary (or speculative) inventories of oil, oil substitutes, or oil-intensive goods. Each option, however, requires an additional cost today in order to reduce future losses during a disruption.[2] In making the investment decision, each individual will balance the added current cost against the expected future benefit. The influence of disruption risks on current investment decisions depends primarily on the likelihood of a disruption and on the expected increase in the price of oil. Individual firms and households will differ in their perceptions of the prospects for, and impact of, a disruption and, consequently, will differ in their response to disruption risks. Marginal changes in consumption habits and investment decisions can be expected to occur throughout the economy.

The extent of individual adjustments, as noted, depends on the balance between current costs and future benefits. This crucial relationship deserves further elaboration because of the resulting implications for the oil import premium. To illustrate, we focus on the difference between the short-run and the long-run demand for oil in figure 4-1. The short-run demand, as indicated in chapter 2, is defined with respect to a specific capital stock, and variations in the quantity of consumption are obtained by varying the utilization rate of that stock. Long-run demand, in contrast, indicates consumption levels at different prices when the capital stock also varies. It is also important to remember that each specific short-run demand curve will intersect the long-run demand curve D at an oil price where the underlying capital stock is optimal at that price.

Short-run demand denoted by SR_N is based on a capital stock that is optimal when the price of oil is P_N, while SR_D is based on a capital stock that is optimal when the price is P_D. For the moment we restrict ourselves to the case in which changes in the capital stock produce parallel shifts in short-run demand. If the price of oil is certain to remain at either P_N or P_D, the appropriate capital stock decision is

---

[2] If no additional cost were required, the investment would be undertaken regardless of the prospect of a disruption.

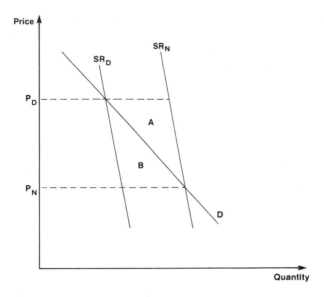

Figure 4-1. Short-run demands for oil at different prices.

unambiguously either SR_N or SR_D, respectively. However, if the price is uncertain between P_N and P_D, neither choice is optimal. The capital stock associated with SR_N will produce losses equal to the area of triangle A (compared to SR_D) when the price rises to P_D; while the capital stock associated with SR_D will produce losses equal to the area of triangle B (compared to SR_N) when the price drops to P_N.

To understand these assertions, notice that the area under long-run demand D and above price P_N represents total profits (or, analogously, consumer's surplus) during a normal period when the capital stock corresponds to SR_N. Similarly, the area between D and P_D is profit (or consumer's surplus) during a disruption when the capital stock corresponds to SR_D. If a disruption occurs when the capital stock is given by SR_N, additional costs are incurred equal to the area bounded by P_D, P_N, and SR_N.[3] Subtracting these added costs from profits under the long-run demand curve leaves net profits (or consumer's surplus) during a disruption equal to the area between D and P_D less the area

---

[3] Note that if SR_N is vertical—meaning that oil consumption is fixed in the short run—the area of additional costs would exactly equal the added expenditure on oil.

of the triangle denoted by A. Compared to net profits that could be earned in a disruption with a capital stock associated with SR_D, there is a net loss equal to the area A.

If no disruption occurs, and the capital stock associated with SR_D is in place, profits (consumer surplus) are less by the area of triangle B than profits that could be earned with the capital stock associated with SR_N. Profits given by SR_D are equal to the area between D and P_D plus the area bounded by P_D, P_N, and SR_D. Thus, by choosing a capital stock associated with SR_N instead, additional profits equal to the area B could have been earned. We conclude that, when the price of oil is uncertain, the appropriate capital stock will depend on how the price is expected to behave in the future.

If, over the economic life of the investment, the price of oil is P_N for a fraction $(1 - \pi)$ of the time and P_D for a fraction π of the time, the optimal capital stock will correspond to a short-run demand for oil that lies between SR_D and SR_N. In the simplest case, individuals will use the expected value of the price of oil, given by

$$P_D + (1 - \pi)\, P_N$$

as the correct price on which to make planning decisions. The short-run demand curve that corresponds to this price will intersect the long-run demand curve at a point where the weighted sum of area A and area B are minimized, where the weights are the probabilities of a disruption and normal period, respectively. That is, the individual will correctly balance current costs and future gains when the marginal cost of using less oil today equals the discounted marginal gain of requiring less oil tomorrow when the disruption occurs.[4]

The new short-run demand curve need not shift parallel to the original curve, and may intersect the long-run demand curve at a planning price that differs from the expected value of current and future prices.[5] The range of possible outcomes will vary among individuals according to the technological options that are available and the flexibility they offer in allowing substitutions of other fuels and inputs for oil when the price of oil rises. For some purposes an investment that allows fuel switching when the price of oil rises may be attractive; for others, the investment options may permit an absolute

[4] This proposition was demonstrated first by Tolly and Wilman (1977), though in the context of a different disruption scenario.

[5] Appendix B discusses in detail the implications of the difference between the expected price and the planning price.

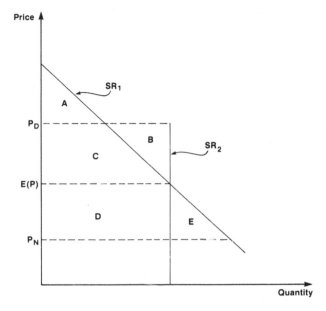

Figure 4-2.   Comparison of rigid and flexible
demands for oil.

reduction in oil consumption but little flexibility in fuel switching
(for example, processes that optimize efficiency with respect to a
specific fuel input level).

The potential tradeoff between investment options that absolutely
reduce oil consumption and those that enhance flexibility in switching
away from oil is of special interest in the context of oil price uncertainty. One source of interest, which we will return to later, is that
market incentives may favor more flexible options, while conventional
instruments of government intervention (for example, tariffs) tend to
distort these incentives in favor of conservation. In other words, intervention may lead to a different and possibly less efficient outcome
than undisturbed market incentives. Another source of immediate
interest is that under price uncertainty some investment options that
are uneconomic at any fixed price become viable.

To see the tradeoff between reducing consumption and increasing
flexibility, and to indicate the possible changes in short-run demand,
refer to figure 4-2. Short-run demand curve SR_1 is intended to refer
to an industrial process that permits flexibility in oil consumption,
while SR_2 refers to an alternative process with a fixed oil consump-

tion requirement. For simplification, SR_2 is drawn so that the demand for oil falls to zero when the price rises above P_D (i.e., SR_2 corresponds to the vertical axis above P_D). This may be interpreted to mean that the plant shuts down temporarily when the price of oil exceeds P_D.

Both curves intersect at $E(P)$, the expected value of P_N and P_D, which is also a point on the long-run demand curve (not drawn). The common intersection at $E(P)$ indicates that the firm, after calculating the expected price of oil in the light of future disruption prospects, can choose between these two distinct capital stock options to establish future oil demand. Both are equivalent when evaluated in terms of the expected price of oil. However, abstracting from differences in capital costs, the flexible option associated with SR_1 is clearly superior to SR_2, when the price of oil is uncertain.

To demonstrate this, suppose that the price is fixed at $E(P)$ with absolute certainty. Suppose further that capital costs are equal for the two processes and that net revenues (gross revenues less the cost of oil) are the same for both options at the price $E(P)$. Net revenues are given by the area $A + C$ for SR_1 and by the area $B + C$ for SR_2. If net revenues are the same, the two areas are equal, and A is equal to B.

Now suppose the price of oil is uncertain: P_N in normal periods and P_D in temporary future (disruption) periods, yet the expected price remains unchanged at $E(P)$. With the rigid process SR_2, net revenues are zero when the price is P_D and $(B + C + D)$ when the price is P_N. With the flexible process SR_1, net revenues are A when the price is P_D and $(A + C + D + E)$ when the price is P_N. Remembering that $A = B$, expected net revenues of the flexible process will be larger than the rigid process by the weighted sum of A plus E, where the weights are the probabilities of P_D and P_N, respectively. Thus, the flexible process will be chosen over the rigid one.

The rigid process will be preferred to the flexible process if the initial conditions are changed sufficiently. For example, if the area of B is sufficiently larger than the area of A, or if the capital outlay for the flexible process is sufficiently larger than that for the rigid one, the rigid process will be preferred.

This example demonstrates that the range of variability of the price, as well as characteristics of the capital stock, can alter the optimal capital investment decision quite apart from the expected value of the price of oil. Indeed, the optimal investment strategy might be inferior when evaluated at any fixed value of the price of oil, yet superior when evaluated over a range of price variations. A more general derivation of the investment decision under alternative conditions is provided in appendix B.

An obvious example of an investment whose sole purpose is to increase flexibility is the installation of dual-firing capability, such as a boiler that can switch from oil to natural gas. Notice, however, that the question of flexibility now falls on the supply of the substitute fuel. Unless the supply of the substitute fuel can increase with the shift in fuel demand, dual-firing capability provides no additional benefits, but serves only to cause the price of substitute fuel to rise enough to reduce the quantity demanded.

It is possible to summarize individual investment decisions in terms of a "planning price" derived from a thought experiment. If individuals respond to price uncertainty by choosing an investment that is optimal with respect to some fixed price, that price may be called the individual's planning price. The individual will invest as if the planning price remained fixed in the future with absolute certainty. This price may lie above or below the expected value of current and future prices, depending on the effect of the investment on the price responsiveness of short-run oil demand. If the investment increases the capability to substitute away from oil at a higher price, the planning price will exceed the expected price. If substitution flexibility is reduced by the investment, the planning price will be below the expected price; and, if flexibility is unchanged, the planning price will be equivalent to the expected price.[6]

The conclusion to be drawn from this discussion is that oil price uncertainty will induce individuals to make capital stock decisions that reduce short-run oil demand, increase the price responsiveness of short-run demand, or a combination of both. The risk element imposed by price uncertainty raises the expected cost of oil to private agents above the normal market price and causes them to consume less oil at both the normal price and at possible disruption prices. We shall see below that this result alters the evaluation of the demand component of the premium discussed in chapter 2, because that premium is measured by the difference between the cost of oil to the nation and the cost to private individuals. The appropriate measure of the disruption component of the premium is also affected by private responses, as discussed in chapter 5.

[6] Note that if the optimal choice under uncertainty would not be chosen at any particular price which is certain to occur, the planning price does not exist.

Responses of Domestic Energy Producers

Domestic oil producers, and producers of substitutes for conventional crude oil, can be expected to respond to the prospects of a disruption because of the additional revenues that a higher price will bring. The analogy with oil consumers carries over to producers, except that the cost of a disruption integrated into investment decisions is now the opportunity cost of forgone revenues and profits. Price uncertainty will alter the optimal capacity of existing production facilities, change the desired rate of production, and make some investments more attractive than they would be when evaluated at a fixed price.

Owners of existing oil facilities will be motivated to install additional surge production capacity to take advantage of higher expected future prices. They will also be inclined to delay or slow current production rates in order to shift the life of existing reserves into the future. Both actions involve higher current costs, in terms of added capital outlays or lower revenues, which must be balanced against expected future gains. The balance will be achieved in the same manner as that described above for consumers, and will vary among individual producers according to technical constraints and the anticipated variation in prices. Of course, the incentive to make these adjustments will be moderated by the anticipation of government actions to reduce windfall gains during a disruption.

The net result of adjustments by producers with existing facilities to the prospect of a disruption is an increase in short-term production capability, and an increase in the responsiveness of output to an increase in the wellhead price. These responses are advantageous to the nation during a disruption because they reduce the absolute loss of oil to the domestic economy, but the gains may be accompanied by some loss of domestic oil output during normal periods (see figure 4-3). The short-run supply curve S_2 is more elastic than S_1, and S_2 gives more output at higher prices and less output at lower prices compared to S_1. Nevertheless, the country may benefit even if there is an increase in import dependence in normal periods because of the decrease in dependence during disruptions.

Exploration and development of new reserves will also receive a boost from the expected gain associated with a supply disruption. The expected stream of future earnings from new reserves will increase with the expected disruption price and its duration. Just as the higher expected price of oil induces consumers to move up to the long-run demand curve and reduce long-run consumption requirements, the

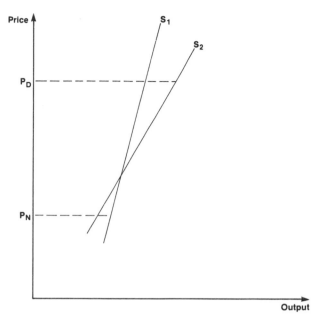

Figure 4-3. Change in short-run domestic oil
supply because of the prospects for a
disruption.

same incentive causes producers to increase long-run output capacity
above that warranted by the price prevailing in normal market
conditions.

Another supply option of considerable interest is investment in
facilities for production of synthetic fuels that can substitute for oil.
It is possible that synthetic fuels plants may be profitable because of
price uncertainty, though they are uneconomic at a normal price.
Typically, these facilities are highly capital intensive and offer little
opportunity for short-run variations in output. Average costs are
minimized when the output rate is near capacity, and capacity is set
by the scale of the initial investment. It is meaningful to analyze
investment decisions for synthetic production in terms of marginal
costs because known reserves of the source of feedstock (coal or oil
shale) are so large that production can be characterized as a renewable
commodity. Production costs, in this view, are governed by conventional operating costs associated with extraction and conversion of the

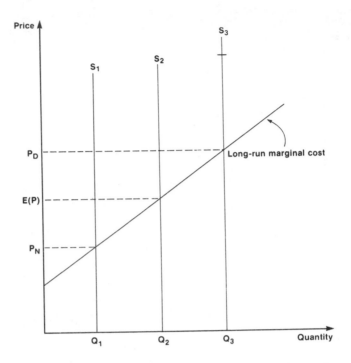

Figure 4-4. Effect of price uncertainty on the scale
of production.

feedstock.[7] The long-run marginal cost of production at a typical
facility is illustrated in figure 4-4, where the curve indicates the cost
of increasing output when all factors of production, including the
scale of the plant, are variable. Long-run marginal cost is assumed
to increase with output as if, for example, increasing returns to scale
are outweighed by decreasing returns to extracting and handling the
feedstock. The assumption that output cannot vary once the scale
is set (except to shutdown) is illustrated by the series of vertical short-
run supply curves S_1, S_2, and S_3, which correspond to output levels
Q_1, Q_2, and Q_3, respectively.

Once the size of the plant is fixed and the price of oil fluctuates
from P_N to P_D, output remains fixed at the predetermined level and
revenues change. For example, if the size of the plant is set at S_1, and
the price rises to P_D, output remains unchanged at Q_1 but revenues

---

[7] This contrasts with investment decisions in nonrenewable resources such as
conventional oil reserves.

increase by the change in price. Revenues could be larger with a larger operation, say at S_2, but there would be losses when the price fell back to P_N. The optimal size plant is S_1 when the price is fixed at P_N, and S_3 when the price is fixed at P_D, but neither is optimal when the price varies from P_N to P_D.

When there is no short-run flexibility, as presumed in this example, the optimal strategy is to calculate the expected price $E(P)$ and set the scale of the plant accordingly (at S_2 in figure 4-4). This choice will maximize the expected value of revenues over the different states of world oil prices. As explained in the preceding section, the expected price is the optimal planning price when short-run shifts in supply are parallel, but not when there is a choice between more or less short-run flexibility. The same considerations apply in choosing among more or less flexible production processes.[8]

A simple example can be used to show that a highly capital intensive production facility, such as a synthetic fuels plant, may be economically viable because of disruption risks, even though it is a losing proposition during normal supply conditions. Suppose the marginal cost curve pictured in figure 4-4 were everywhere above P_N (the normal price), indicating that it is not possible to build a plant of any size that is profitable at this price, yet below the expected price $E(P)$ for some range of output, so that profits earned during periods when the price is high are sufficient to offset losses during normal periods. The facility would operate full time at capacity even though capital costs were not fully recovered during normal periods, as long as operating costs were less than the normal price. By operating full time, the synthetic fuels plant would displace imports in both normal and disrupted periods. The primary benefit of the plant to society does not derive from the ability to replace imports in a disruption, but from a supply of oil that is cheaper on average than that available in the world market. This benefit arises because less wealth is transferred to foreign producing countries during a disruption.

To summarize, the prospect of a disruption increases the potential returns to investment in production of domestic oil and oil substitutes. The nature of the investment and its effect on domestic supply will vary according to technical constraints and individual perceptions of world market conditions. In some cases current production will fall and in others it will rise, but in all cases the incentives work to increase domestic oil supply in a disrupted market.

[8] See appendix B for details.

Private Incentives to Hold Inventories

In addition to investments in capital stocks, private agents have the option to invest in additional inventories of crude oil and products, or in oil-intensive commodities that may be severely affected during a disruption. Both oil producers and consumers have an incentive to build inventories, either to use for their own purposes or to sell to others. In either case, the opportunity cost of oil in a disruption is its market price and the incentive for stockpiling comes from the expected increase in the price.[9]

Private investors will be inclined to build an oil stockpile as long as the cost of adding another barrel is less than the expected appreciation in the price. This strategy will maximize the total expected profit and determine the optimal size of the inventory, which will therefore rise with the probability of a disruption and with the expected disruption price. Conversely, the size of inventories will decline as the prospects for a disruption dissipate.

The spread between normal and disrupted prices is the source of the private incentive to stockpile. The additional benefit of private stockpiling to society is the reduction in the price spread achieved by transferring oil from normal to disrupted periods. Building inventories in normal supply periods will tend to raise the normal price, while sales from inventories in a disruption will tend to reduce the disrupted price. This narrowing of the price spread as inventories grow also provides the market signal that limits the total amount of inventory building. Similarly, inventory building affects, and is affected by private investments in capital stocks, described above. All of these options alter the supply and demand for oil, and fundamentally affect the demand for oil imports in advance of and during a disruption. How these adjustments affect market prices and, in turn, how market prices affect private adjustments, is the subject of the next section.

Private Adjustments and the Market for Imports

The individual responses to disruption risks just described will collectively alter the structure of domestic supply and demand for oil, and therefore the demand for oil imports. The determination of their

---

[9] We are ignoring inventories required for normal, on-going business operations and concentrate on those held in anticipation of large price movements not encountered in the ordinary course of business.

effect on current and future market prices requires, in addition, some assumption about the characteristics of world oil supply in normal and disrupted periods. Import supply and the demand are introduced first, followed by a discussion of the determinants of equilibrium market prices. Based on this analysis, we reconsider the demand component of the premium in the next section.

The Demand for Imports

The demand for U.S. oil imports, as explained in chapter 2, is the difference between domestic supply and demand for oil. Both schedules, moreover, have short- and long-run counterparts. The influence of disruption risks on private investment decisions is recorded in terms of shifts in short-run supply and demand schedules along their long-run counterparts, because changes in capital stocks are already embodied in the long-run curves.[10]

The effect of private adjustments on oil import demand is illustrated in figure 4-5. Starting with the normal world price P_N and no risk of disruption, optimal investment decisions would locate the short-run domestic supply and demand schedules at SRS_N and SRD_N, respectively, and the corresponding short-run oil import demand curve at SR_N. Adding disruption risks induces changes in private investments, causing SRS_N to shift to the right and SRD_N to shift to the left, and causing both curves to become more price responsive, as indicated by SRS_* and SRD_*, respectively. The corresponding short-run import demand curve shifts from SR_N to SR_*, reflecting a reduction in demand and an increase in price responsiveness compared with the initial position.

The new short-run curves intersect their respective long-run schedules at the price P_*. This price is the market aggregate of individual planning prices. The market aggregate has no particular significance for individual decisions, because some individuals will have higher and others lower planning prices than the aggregate. For example, figure 4-6 aggregates two individual sets of short- and long-run de-

---

[10] Technically, the use of long-run demand and supply curves implies that flexibility is limited to a choice of capital stocks embodied in the long-run demand curve, and excludes the possibility examined earlier that there are options that would be chosen only when the price of oil is uncertain. The simplification is not important in the discussion of a market equilibrium, but is important in the analysis of tariff policy.

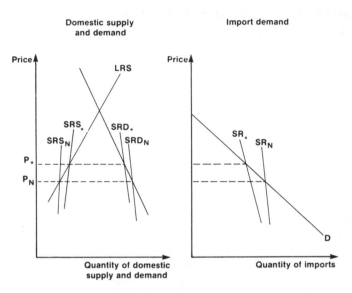

Figure 4-5.   Private adjustments to price uncertainty
and the demand for oil imports.

mand curves, denoted by subscripts 1 and 2, to obtain the corresponding market schedules, denoted by the subscript M. The market
planning price P_M falls between the two individual planning prices,
P_1 and P_2, giving a market outcome (in this example) that does not
correspond to any individual planning price on which participants
base their consumption decision. The distinction becomes important
later on when we discuss government intervention designed to adjust
individual planning prices. A tariff, for example, will adjust the market and all individual participants in the same direction, while overall
efficiency in the use of oil resources may require some discrimination
among participants.

The market planning price is significant, however, with respect to
the collective demand for oil and oil imports. The aggregation of
individual responses to price uncertainty determines the level of oil
import demand. The aggregate planning price is determined from
equilibrium market prices in both normal and disrupted supply
periods, though equilibrium outcomes cannot be deduced without
introducing world supply conditions in both periods. Supply is introduced next, and market equilibrium is discussed in the following
section.

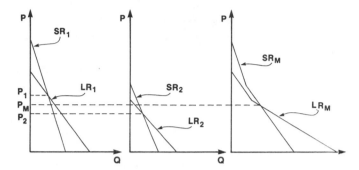

Figure 4-6. Individual planning prices and the intersection of long-run and short-run market demand curves.

The important conclusion reached so far, indicated by the position of SR_* relative to SR_N, is that the private market will adjust to disruption risks by regarding the expected price of oil as higher than the normal market price. Individuals will consume less and produce more oil than the amounts corresponding to the actual market price.

The Supply of Oil Imports

The supply of oil imports to the United States is the difference between non-U.S. supply and demand, as described in chapter 2. Our earlier discussion of long-run (that is, normal) import supply emphasized the importance of assumptions about the behavioral relationship between the world price and the quantity of oil available to the United States, and that uncertainty about the relationship cannot be expressed simply in terms of the size of the price elasticity. Keeping that discussion in mind, we will assume for the purposes of this section that normal supply corresponds to the conventional view of an upward-sloping schedule, and remember later that alternative constructions are plausible. Normal supply and short-run import demand combine to establish the normal market price, where the position of the short-run demand curve depends on private responses to disruption risks.

Supply behavior during a disruption is also subject to considerable uncertainty. Past history provides some guidance, though future disruptions need not resemble those of the past. The first disruption in 1973 took the form of an embargo aimed primarily at the United States, plus a reduction in the total volume of output. The second disruption in 1979 involved a reduction in output caused by internal political events in Iran, and the disruption in 1980 was due to the war between Iran and Iraq. Whatever the motivation in each case, the world oil market operated to spread the resulting supply shortages across all importers. Supplies were rapidly reallocated to countries that were willing to pay the higher price established after the disruption.

This experience suggests that the supply curve for U.S. imports in a disruption should not be specified as a fixed quantity, but as a variable amount which increases with the offer price.[11] A positive relationship between price and quantity seems most plausible for two reasons: exporters not associated with the disruption are willing to increase output at higher prices, and supplies going to other importers will be bid away at higher prices. Consequently, we will assume that the disrupted supply curve is upward sloping.[12] Compared with the assumed normal supply curve, disrupted supply lies everywhere to the left and is less price elastic (see S_N and S_D in figure 4-7).

Market Equilibrium

Combining the supply and demand schedules described above gives an overall picture of equilibrium conditions in the oil market (see figure 4-7). In particular, we can compare equilibrium conditions in normal and disrupted states and show how the introduction of disruption risks alters the normal equilibrium condition.

In the absence of any risk of a supply disruption, equilibrium in the market occurs at the intersection of long-run import demand D and import supply S_N. This is the straightforward outcome of independent actions on both sides of a competitive market. Introducing disruption risks means that private agents will undertake the kinds of investments described earlier that reduce the demand for imports in both normal and disrupted states. If disrupted supply shifts to S_D, the disruption price will be determined by the intersection of

[11] Changes in the structure of the world oil market could make absolute quantity restrictions more plausible in the future. As producing countries supplant oil companies in downstream activities, origin and destination restrictions are easier to enforce. For a discussion of recent developments, see Neff (1981).

[12] A backward-bending supply curve is less plausible in a disruption than in normal (long-run) periods because of the relatively greater importance of diversions away from non-U.S. importers in a disruption, and because the desire to postpone production into the future is less plausible in the short-term context of a disruption.

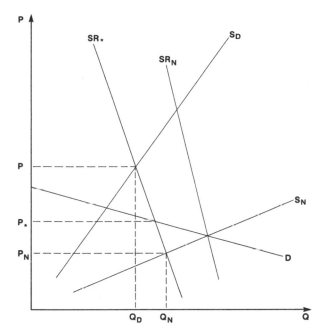

Figure 4-7. Market equilibrium prices in normal and disrupted periods.

short-run demand prevailing at the time of a disruption and S_D.

The effect of disruption risks on short-run demand is pictured in the figure by the shift from SR_N to SR_*. Note that the effect of private adjustments embodied in SR_* is to lower the normal market price (P_N) and the disrupted market price (P_D), compared with their respective equilibrium positions given along SR_N. This comparison illustrates the effect of private expectations about future market conditions on both the current and future market outcomes. Failure to account for these adjustments, by implicitly assuming that the private sector is completely myopic, can lead to an incorrect interpretation of the normal market equilibrium and an incorrect forecast of the future equilibrium.

The normal market equilibrium will be incorrectly interpreted if the point corresponding to the price P_N and quantity of imports Q_N is perceived to lie on the long-run demand curve for imports. Instead, the quantity of imports is determined by short-run demand, and short-run demand is in turn determined by a higher planning price (given by P_*) which takes into account the anticipated price of oil in a disruption. This means that the calculation of the demand component of the premium (as in chapter 2) cannot be determined from estimates of long-run demand alone, but requires estimates of short-run demand as well. The next section demonstrates how the two demand curves determine the premium.

It is more difficult to estimate demand curves from market data because of private adjustments to disruption risks. Because consumption points do not fall along a long-run demand curve, those observations cannot be used to estimate long-run demand directly. An indirect procedure is required, based on estimates of short-run demand and on adjustments in capital stocks. Unfortunately, estimates of $SR*$ cannot be obtained from historical data, with the possible exception of that following 1978, because of the absence of experience with large price jumps followed by periods of normalcy long enough for the private sector to make adjustments to disruption risks. Using earlier information to estimate demand and predict prices would overstate both the price and the quantity of imports that would occur in a disruption. Similar biases would result from engineering-economic calculations of optimal imports at various prices, if those calculations were based on the assumption that private individuals are myopic about the future.

It is clear from figure 4-7 that the location of $SR*$ is critical to the determination of both normal and disrupted equilibrium prices. Estimating the location of $SR*$ also presents a difficult analytical problem because the location is determined jointly with the normal and disrupted prices, that is, the location must be consistent with both equilibrium prices. The required consistency means that individual private agents cannot take the normal and disrupted prices as fixed outcomes determined by exogenous events, but must anticipate them on the basis of some perception of overall market conditions. Specifically, the correct outcome requires that individual private agents take into account in their investment decisions the expectations and actions of all other individuals, including the exporting countries, and predict aggregate market behavior.

One approach to the analysis of market behavior in this context, known as "rational expectations," assumes that individuals make decisions on the basis of a probability distribution of future prices that is consistent with a market equilibrium.[13] The probability distribution

[13] The term "rational expectations" may be interpreted to mean that people are rational in acting in their own best interests, and that they will do so by forming expectations about future events using all available information in the most efficient manner. For detailed discussions of this approach, see Muth (1961), Grossman (1980), and Lucas and Sargent (1981).

assimilates information on the probability of a shift in supply during a disruption and on the level of short-run demand for oil when the price rises. The equilibrium price in a disruption is assigned a probability equal to that of the disruption. Disruptions of differing degrees of severity would be assigned different disruption prices (or price paths), each with its own probability.

As the probability of a disruption (or its severity) increases, rational participants in the oil market will make adjustments that will tend to reduce the quantity of imports and the world price in both normal and disrupted conditions. The tendency to adjust in the direction indicated in figure 4-7 seems beyond dispute, but whether the adjustments will be optimal is a source of doubt and concern. One concern, deferred to the next section, is whether private agents can forecast future equilibrium prices. The second, discussed in chapter 5, is whether the adjustments made by the private sector are socially optimal.

Before closing this section, it is of interest to provide a quantitative example of the adjustments illustrated in figure 4-7. We use a linear simulation model of the oil market described in appendix A. With linear supply and demand curves, and parallel shifts in short-run demand curves, the optimal adjustment in short-run demand is given by the curve which intersects long-run demand at the expected value of prices in normal and disrupted states of the market.[14] The initial conditions, key assumptions, and results are given in table 4-1.

It is assumed that long-run demand and normal supply intersect at a price of $35 per barrel and quantity of imports of 7 million barrels/day (mmb/day). This is the market equilibrium when no disruption is anticipated. At the initial equilibrium, the assumed price elasticity of long-run supply is 4.0; for disrupted supply it is 0.14; for long-run demand, -0.5; and for short-run demand, -0.10.[15] A disruption is defined as a reduction of 2 mmb/day in the quantity of imports available to the United States at the initial price of $35 per barrel. The effect of private adjustments on market outcomes is recorded at three disruption probabilities (0, 0.1, and 0.3), to compare the assumption of complete myopia with that of perfect foresight and to show how the adjustments change with the probability of a disruption.

---

[14] This example is therefore a special case of the adjustments discussed in this chapter and in the general model analyzed in appendix B.

[15] The elasticities will change with movements along the curves, that is, the elasticity of demand will rise with the price, but the changes remain within a reasonable range, as indicated in appendix A.

Table 4-1. Effect of Private Adjustments on Market Equilibria with
Alternative Disruption Probabilities[a]

	Probability of a disruption		
	0.0	0.1	0.3
Normal quantity	7.00	6.70	6.30
Normal price	35.00	34.62	34.12
Expected price	35.00	38.88	43.99
Disrupted quantity	6.00	5.84	5.64
Disrupted price	85.00	77.23	67.02

[a] *Assumptions*:

Normal price	= $35.00/bbl
Normal quantity	= 7.00 mmb/day
Disrupted quantity	= 5.00 mmb/day
Normal supply elasticity	= 4.0
Disrupted supply elasticity	= 0.14
Long-run demand elasticity	= −0.5
Short-run demand elasticity	= −0.10

If private agents are completely myopic about the prospects for a disruption (zero probability), there is no adjustment in short-run demand and the price rises from $35 to $85 per barrel in the disruption. Consumption declines at the higher price and the quantity of imports falls from the normal level of 7 mmb/day to the disrupted level of 6 mmb/day. If the probability of a disruption is perceived to be larger than zero, the impact of a disruption is reduced. At a probability of 0.1, the expected price rises to $38.88 (or $4.24 above the actual normal market price) and normal imports fall to 6.7 mmb/day. The same disruption now raises the world price to $77.23, or $7.77 less than the myopic case, and imports fall to 5.84 mmb/day, a decline of 0.86 mmb/day. If the probability of a disruption is 0.3, the expected price is $43.99 (or $9.87 above the normal market price) and the disruption price rises to $67.02 (or $32.90 above the normal price). Notice that the expected price rises and the disruption price falls as the disruption probability increases, thereby reducing the impact of the price change on the private sector. The difference between the expected price and the disruption price is $50 per barrel when the private sector is completely myopic, but this difference falls to $23.03 if the probability is 0.3.

A comparison of the figures derived under the assumption of myopic expectations with those assuming some foresight shows the importance of private adjustments in an analysis of the relationship between the social and private costs of oil and in estimating the impact of a disruption on the economy. The effect of private adjustments on equilibrium prices is determined in this example by the assumed price elasticities of normal and disrupted supply. The reader is cautioned to remember that the size of the elasticities is not the only source of uncertainty in this analysis. A deeper question is whether supply behavior can be summarized with an elasticity at all.

Private Adjustments, the Demand Component, and the Optimal Tariff

Chapter 2 derived the demand component of the premium and the associated optimal tariff under the assumption of no disruption risks and a stable relationship between the quantity of U.S. oil imports and the world price. As indicated above, the size of the demand component declines when the private sector adjusts to disruption risks. This section reexamines the demand component in the light of private adjustments to disruption risks, first qualitatively, and then quantitatively using our linear simulation model of the oil market.

With the introduction of two possible states of supply, the demand component may be defined with respect to either a disruption or a normal period. For comparison with the demand component in chapter 2, this section focuses exclusively on the normal period where the premium is intended as a guide to import policy in normal supply periods. The demand component of the premium derived in chapter 2 is illustrated in figure 4-8 by the difference between the normal long-run supply of imports S_N and the landed cost of imported oil $S_N + t$. The difference between the two curves is the size of a tariff, which raises the domestic price by enough to equate the domestic price with the marginal social cost of imports; that is, $S_N + t$ is the marginal social cost of imports. In the absence of disruption risk, the optimum tariff raises the domestic price to P_t, and lowers the world price to P_w. The private sector adjusts to the tariff by moving from the position indicated by the short-run import demand curve given by SR_N to that given by SR_t.

The possibility of a supply disruption means that the world price will be higher than P_w for some future period and that the corresponding domestic price will be higher than P_t. These facts, integrated into decisions of private agents, imply that planning prices will exceed

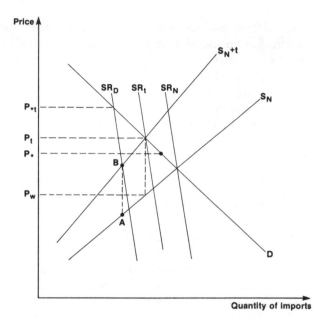

Figure 4-8. Effect of private adjustments to
disruption risks on the demand
component of the premium.

P_t and that short-run demand will shift to the left of SR_t. The original
tariff is now too large because any leftward shift in short-run demand
reduces the size of t by narrowing the distance between $S_N + t$ and
S_N.[16]

The tariff should not be fixed on the basis of SR_N but on the basis
of a short-run demand curve to the left of SR_N. This is true, as
demonstrated above, because private agents make investment decisions on the basis of an oil price that is higher than the normal
world price. Suppose that before the tariff is imposed, the market
planning price is P_*. This price now becomes the appropriate initial
position on which to determine the tariff that closes the gap between
the marginal cost of imports and the world price.[17]

---

[16] This assumes that the market price is an increasing function of net import
supply to the United States, and that the slope of this function is constant or
increasing in the level of imports. The alternative of a decreasing function is
regarded as implausible.

[17] P_* may be above P_t with no effect on the argument for a tariff. The higher
P_*, the smaller the optimum tariff.

The marginal rule for determining the optimum tariff in the presence of disruption risks requires, as before, an import tax that equates the landed price of oil to private individuals with the marginal cost of imports to the country, but a second condition is now required because of the difference between the market and the planning prices. Without disruption risks, there is no difference between the two, and short-run demand equals long-run demand at the landed price. With disruption risks, there is a risk element included in private decisions that drives a wedge between the landed price of oil and its true cost for long-term planning. This risk element means that investment decisions will be determined by a planning price while actual consumption will be determined by the landed price. The equilibrium condition must satisfy both short-term consumption and long-term investment conditions as reflected in short- and long-run demand curves. The short-run condition is satisfied when the landed price equals the marginal cost of imports and the long-run condition is satisfied when the short-run curve intersects the long-run curve at the planning price. The optimum tariff is that amount which satisfies both conditions.

The equilibrium condition with disruption risks is illustrated by the short-run demand denoted by SR_D in figure 4-8. The tariff is represented by the distance from point A to point B, which satisfies the requirement that the landed price of oil equal the marginal cost of imports to the country. At the same time, the tariff adjusts the planning price to $P*_t$ (equal to the landed price plus the disruption risk element) so that the correct short-run demand curve intersects the long-run demand curve at this price, satisfying the condition that the long-run marginal value of oil and planning price be equal. The planning price $P*_t$ must be interpreted cautiously at the market level because it is an aggregation of various individual planning prices and it possesses no inherent welfare significance.[18] It is, however, a useful construct to gain some understanding of how the demand component of the premium is affected by private adjustments to disruption risks. The same conclusions emerge from a more general treatment of planning prices in appendix B.

The equilibrium location of the short-run import demand curve is determined by the planning price $P*_t$ and long-run import demand D,

[18] Except in the unlikely special case where the planning price for each individual equals the expected value of current and future prices, so that the sum of individual short-run demand curves yields a market curve that intersects the long-run market demand curve at the expected price.

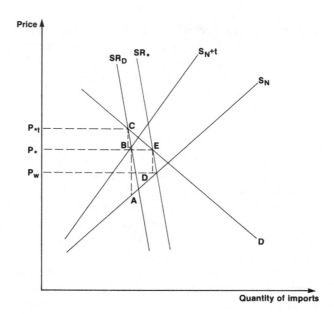

Figure 4-9.   Effect of a tariff on the expected cost of
oil imports.

while the quantity of imports is determined by the landed price and
short-run import demand (at point B). Notice that the tariff drives
down the normal world price (to point A) yet increases the expected
cost (to P_{*t}). The expected cost of imports rises because any downward movement in normal and disrupted prices caused by the tariff
is smaller than the size of the tariff.[19]

The tariff will alter private expectations about the price of oil in a
disruption and thereby alter the risk element that enters private
planning decisions. Although the disruption price declines, the risk
element in the planning price may rise or fall with a tariff. The effect
of a tariff on the risk element is demonstrated in figure 4-9, which
reproduces figure 4-8, with the focus on private planning prices before
and after the imposition of a tariff. Before a tariff is imposed, the
planning price (or expected cost) of imported oil is P_*. Assuming the
private sector adjusts completely to expectations about disruptions,
short-run import demand is given by SR_*. Short-run demand and

---

[19] Recall from chapter 2 that the world price could fall by more than the
tariff, or rise with the tariff, if normal supply is backward bending. These possibilities are avoided here by assuming that supply is upward sloping.

import supply determine the market price P_w and the volume of imports. The difference between P_* and P_w is the risk element associated with the probability of an increase in the price of oil in a disruption. This difference is also indicated in the figure by the distance from point D to point E.

A tariff (indicated by the vertical distance from point A to point B) causes short-run demand to shift to SR_D, consistent with the new expected cost of oil P_{*t}. The difference between the landed price (at point B) and expected cost (at price P_{*t}) is shown by the vertical distance from point B to point C. A comparison of the distance from B to C with the distance from D to E gives the effect of the tariff on the risk element incorporated in the expected cost of oil imports. Normally, one would expect the risk factor to decline with a tariff, because import demand is reduced, but the outcome is not entirely unambiguous. The risk of a disruption is determined by the difference between normal and disrupted prices, not just their absolute levels, and by their respective probabilities. A tariff may reduce both normal and disrupted prices, but may not narrow the price spread. The price spread will narrow if the tariff-induced shift in import demand measured at the disrupted price is equal to or greater than the shift measured at the normal price, and if disrupted supply is less price elastic than normal supply. Both conditions are likely to hold, but are still unknown. In addition, the probability of a disruption may decline with a tariff, if one accepts the thesis that the probability is positively related to the volume of imports. This thesis, however, is questioned in chapter 5, where it is recalled (from chapter 2) that a tariff may provide the impetus for a supply disruption.

It is of interest to provide quantitative measures of the relationships described in this section, using the linear simulation model of the oil market described in appendix A. The results are presented in table 4-2, along with initial conditions and parameters.[20] The first column gives the results of the model when the probability of a disruption is zero. The results are equivalent to those examined in chapter 2, where the calculated demand component (tariff) is $7.88 with the assumptions listed. Increasing the probability of a disruption reduces import demand, as reflected in the table by the reduction in the quantity of imports in both normal and disrupted states, and by

---

[20] Because the assumptions are identical to those examined earlier in table 4-1, the two tables may be compared to show the effect of a tariff on private adjustments.

Table 4-2. Effect of Private Adjustments to Disruption Risks on the Demand
Component of the Premium Using Various Disruption Risks[a]

	Probability of a disruption		
	0.0	0.1	0.3
Optimum tariff	7.88	7.67	7.40
Normal quantity	6.30	6.14	5.92
Normal price	32.00	31.60	31.04
Expected price	42.00	44.11	47.02
Disrupted quantity	5.72	5.64	5.52
Disrupted price	71.00	66.77	60.96

[a] *Assumptions:*

Normal price	= $35.00/bbl
Normal quantity	= 7.00 mmb/day
Disrupted quantity	= 5.00 mmb/day
Normal supply elasticity	= 4.0
Disrupted supply elasticity	= 0.14
Long-run demand elasticity	= −0.5
Short-run demand elasticity	= −0.10

the increase in the expected price of oil. The optimum tariff therefore declines with an increase in the probability of a disruption.[21]

The combined effect of a tariff and private adjustments is illustrated by comparing table 4-2 with table 4-1. With complete myopia and no tariff (in table 4-1), the disrupted price increases to $85; with private adjustments and a tariff (in table 4-2), the disrupted price rises to less than $61 when the probability of a disruption is perceived to be as high as 0.3.

The Efficiency of Private Expectations

The analytical importance of private adjustments to disruption risks is by now clear, but two questions of practical importance remain: can the private market anticipate the price of oil in a disruption and, if not, can government intervention correct for deficiencies in private expectations by adjusting the price of oil? The answer to the first question is unknown but, we believe, the burden of proof falls on the skeptic. The answer to the second question, we will argue, is no.

---

[21] The modest reduction in the optimum tariff must be interpreted with caution, because it is the result of a modest shift in the short-run demand curve, as indicated by the minor changes in expected quantities.

The economics literature is divided on the possibility that the private sector will undertake optimal preparations for a disruption using complete information about the probability distribution of future prices. The rational expectations approach to market analysis assumes that the market will work efficiently toward an optimal equilibrium.[22] Important negative results on market efficiency in the presence of uncertainty are given by Radner (1968), Stigum (1969), and Svensson (1976). One particularly troublesome result from their work is that markets are not likely to work efficiently in the presence of speculative behavior; that is, when investment decisions are based on expected appreciation in the market value of the investment (that is, speculation in oil inventories).[23]

The same kinds of investment decisions are pertinent to the discussion in this chapter. In particular, it seems implausible to believe that the information requirements necessary for efficiency can be fulfilled. To be optimal, investments in energy-associated capital stocks made prior to a disruption must be based on prices that will prevail in a disruption and on the probabilities that they will occur. However, the investment decision, once made, will affect future prices and probabilities. The problem is that individuals making decisions at one point cannot observe directly each possible future state of the world nor can they make binding contracts at a different set of prices that are contingent on future states.[24]

Future oil prices are uncertain because the characteristics of future oil supply are uncertain and because the market outcome conditional upon the state of supply is uncertain. The combination of both uncertainties makes it difficult to define an efficient market outcome and undermines confidence in hypotheses that private markets will under-

[22] See Lucas and Sargent (1981), and the references cited therein.

[23] See Burness, Cummings, and Quirk (undated), and Stiglitz (1974). Blanchard and Watson (1982) present interesting remarks on the possibility of price "bubbles," where speculation is based on self-fulfilling expectations that generate a price increase far greater than justified by underlying market conditions.

[24] Arrow (1964) demonstrates that market efficiency is assured if it is possible to make trades contingent on both the state of the world and the date. Arrow argues that a securities market in which it is possible to buy a security whose value depends on the state of the world also supports an efficient allocation, but Nagatani (1975) demonstrates convincingly that remaining uncertainty about spot commodity prices makes Arrow's definition of optimality in a securities market questionable. Nagatani bases his argument on the distinction between uncertainty about prices and uncertainty about states of the world, as introduced by Radner (1968).

take optimal preparations for a disruption. On the other hand, it is not clear that the concept of "correct" expectations is meaningful. Individual expectations will be diverse, to be sure, because they are based on different information and because they refer to unique events with no exact historical parallel. But this is not to say that they are wrong, individually or collectively, as they become embodied in market performance.

The justification of government action intended to "correct" private anticipations requires an argument that private expectations are systematically biased toward excessive optimism or pessimism, and that government expectations are less biased. Private expectations may be biased for several reasons, including attitudes toward risk, regulatory or institutional constraints that distort private incentives, and incomplete or unevenly distributed information. Whether these arguments are sufficiently strong to warrant governmental action is a matter that should be investigated before action is taken. Furthermore, the requirement that government expectations be less biased than private expectations should create some skepticism about the rationale for intervention. The next chapter returns to this topic. It explores potential reasons for government intervention to enhance preparations for a disruption, and the implications of alternative policy instruments.

If it is believed that private expectations about disruptions are too sanguine, there remains the practical question of what the government can do about them. Based on the analysis in this chapter, we would argue that the government cannot alter private expectations by adjusting the price of imported oil without the danger of a serious loss of efficiency in the domestic economy.

Suppose, to be specific, the government imposes a tariff on imports to raise the price at which private agents make current investment decisions. Although the tariff may be successful in raising the expected cost of oil, and will reduce the quantity of imports today and in the future, it also distorts private incentives in three distinct ways that could reduce efficiency. First, the tariff will force unnecessary reductions in the use of oil in normal periods when it is cheap, so that capital stocks will be underutilized even if they are optimal with respect to the "correct" expected price of oil. Second, the tariff will not encourage, and may discourage, investments that address the potential variation between current and future oil prices by enhancing substitution flexibility for oil when a price shock occurs. Third, a tariff adjusts all private agents in the same direction regardless of their initial expectations about future prices and the considerations on which investment decisions are based. For a variety of reasons, individuals will value oil differently, will evaluate precautionary (and speculative) investments differently, and will assess future risks differently. The "correct" price is unique to the individual private agent and a single price cannot be correct for all individuals. A tariff will therefore force some individuals to reduce consumption (or increase oil production) more and others less than necessary. Though the deviations from the average may be offsetting in terms of the quantity of aggregate consumption and imports, they are cumulative in terms of losses in efficiency. These distortions caused by a tariff will arise again in the next chapter.

Conclusions

This chapter has demonstrated that private agents may be expected to respond to the risks of a disruption by taking actions that will improve their welfare should a disruption occur. At the market level, these adjustments tend to reduce the quantity of imports, the prospective price of oil in a disruption, and the impact of a price shock on the economy.

They also affect the oil import premium, first, by reducing the demand component from whatever level is judged appropriate in the absence of disruption risk and, second, by reducing the potential role of the government in preparing the economy for a disruption. Private behavior will be affected by government intervention, indicating that the rationale for government actions must be evaluated jointly with the expected results.

The thesis of this chapter is that the presence of disruption risks does not alone justify government intervention. The rationale for such action must be based on some deficiency in private preparations. The next chapter explores a number of possibilities and focuses on their relationship to the oil import premium and import policy. The interaction between the public and private sectors described here provides the mechanism for evaluating the combined effect of policies designed to lower world oil prices and reduce the cost of supply disruptions.

5

Disruption Costs and the Premium

Disruption costs that are anticipated and adjusted to by private agents, as described in chapter 4, do not constitute an argument for an oil import premium. Government intervention cannot improve on the efficiency with which the private sector responds to these incentives. On the other hand, it may be argued that the private sector does not fully anticipate all disruption costs, that the prospects for a disruption are systematically underestimated, or that the incentives to prepare for a disruption are somehow distorted and work against the appropriate actions. If any of these arguments is correct, there is a rationale for intervention and possibly, though not necessarily, an additional element that should be included in the import premium. The import premium is affected if the market distortion is related to the quantity of imports and if a reduction in imports in normal (predisruption) periods will remedy the distortion.

Our objectives in this chapter are as follows. First, we explore the arguments for intervention to determine which arguments provide reasons for including additional elements in the import premium. Second, we address the question of whether a tariff is an appropriate instrument to correct the market distortion in each case. Third, we determine how these arguments for intervention, to the extent they are valid, combine with the demand component and private adjustments to jointly determine the optimal level of oil imports. The final section presents results from our oil market model to illustrate how the demand and disruption components interact.

Rationales for Intervention

A supply disruption imposes three kinds of costs on the economy: (1) a reduction in income because of wealth transferred abroad; (2) a reduction in domestic output and consumer welfare because less oil is consumed; and (3) further losses in national income because nonoil markets cannot adjust efficiently to an oil price shock. The first two categories of costs are borne directly by private agents and may be anticipated as described in chapter 4. If the private market underestimates the probability that these costs will occur, or if the private sector does not act on its expectations, there is a potential rationale for government intervention. Another rationale is provided by the demand component during a disruption (analogous to the demand component in normal supply conditions), because the disruption price increases with the level of oil imports. The fourth rationale centers on category (3) above, termed the "indirect macroeconomic costs" of a disruption. Each argument is discussed in turn.

Underestimating the Prospects for a Disruption

It is sometimes argued that private agents have less complete or less accurate information about the prospects for a disruption than the government, and that government action is therefore required to make up for deficiencies in private planning. This argument may be true, but we are unable to cite convincing evidence or logic to support the claim. Although it is costly to gather information, and the government can take advantage of potential economies of scale in producing information, it does not follow that the government will (or should) be any less sanguine about disruptions than the private sector.

However, a case can be made on other grounds that the private sector will systematically undervalue the role of increased imports in the expected cost of disruptions. This argument is based on the spillover effect that individual actions have on security of supply, and is analogous to the effect of import demand on the world price. Even if individual private agents exhibit no systematic bias in their beliefs about the probability of a disruption, market outcomes will not fully account for the effect that U.S. import levels have on the probability and size of disruptions. The collective effect of import demand on security of supply is a social cost that is not taken into account in individual import decisions. As a consequence, the argument goes, imports will be larger than socially desirable because the full risk of disruptions is not integrated into planning decisions.

There are three main elements in the relationship between the volume of imports and the likelihood of disruptions. One is that larger imports make the United States a better target for a strategic disruption decision, because such decisions are thought to be influenced by the harm they would inflict. The second element is that the greater part of increases in imports is thought to come from insecure sources (e.g., Persian Gulf), thus increasing the proportion of insecure oil in world trade.

The second element of the argument is particularly important because it accounts for the probability of disruptions caused by internal strife, internecine conflicts, and other regional tensions, and because it embodies the notion that the potential size of a disruption is related to the amount of insecure oil imported. The argument hinges on the assumption that changes in import demand will be absorbed for the most part by producers in unstable countries (e.g., those in the Persian Gulf). During 1981 and 1982, Saudi Arabia did seem to operate as the residual supplier, aided at times by smaller producing states. When changes in oil demand threatened to increase or decrease official prices by more than desired, Saudi Arabia altered production rates to stabilize the market. Thus, with slack demand in 1982, Saudi production declined below 6 million barrels per day and its share of total supply was substantially less important than in earlier years when production exceeded 11 million barrels per day.

Saudi Arabia could tolerate large fluctuations in production rates because marginal costs of production are low and its financial resources are large. Nevertheless, long-run reductions in import demand cannot be absorbed without limit by Persian Gulf countries with lower production costs. If, as in recent years, these countries attempt to maintain the world price by reducing output, they will leave an increasing share of the market to higher cost, non-OPEC producers. High marginal cost producers, in contrast, require rising world prices to expand production and will be more sensitive to changes in price incentives. If Persian Gulf countries fail to maintain the world price by reducing production in line with demand, the proportion of secure supplies may fall. In this event, limitations on imports, by depressing price incentives, may actually contribute to overall insecurity (Blankenship and coauthors, 1980).

The third element in the relation between import levels and insecurity concerns the amount of excess capacity in the world market and the ability of the market to absorb a disruption without a large price increase. A reduction in import demand may indeed create excess capacity, but the benefits in terms of reducing the probability and severity of a disruption are likely to be transitory. A permanent reduction in demand is likely to be matched in time with a reduction of operating capacity because of the cost of maintaining excess facilities. Moreover, there is no guarantee that the excess capacity would not occur in precisely those countries most susceptible to a disruption.

Another point stressed in chapter 2 is the potential for retaliation following a decision to restrict imports. Tensions in the oil market could increase rather than ease as a result of intervention. The conclusion reached in chapter 2 is pertinent here: while increased imports may impose a cost on society in the form of greater insecurity, actions to reduce imports may increase rather than reduce those costs, depending on the behavior of OPEC members.

These considerations suggest that the relationship between import levels and the prospects for a disruption is ambiguous. A reduction in imports may make disruption more or less likely. A definite case may emerge as understanding of the dynamics of supplier behavior improves, but in the meantime, we tentatively suggest that this factor does not contribute to the premium.

Failure to Respond to Expectations

While private agents may foresee a disruption, and may understand the potential advantages of acting on their expectations, other considerations may remove or otherwise distort the incentives to act. The main culprit is usually identified as the government, because existing or expected regulations interfere with incentives. For example, regulations that allocate available oil supplies during a disruption destroy incentives to prepare for a shortage by usurping the benefits of such actions and distributing them to individuals whose lack of initiative has left them with shortages. It is important to keep in mind the fact that the distortion need not be related to an explicit set of regulations, but can be produced by expectations about institutional behavior in a crisis. The fact that allocation regulations were implemented in previous supply disturbances adds force to these expectations. Government announcements that there will be no allocations in a crisis carry little weight if the political system and institutional behavior are molded to the contrary.

If the private market is prevented from acting optimally because of expected intervention, it may seem more appropriate for the government to seek ways of removing perverse expectations rather than new ways of intervening in the market. On the other hand, this may be an overly simplistic attitude because of the multiple and sometimes inconsistent objectives of government policy. In particular, the need to balance equity and efficiency considerations may result in seemingly inconsistent policies to motivate the private sector yet moderate over-all distributional results.

Such considerations are difficult to evaluate when it comes to as-signing a specific value to the oil import premium. Distortions created by government policy are likely to be highly specific and uneven in their significance, while an import premium implies a uniform cor-rection across all sources and uses of oil that may be inappropriate in specific cases. There is also the question of what an associated premium means for government policy. A tariff on oil imports, for example, will not correct the source of the distortion, although it may reduce its significance by reducing the cost of a disruption. An oil stockpile, in comparison, will achieve the same benefit more directly by reducing the impact of a disruption and the significance of market errors in evaluating or responding to disruption risks.

Marginal Cost of Oil During a Disruption

The argument that the marginal social cost of imported oil exceeds the price is as valid during a disruption as during a normal supply period, and is subject to similar uncertainties about supply behavior. The arguments given in chapter 2 need not be repeated here. It may be argued further that the discrepancy between marginal cost and price is larger during a disruption than during normal supply condi-tions because the disrupted price will be higher than the normal price, and because disrupted supply will be less price elastic. If this is cor-rect, the premium attached to imports in a disruption will be larger than that on normal imports.

To illustrate the argument, figure 5-1 shows disrupted supply S_D to the left of and steeper than normal supply S_N, reflecting the idea that for any level of imports the disrupted price is higher than the normal price, and the slope of the supply curve is steeper. With short-run demand given by S_R, marginal cost and the domestic price would be equated with tariff t_N in normal periods and tariff t_D in disrupted periods. The required tariff is larger during a disruption and the dis-ruption tariff is more effective in reducing the world price. The cross-hatched areas show the potential wealth transfers which the tariff retains in the United States at the expense of oil-exporting countries.

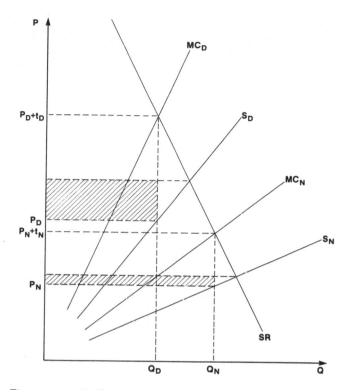

Figure 5-1. Difference between marginal cost and price with normal and disrupted supply curves.

The perception that import supply conditions during a disruption will be such that a tariff will be highly effective in reducing the world price (or, more appropriately, in moderating the increase in the world price during a disruption) is the basis for recommending a "disruption tariff." Such a tariff would reduce the impact of a disruption by reducing the wealth transfer to oil-exporting countries. Balanced against this gain is the potential cost a disruption tariff might create by further increasing the domestic price of oil. As argued in the next section, the jump in the world price in a disruption causes dislocations throughout the economy that reduce domestic income, quite apart from the effect of the wealth transfer. A disruption tariff may reduce the wealth transfer but, by increasing the domestic price, also exacerbate the macroeconomic dislocations. Consequently, there is a trade-off that makes the disruption tariff a questionable policy option.[1]

[1] This conclusion is supported by estimates given in Gilbert and Mork (1981) and Fry and Hubbard (1981).

Because of the undesirable side effects of a disruption tariff, the question arises whether a tariff implemented in normal periods can be designed to satisfy the combined objective of reducing the normal world price and the wealth transfer during a disruption. In broader terms, the question is whether the premium on oil imports in normal periods should be increased to account for wealth transfers during a disruption. Our analysis in the following sections points up an important distinction between the premium and the tariff: we conclude that the wealth transfer in a disruption should not be included in the design of a long-run tariff policy, and that a nontariff policy instrument is required to address the wealth transfer problem. This is where the strategic petroleum reserve comes into the picture. In analyzing the premium and in designing import policy, it is important to distinguish between the two primary reasons for a divergence between private and social costs in a disruption—that associated with the wealth transfer and that associated with the macroeconomic dislocation—and how a tariff may be expected to work in addressing these problems. The effect of a tariff on private investment decisions, discussed in chapter 4, will play an important role in this analysis. Before going into the arguments, it is necessary to describe the macroeconomic dislocations and how they arise.

Indirect Macroeconomic Costs of a Disruption

The fourth source of a discrepancy between social and private costs of a disruption is the macroeconomic dislocations that accompany an oil price shock. The potential losses in income and output that result are in addition to the losses associated with the wealth transfer abroad and those associated with reduced oil consumption during a disruption. The latter two kinds of economic costs are in principle already incorporated into private costs, and the private sector will (to some degree) act to reduce them. The macroeconomic costs referred to in this section, because they arise from disequilibrium market conditions, are by their very nature external to the process by which the private sector anticipates and adjusts to market signals. The costs occur because nonoil markets do not always immediately and completely adjust to a sudden jump in the price of oil. When markets do not clear, there are shortages and surpluses that compound each other when traced throughout the economy, and that tend to reduce efficiency in the use of all resources. Aggregate productivity declines and is accompanied by reductions in employment and output.

The dislocations are caused by changes that occur on both the supply and demand sides of the economy. The supply side is by far the most important because the causes of the problem are less amenable to correction and because demand-side changes largely affect aggregate production. We thus start with, and put more emphasis on, the supply-side dislocations.

The failure of nominal wage rates to decline in response to an oil price increase is usually regarded as the heart of the supply-side adjustment problem.[2] A sudden increase in the price of oil will be followed by a sudden reduction in the demand for labor because labor is used in combination with oil in producing goods and services, and a reduction in the use of oil lowers the marginal productivity of labor. The reduction in labor productivity is equivalent to a reduction in the demand for labor services. If nominal wages are insensitive to a decline in demand for labor services, firms must trim their wage costs by reducing the level of employment. The reduction in employment implies a reduction in output in addition to that directly caused by an increase in the price of oil: it is caused by a rigidity in the nominal wage rate.

A reduction in nominal wages (and in other resource prices) could offset the increase in the oil price and help stabilize average production costs. In an ideal world, characterized by perfectly flexible wages and prices, average production costs need not rise with the oil price. Similarly, an oil price shock need not cause inflation if input costs adjust and if final product prices reflect both production costs and shifts in demand. If prices and wages are rigid, some markets will experience excess supplies and others excess demands, preventing resources from flowing to their most efficient uses. The end result is likely to be an inflationary process rather than a one-time adjustment to the higher relative price of oil. A corollary is that real wages will fall.

The decline in real wages will moderate the need for involuntary unemployment, but less efficiently than adjustments in nominal wages. The reason is simple. Nominal wage adjustments can be made differentially by sector in order to ensure an equality between wages and labor productivity in that sector. Real wage adjustments, in contrast, occur across all sectors by the same inflationary factor and do not allow real wages to align with differential values of marginal productivity. Consequently, a decline in real wages still implies that the

[2] For example, refer to Hall and Pindyck (1981), and Gilbert and Mork (1981).

economy will not operate efficiently, and total employment and output will fall below potential levels.

Rigidities may be expected to show up in commodity markets as well. Traditional supplier-buyer relationships will be disrupted as shortages develop among some commodities and excess supplies develop for others. Firms with excess supplies must look for new markets, which in some cases may mean previously unexplored regions and new uses. Imperfect information about alternative possibilities (another form of market imperfection) slows the reallocation of resources among these uses. Inventory building may be expected to occur in some cases before a reduction in output or prices. Firms experiencing excess demands may be reluctant to adjust their prices immediately because of uncertainties about marketing potential, including fears of upsetting traditional markets. Thus, inventories may be drawn down or delivery time increased before a market-clearing price is established. Consequently, throughout the economy, prices will not immediately adjust to reflect excess supplies and demands, and the cost of adjustments will not be immediately internalized in private decisions.

In addition to these direct supply-side effects, an oil price shock can change the level and composition of aggregate demand.[3] Aggregate demand can decline temporarily because of a lag between receipts and expenditures when income is redistributed. Income will shift from domestic oil consumers to foreign oil producers and, to the extent domestic supply prices are allowed to rise in a disruption, to domestic oil producers. Also, because of various taxes, income will shift from consumers to the government. A time lag between the receipt of new income and subsequent expenditures would cause a temporary leakage from the income stream and could depress output and employment.

The leakage may be quite short for transfers to the government and perhaps even for domestic oil producers, but could be quite lengthy for the extra income flowing to foreign producers. The problem can be corrected easily in principle, simply by altering the timing of federal government receipts and expenditures to offset the temporary reduction in domestic and foreign demand. Tax receipts could be temporarily deferred, or expenditures temporarily increased, to be made up later when respending of oil revenues begins. Although it is easy in principle, altering government receipts and expenditures is some-

---

[3] See Horwich (1981).

times difficult in practice. Nevertheless, the problem is amenable to conventional monetary and fiscal stabilization policies, unlike the other market adjustment problems described in this section.

Changes in the distribution of income also lead to changes in the composition of aggregate demand. Foreigners will spend their additional oil earnings on a different array of goods than domestic oil consumers who have lost income, as will domestic oil producers and possibly even the government. At the same time, changes in relative commodity prices throughout the economy will cause domestic consumers to alter the composition of their purchases. Energy-intensive products, for example, will be among the products with the most rapid increases in relative commodity prices and possibly the most important reductions in consumption.

Changes in the level and composition of aggregate demand will exacerbate the supply-side problems described earlier because they will require a reallocation of resources from one use to another. The reallocations cannot be performed efficiently unless resource prices alter quickly and in line with market-clearing requirements. With wage and price rigidities, the necessary adjustments will not occur and the shifts in demand will cause additional losses in total production and employment. Notice that the cause of the problem in this case is on the demand side of the economy, although the loss of income results from dislocations in production.

To summarize, prices and wages will not respond immediately to an oil price shock by reallocating resources. Markets will be in temporary disequilibrium as excess supplies and demands develop and the economy will be operating less efficiently as a result. Bottlenecks will occur in some markets and excess capacity will develop in others. Total employment will fall, while employed resources will be used less efficiently. All of this amounts to a reduction in potential output because of a supply disruption, and the reduction is in addition to that directly related to the consumption of imported oil. Moreover, the losses in output cannot be averted by using monetary and fiscal stabilization policies, except insofar as the level of aggregate demand is reconstituted to avoid leakage from the income stream.[4]

How do these costs relate to the oil import premium? In the strictest sense they do not because they are caused by inefficiencies in nonoil markets, not by the oil price. The best corrective approach

[4] The change in the relative price of oil and the necessity for changes in wages and nonoil prices cannot be avoided through the use of monetary and fiscal policy.

(i.e., one that gets at the source of the problem) would require policies that enable markets to work better. Unfortunately, there are no promising policy options that will directly enhance wage and price flexibility. At the next level, adjustments to higher oil prices could be facilitated by actions which alter the returns to other factors of production, but it is difficult to come up with a plausible option other than a reduction in payroll taxes. It is not realistic to count on payroll tax adjustments because it is unlikely that the changes could be implemented as rapidly as required after a disruption occurs, nor targeted in a way to deal effectively with the situation in different sectors of the economy.

The lack of feasible options forces one to turn attention from the source of the problem, market rigidities, to its stimulus, oil prices. This is where the premium comes into the picture, but not in a direct and unambiguous way because the costs do not depend only on the quantity of oil imports. Of the factors that generate market dislocations, only the distributional effects produced by the transfer of income to foreigners are directly related to the quantity of oil imports. These indirect costs of course increase the desirability of reducing wealth transfers during a disruption. Domestic income transfers, and inefficiencies caused by rigid wages and prices, are related to the level of total domestic oil consumption, not to the quantity of imports. The losses in output and employment would occur whether the United States were a net oil importer or exporter. They are related to the quantity of imports only to the extent that total consumption depends on imports.

The distinction between consumption and imports is important for measuring the premium and for using the premium to recommend policy. Although the macroeconomic costs involved imply a divergence between social and private costs, this divergence is a function of the quantity of imports only when changes in imports equal changes in total consumption. The level of domestic consumption, rather than the level of domestic oil production, should be the focus of policies aimed at minimizing the dislocations in nonoil markets. For example, an increase in domestic oil supply that replaces imports and leaves total consumption unchanged will not reduce macroeconomic costs of a disruption except for those determined by the size of the wealth transfer abroad. Policies that reduce the importance of oil in the economy, or promote flexibility in substituting away from oil in a crisis, will be more effective in controlling macroeconomic costs than policies that focus on long-run supply enhancement.

Disruption Costs and Tariff Policy

There are two robust reasons for government intervention to reduce the costs of an oil supply disruption: limiting wealth transfers abroad and reducing dislocations in nonoil markets. This section explores the advantages and disadvantages of using an oil import tariff as a way of reducing both kinds of costs. The policy issue is one of balancing tradeoffs because the two objectives are sometimes in conflict. A disruption tariff is the best way to reduce the wealth transfer, but it will exacerbate the macroeconomic dislocations; a tariff in normal periods will reduce oil dependence and dislocations in a disruption, but will not correctly balance savings in wealth transfers abroad with the cost of reducing imports. This conflict in objectives suggests that more than one policy instrument is required, and leads us to consider the complementary relationship between a tariff and the strategic petroleum reserve. Before doing that, however, it is necessary to examine in closer detail what may and may not be accomplished with a tariff.

Integrating Disruption Costs and the Demand Component

To get at the essence of the tradeoff between macroeconomic dislocations and the wealth transfer, we introduce a simple three-period dynamic optimization model of the economy.[5] In the first period, private agents make investment decisions that determine the capital stock and the short-run demand for oil in the last two periods. Investment decisions will be determined by the prices of oil in the second and third periods which, in turn, depend on normal or disrupted supply conditions and the size of the import tariff. To assure proper sequencing of the dynamic process, we assume that normal supply conditions prevail in the second period and that a disruption occurs in the third period with probability π.[6] The government will set the import tariff in the last two periods at levels that will maximize national income, and is presumed to announce the tariffs in the first period in order to assure that the optimal capital stock is put in place before consumption begins. This assumption enables us to focus on the effect of a tariff on private investment decisions. We also assume, for the moment, that the country has no domestic production of oil

[5] Appendix B describes the model in detail.

[6] This simplification enables us to avoid following other branches of a decision tree, and does not affect the conclusions.

so that measures of oil consumption are equivalent to measures of oil imports. The importance of this assumption for import policy will be explored in the next section.

To focus on the variables of interest, we suppose that total domestic output is a function of the capital stock and the quantity of oil consumed (or imported). Potential output in a normal period is given by $F(K,Q_N)$, where K is the capital stock and Q_N is normal oil consumption, and potential output in a disruption is given by $F(K,Q_D)$, where the quantity of oil consumption changes to Q_D. The objective of society is to maximize expected net national income over normal and disrupted supply periods, where expected net national income is equal to expected potential output less payments for oil and capital and any macroeconomic dislocations caused by a change in the price of oil. Payments for oil and capital reduce income to other factors of production, and macroeconomic dislocations reduce actual production below potential production.

With oil consumption equal to oil imports, the social cost of imports is measured by the wealth transfer abroad (i.e., price times quantity) and the macroeconomic dislocations. The relationship between oil imports and dislocation costs may be expressed in several plausible ways, and different specifications can alter optimal import policy in the presence of domestic oil production. For the moment we express dislocation costs by $M = M(Q_N,Q_D)$, which is some function of oil consumption, and return to this question in the next section.

In the first period of our decision process, when the tariff policy is announced and private investments are made, it is known that the probability of a disruption in the second period is zero and in the third period is π. The capital stock chosen is that which equates the expected value of the marginal product of capital (over all future periods) with the two-period rental price of capital. This capital stock is optimal if optimal oil consumption decisions are made in periods two and three.

Of interest is how the optimal oil consumption decisions are made in the normal second period and the disrupted third period. In a normal period, the difference between current benefits and costs of oil consumption is given by $F(K,Q_N) - P_N Q_N$; while the possibility of future macroeconomic costs has a present value of $\pi M(Q_D,Q_N)$, where Q_D is the quantity of imports in the next period if there is a disruption.

Thus, the first-order condition for optimal oil consumption in the second (normal) period is[7]

$$F_2(K,Q_N) = P_N + P'_N Q_N + \pi M_1(Q_N,Q_D)$$

If a disruption fails to occur in the third period (and in subsequent periods), a similar decision on oil consumption will be made.

If there is a disruption in the third period, the net benefits of oil consumption are given by

$$F(K,Q_D) - P_D Q_D - M(Q_N,Q_D)$$

The first-order condition for optimal oil consumption is then

$$F_2(K,Q_D) = P_D + P'_D Q_D + M_2(Q_N,Q_D)$$

The term $M_2(Q_N,Q_D)$ is the increase in macroeconomic cost that results from a decrease in consumption. To avoid this cost, the country should be willing to buy oil at a price that exceeds the disrupted market price. The marginal value of oil, in other words, is equal to the sum $F_2(K,Q_D) + M_2(Q_N,Q_D)$. The condition for optimal imports in a disruption therefore states that the marginal value of oil in consumption must be set equal to the marginal social cost of imports given by $P_D + P'_D Q_D$.

Unless a tariff is imposed on oil imports, private agents will base their consumption decisions on the private value of oil and the market price, not on the marginal social value of oil and the marginal cost of imports. Accordingly, the tariff in a normal period should be set at

$$t_N = P'_N Q_N + \pi M_1 \tag{5-1}$$

and the tariff in a disruption should be set at

$$t_D = P'_D Q_D + M_2 \tag{5-2}$$

[7] Numbered subscripts refer to partial derivatives with respect to the order of variable in parentheses and the prime denotes the derivative of price with respect to quantity. Details are given in appendix B.

In both expressions the first term is the demand component of the premium, which measures the reduction in the wealth transfer abroad by imposing a tariff.[8] This term is positive if the supply curve is upward sloping.[9] The second term measures the change in dislocation costs as a result of a change in oil consumption in each supply state. This term will be positive in a normal period because the effect of a disruption on macroeconomic costs increases with the importance of oil in the economy; it will be negative in a disruption because dislocation costs decline as oil consumption increases in a disruption.

A number of preliminary observations can be made so far. First, it is clear that the same tariff will not in general be optimal in both normal and disrupted supply states. The tariff will differ because of conditions that govern the wealth transfer and the macroeconomic dislocations. Second, the addition of disruption costs increases the appropriate tariff above the demand component argument in normal periods, and reduces the appropriate tariff in a disruption. The addition of macro costs, in effect, shifts a portion of a disruption tariff into normal periods, but the increase in normal periods is smaller than the decrease in disruptions because macro costs are discounted by the probability of a disruption in the first case and not in the second. Third, it is not necessarily true that a zero tariff is optimal during a disruption because the magnitude of the tariff depends on the tradeoff between the wealth transfer and dislocation costs. The dislocations could in fact be so important that a subsidy on imports is warranted in a disruption, or they could be so unimportant that a large tariff is warranted. Unfortunately, too little is known about the problem to be able to make a more definitive conclusion.

The final observation concerns the effect of the tariff on the initial capital stock decision. The optimal tariffs in each supply state are presumed to be announced in advance to ensure that the private sector receives the correct price signals on which to make investment decisions. Any choice of tariffs will of course raise the expected cost of oil and make the private sector more conservation minded. The primary issue in this regard, as emphasized in chapter 4, is the effect of tariff policy on choices among investment options that are more flexible in the use of oil as the price increases. We concluded earlier

---

[8] More precisely, the term measures the savings in wealth transfers net of deadweight losses in the domestic economy. See chapter 2 for a discussion of these terms.

[9] It could be negative if, for example, supply is backward bending, as noted in chapter 2.

that the wider the spread between normal and disrupted prices, the greater the incentive to invest in flexibility.

A tariff that remains fixed over both normal and disrupted supply periods may be expected to narrow the range of price uncertainty.[10] A fixed tariff may be expected, therefore, to bias private investments toward less flexibility and reduce the ability to respond to an increase in the price of oil. This consideration adds force to the argument that tariffs should be different in normal and disrupted periods. In particular, it is incorrect to calculate a single tariff on the basis of the weighted average of social costs in a disruption and in a normal period.[11]

The Specification of Dislocation Costs

A significant assumption underlying the foregoing model is that the country produces no oil from domestic sources. This assumption is important to the specification of dislocation costs because if there is domestic production, a distinction must be made between oil consumption and oil imports. This distinction can affect the design of oil import policy, depending on the relationship among oil consumption, imports, and dislocation costs. We have explored a number of alternative plausible specifications of dislocation costs and find that the most important implication of domestic production for import policy depends on whether dislocation costs are proportional to the level of oil consumption in the economy.

To demonstrate this conclusion, we start with the simplest and most straightforward specification of macroeconomic dislocations:

$$M = M(Q_N - Q_D) \tag{5-3}$$

which states that dislocations are a function of the difference between normal and disrupted oil consumption. The derivatives appearing in equations (5-1) and (5-2) above become

$$M_1 = -M_2 = M' \tag{5-4}$$

[10] This will occur if a tariff reduces the risk element in planning prices, as discussed in chapter 4.

[11] This error is implicit in studies that recommend tariffs on the basis of the sum of social costs in normal and disrupted periods, and is very common in the literature, as noted in the survey by Broadman (1981). See Kline (1981) for an explicit example.

The demand component in a disruption is reduced by the change in macroeconomic costs while the demand component in a normal period is increased by the same term deflated by the probability of a disruption. Note that the average price received by domestic oil producers over both periods is unaffected by macroeconomic costs because the increase in the price of oil received in normal periods is equal to the reduction in the expected price received in a disruption. Thus, the modification of the tariff for macro costs does not alter long-run production incentives, and this result follows from specification (5-3) where macro costs do not depend on the level of domestic production.

Short-run increases in domestic production in a disruption can reduce macro costs, however, as indicated by equation (5-4). If short-run supply will respond to price changes, it follows that macro costs can be further reduced by widening, rather than narrowing, the price spread received by producers. If, on the other hand, short-run flexibility is not significant, there is no practical reason to differentiate between short-run and long-run price incentives to domestic production.[12]

To promote flexibility in energy supply, and to provide sufficient conservation incentives to consumers, the tax on consumption should differ from the return to producers. Specifically, equations (5-1) and (5-2) now apply to oil consumption, while only the terms measuring the demand component should apply to oil production. Deleting the disruption component means that producers should receive a smaller price increase in normal periods and a larger price increase in a disruption, compared with the prices paid by consumers. Note that the effect of this change reduces gains to producers in normal periods, but enhances the incentive to increase supplies in a disruption by widening the price spread. The incentive will act to increase output in a disruption by shifting normal production into the future, by increasing inventories of crude oil, and by encouraging investments in short-term production flexibility.

While theoretically pleasing, serious practical problems arise with attempts to distinguish between producer and consumer prices. Achieving the correct result requires a high degree of administrative flexibility and discretion. For example, import tariffs calculated by equations (5-1) and (5-2) would raise consumer prices to the full amount, while a supplementary excise tax on sales of domestic crude

---

[12] The National Petroleum Council (1980) indicates that short-run surge production capacity is insignificant in the United States.

oil in normal periods and a supplementary subsidy on domestic oil in a disruption are required to adjust the return to producers.[13] The excise tax would equal the disruption component deflated by the probability of a disruption, while the subsidy would equal the full amount of the disruption component. The combination of a variable tariff with a sometime excise tax and sometime subsidy stretches the limits of administrative feasibility.

The practical problems continue, however, because undesirable side effects arise with multiple prices for the same good. For example, oil consumers that can switch from oil to another fuel may reduce oil consumption without adverse macroeconomic consequences.[14] These consumers, it may be argued, should not be penalized by paying a tariff that includes a disruption component, but should be encouraged relative to other oil consumers. The problem of multiple prices is even more acute for utilities, because utilities are both oil consumers and energy suppliers and some possess fuel switching capability. Making distinctions such as these in the tax schedule indicates the many problems that can arise when a system of multiple prices is contemplated. We conclude that the advantage of multiple prices for encouraging short-run production flexibility is not likely to be worth the trouble.

This discussion is couched upon the specification of macro costs posited in equation (5-3). Suppose we modify the specification so that the cost function is proportional to the quantity of domestic consumption, as in

$$M = M(Q_N - Q_D)Q_N \tag{5-5}$$

indicating that macroeconomic costs increase with the change in consumption and with the initial level of consumption. In this case, the partial derivatives inserted into the tariff equations become

$$M_1 = M + M'Q_N \tag{5-6}$$

$$M_2 = -M'Q_N \tag{5-7}$$

The differences with the outcomes in equation (5-4) above are apparent. The cost term in the normal period is no longer symmetric

---

[13] Alternatively, instead of import duties, equations (5-1) and (5-2) give the appropriate excise taxes on consumption, to be supplemented by subsidies to producers equal to the demand component in normal and disrupted periods, respectively.

[14] This is true if supply of the alternative fuel is sufficiently elastic to avoid a price increase with the switch in demand.

with that in a disruption and, more important, equation (5-6) now depends on consumption levels as well as changes. The implication for energy policy is that greater dependence on oil, whether the oil comes from domestic or foreign sources, makes the economy more vulnerable to a price shock in a disruption. Even greater emphasis is now placed on the desirability of reducing normal consumption, and correspondingly less emphasis on the desirability of larger domestic production.

This view of macroeconomic dislocations leads to the conclusion that domestic production deserves no additional price support in normal periods beyond that implicit in the demand component, and that domestic consumption deserves to be taxed according to the combined demand disruption components. Instead of a tariff, the appropriate instrument is an excise tax because it raises the price to consumers without increasing the return to producers.[15]

To summarize our discussion, the presence of domestic production raises the question whether the premium on oil imports should be applied equally to domestic production and consumption. When macroeconomic dislocation costs are viewed as proportional to the quantity of normal consumption, the distinction becomes very important and the premium is applied to consumption but not production. When costs are not proportional to the level of consumption, the distinction between producer and consumer prices is less important and perhaps not worth practical consideration. Although these conclusions are drawn from a simple specification of macro costs, expressed as a function of the difference between normal and disrupted consumption, appendix B demonstrates that they are equally valid with other plausible specifications, including consumption levels and price differences in both supply states.

Factors Affecting the Magnitude of the Tariff

The foregoing model demonstrates that the demand and disruption components combine to determine the tariff, but it does not reveal how the two components interact. For example, the demand com-

---

[15] An excise tax discourages investments in flexibility relative to a variable tariff. This result may be desirable if in fact the supply of substitute fuels is highly inelastic in the short run. In this case, widespread introduction of fuel switching capability makes alternative fuels closer substitutes for oil and increases the impact of an oil price shock on other fuel prices. This topic is analyzed in Mork (1981b).

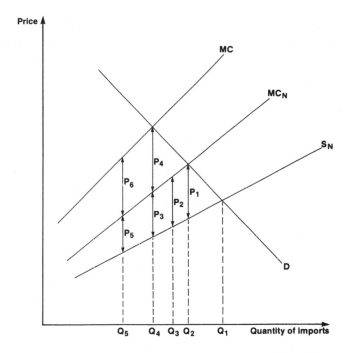

Figure 5-2. Comparing optimal tariffs under alternative assumptions.

ponent imposed in normal supply periods will also reduce disruption costs by encouraging conservation, and thus reduces the contribution of disruption costs to the size of the tariff. Conversely, the disruption component of the tariff may produce joint benefits to the U.S. economy by lowering the normal world price of oil and reducing the contribution of the demand component to the tariff. These interactions suggest that the magnitude of the tariff should be larger than that required to implement either the demand or the disruption component, but smaller than the sum of the two calculated independently.[16] Moreover, as explained above, the magnitude of both components also depends on private adjustments to the risk of a disruption.

The interrelationships among these separate elements may be illustrated with figure 5-2. Long-run import demand is given by D, long-run "normal" supply by S_N, and the corresponding normal marginal cost of imports is MC_N. These curves are taken from the analysis in chapter 2 where supply is assumed to be upward sloping. The rela-

[16] This assumes that import supply has a slope that is constant or increasing in the quantity of imports.

tionship between the quantity of imports and disruption costs is represented by the difference between MC_N and MC. These additional marginal costs represent the contribution, if any, of larger imports to the probability or size of a disruption, and the contribution of larger imports to macroeconomic dislocation during a disruption. The last element will increase with the quantity of imports if changes in imports are the result of changes in total domestic consumption.

Assuming to begin with that there is no risk of a disruption, the free trade quantity of imports is Q_1 and the optimal tariff (as determined in chapter 2) is given by the distance labeled P_1. The optimum quantity of imports is Q_2. Introducing disruption risks, P_1 is no longer optimal, but the correct value depends on private adjustments to risk and the importance of external disruption costs. If the private sector correctly anticipates all disruption costs (i.e., there are no additional externalities to account for above MC_N), the optimal tariff falls to P_2 as determined in chapter 4. Underlying this result is the fact that the true price of oil to the private sector is greater than the market price. Consequently, as demonstrated in chapter 4, the optimal tariff is smaller than P_1 and the new optimal quantity is smaller than Q_2.

If external disruption costs are included, but private responses to disruption costs are ignored, the tariff is determined by the intersection of long-run demand and external marginal import costs. The tariff would equal the distance $P_3 + P_4$ and optimal imports would be Q_4. Of the total tariff, P_3 represents the demand component and P_4 the disruption component. Notice that P_3 is smaller than the discrepancy between marginal costs (on MC) and price (on S_N) at either Q_2 or Q_1. This reflects the argument that adding the disruption component (P_4) to the tariff reduces the size of the demand component (to P_3). The disruption component includes only external disruption costs in this case, with no allowance for errors in forecasting costs borne directly by the private sector. If expectations errors are to be corrected by adjusting the domestic price, P_4 would be larger.

Private responses to disruption risks, as discussed in chapter 4, will reduce normal oil demand relative to long-run demand, and reduce the appropriate premium. This is shown by the shift to $P_5 + P_6$, and the reduction in the quantity of imports to Q_5. Of course, the less sensitive private responses are to disruption risks, the smaller the leftward shift in the optimum quantity and the smaller the reduction in the optimal tariff. This exercise emphasizes the importance of correctly assessing the actions of the private sector, and the size of the discrepancy between social costs and the price, in establishing the tariff.

Notice that the size of the import premium varies with the level of imports and that the optimal tariff equals the value of the import premium calculated at the optimal level of imports. Furthermore, the components of the premium are additive and sum to equal the optimum tariff only at the point of optimal imports. At this point, the offsetting influences of the separate components are taken into account. Each component taken alone will yield a smaller tariff and a larger level of imports compared with the optimum and, if added together without recognition of their offsetting influences, will yield a larger tariff and smaller level of imports compared with the optimum. These observations reinforce the conclusion reached above that calculations of the optimum tariff require predictions about private supply, demand, and investment responses to changes in the current and future price of oil.

Another feature worth emphasizing is the relationship between the tariff which accounts for all disruption costs and private adjustments ($P_5 + P_6$), and the tariff when there is no risk of a disruption (P_1). As indicated in figure 5-2, it is conceivable that P_1 could be a close approximation of the more complicated measure, depending on the slopes of the curves. This is an intriguing question to pursue because it suggests that, because of the joint characteristics of the elements of the premium, it may be unnecessary to try to develop the complex information required to account for both demand and disruption components. What is required instead is some idea of the robustness of P_1 as an estimator for $P_5 + P_6$. That is, under what range of assumptions about normal supply behavior, about the probability of a disruption, and about the discrepancy between internalized and external disruption costs will the simple demand component approximate the total?

To address this question, we have used our simple oil market simulation model to calculate optimal tariffs under different assumptions (see appendix A for a description of the model). External disruption costs are included in the model by assuming that the marginal social value of a barrel of oil lost in a disruption is proportional to the disrupted price (as given by short-run demand).[17] This is the simplest

---

[17] This assumption is equivalent to the specification of macroeconomic dislocation costs given by equation (5-3). See appendix A for a proof.

way of positing a relationship between private and social marginal value of oil that is consistent with the intuitive notion that bigger disruptions cause greater macroeconomic damage. The private marginal value of oil is assumed to equal the market price, while social marginal value is somewhat higher if macroeconomic costs increase with the level of consumption. Private expectations are handled in the manner described in chapter 4. A summary of comparative results is presented in table 5-1.

Tariffs are calculated under two assumptions about disruption costs to illustrate the importance of deviations between social costs and the price. The assumptions are expressed as factors of proportionality (including 1.1 and 2.0), where the figure 2.0 implies that the social cost of a disruption is twice as large as the loss of consumer surplus. Tariffs are also calculated under two disruption probabilities (0.1, 0.3), and three long-run import supply elasticities (2.0, 4.0, and 8.0).

The rather large supply elasticities deserve an explanation. To begin with, as argued in chapter 2, an elasticity as large as 2.0 is plausible even if supply from oil-exporting countries is unresponsive to price because of the elasticity of demand by other oil-importing countries. In addition, large import supply elasticities are required to find a case in which the disruption component is large relative to the demand component. Elasticities smaller than 2.0 simply increase the importance of the demand component relative to the disruption component, and reinforce the conclusion that a tariff based on the demand component alone is sufficient. As demonstrated below, the likelihood of a serious error in estimating the size of the tariff increases with the elasticity of import supply.

The estimates are separated into three groups according to the assumed supply elasticity. Line 1 in each group gives the tariff associated with the "pure" demand component (from chapter 2) when there is no risk of disruption. The second line gives the adjusted demand component when it is assumed that private agents fully adjust to expected private costs of a disruption (from chapter 4). The third line gives the amount of the tariff required to internalize the macroeconomic dislocation costs of a disruption in the normal price of oil. Note that the tariff rises with the probability of a disruption and with deviations of social from private costs. The last line in each set gives the optimal tariff required to account for both demand and disruption components, as jointly determined when private agents are assumed to adjust fully to anticipated costs of a disruption.

Interpretations of the numbers in table 5-1 should concentrate more on relative than on absolute magnitudes. Absolute magnitudes

Table 5-1. Optimal Tariff Measures Under Alternative Conditions[a]
($/bbl)

Tariff measure	Ratio of social to private costs[b]			
	1.1		2.0	
	Disruption prob.		Disruption prob.	
	0.1	0.3	0.1	0.3
A. Supply Elasticity = 2.0				
1. Demand component (no disruption risk)	14.58	14.58	14.58	14.58
2. Demand component (with private adjustment to disruption risk)	14.40	14.14	14.40	14.14
3. Disruption component (to internalize macro costs only)	0.48	1.38	3.92	8.62
4. Demand and disruption components (jointly determined)	14.53	14.54	15.47	16.73
B. Supply Elasticity = 4.0				
1. Demand component (no disruption risk)	7.88	7.88	7.88	7.88
2. Demand component (with private adjustment to disruption risk)	7.67	7.40	7.67	7.40
3. Disruption component (to internalize macro costs only)	0.47	1.31	3.78	8.05
4. Demand and disruption components (jointly determined)	7.92	8.15	9.76	12.10
C. Supply Elasticity = 8.0				
1. Demand component (no disruption risk)	4.13	4.13	4.13	4.13
2. Demand component (with private adjustment to disruption risk)	3.99	3.80	3.99	3.80
3. Disruption component (to internalize macro costs only)	0.46	1.28	3.70	7.74
4. Demand and disruption components (jointly determined)	4.33	4.77	6.75	9.77

[a] See appendix A for a full discussion of the model and assumptions. The initial conditions are a world price of $35, imports of 7 mmb/day, and a disruption of 2 mmb/day at the initial price.

[b] Ratio of the marginal social value to the demand price (as given by the short-run demand curve) for import quantities lost during a disruption.

will vary with the set of assumptions employed, while the relative magnitudes tend to hold over a wider range of assumptions (as indicated by the tables in appendix A). The important relationship to consider first is that between the sum of lines 2 and 3, and line 4:

the sum of the demand and disruption components calculated sep-
arately is always larger, as expected, than the two components determined simultaneously. Moreover, the discrepancy increases with the
probability of a disruption and with the importance of macroeconomic
dislocation costs.

The second relationship to consider is that between line 1 and line 4,
where line 1 is the simplest interpretation of the oil import premium
and line 4 is the most complicated. Line 1 may be below or above
line 4, depending on the perceived importance of disruption risks and
the long-run supply elasticity. Note that the demand component
alone is a reasonably close approximation of the combined demand
and disruption components across the range of supply elasticities,
when dislocation costs do not deviate widely from private costs. When
dislocation costs are large, the demand component consistently under-
states the combined tariff, and the understatement gets larger the
more elastic the world supply of oil. We conclude from these observations that the demand component alone is a conservative estimate of
the full optimal tariff, and that the likelihood of a serious estimation
error occurs when supply is very elastic.

Finally, as two alternative approximations of the full tariff (line 4),
the demand component alone (line 1) is closer over a wide range of
assumptions than the sum of individual elements (lines 2 plus 3).
The simplest approximation of the optimal tariff is superior in all
cases represented in the table except, again, where world supply is
highly elastic and the risks associated with a disruption are most
severe.

The difficulty of identifying and separating external macroeconomic
costs of a disruption with existing economic models, the diversity of
assessments of the probability of disruptions, the economic costs of
suddenly imposing a large tariff, and the implications of table 5-1,
lead us to conclude that the demand component alone is a justifiably
conservative estimate of the total premium. However, even this conclusion depends critically on the assumption of a well-behaved
upward-sloping supply curve.

An alternative to the conventional supply assumption recalled from
chapter 2 is the backward-bending supply curve. Comparing this
view of supply behavior with the conventional view assumed above,
we conclude that the objective of reducing the normal world price
with a tariff is no longer compatible with that of preparing for a disruption. Rather, a tariff forces a tradeoff between the two. This conclusion becomes apparent when it is recalled from chapter 2 (especially

figure 2-6) that there are two possible equilibrium positions peculiar to a backward-bending supply curve, one unstable and one stable, which serve to differentiate it from the conventional upward-sloping curve. With the unstable equilibrium position, a tariff reduces the quantity of imports but raises the world price; with the stable equilibrium position, a tariff reduces the world price but increases the quantity of imports. Of course, a tariff is still a desirable policy option if it is expected to produce an even larger reduction in the world price, even though the economy becomes more dependent upon oil, but another policy instrument is required to prepare for a disruption.

Conclusions

This chapter has explored several reasons why oil supply disruptions may produce costs to society that are not reflected in market prices. While these discrepancies may provide a rationale for government intervention, they are not all directly related to the quantity of imports. Consequently, their contribution to the oil import premium is sometimes ambiguous. Furthermore, a tariff on imports will not correct all discrepancies between social costs and the price. Under favorable assumptions about supply behavior, a tariff may achieve joint benefits by reducing the world price and the quantity of imports. However, a tariff implemented in advance of a disruption produces only a rough approximation of the incentives required to stimulate proper actions in the private sector. A tariff implemented during a disruption produces adverse side effects and should not be considered without a better idea of the nature and importance of potential macroeconomic dislocations.

The joint benefits achieved by a tariff tend to reduce its recommended size compared with the sum of demand and disruption components of a premium. Under a wide range of assumptions, including the assumption that import supply is positively related to the price, the demand component alone will approximate the jointly determined tariff. Furthermore, incorporating the disruption component into the tariff provides an additional incentive for both conservation and domestic production even though larger domestic output may not serve to reduce the macroeconomic impact of a disruption. Consequently, adding a disruption component to the tariff will stimulate domestic production that has a cost greater than its benefit.

There are also specific investments that may be made in anticipating a disruption that a tariff does not encourage, or does not encourage efficiently. The most important example is stockpiling; when released during a disruption, stockpiled oil provides benefits without distortionary side effects. The next chapter discusses the use of stockpiling in conjunction with a tariff. Our objective is to show how stockpiling relates to the size of the premium, the size of the tariff, and the quantity of imports.

6

Petroleum Reserves and Oil Import Policy

Our evaluation of an oil import tariff as the instrument intended to implement the oil import premium has reached mixed conclusions. While it is the appropriate instrument to deal with the demand component of the premium, a tariff can only imperfectly address the problems raised by disruption risks. To be sure, a tariff can help prepare the economy for a disruption, but the benefits to be gained are always accompanied by potentially serious costs that make the net benefits questionable. The possibility of a negative outcome is most likely for a tariff imposed in a disruption, because the benefit of reducing wealth transfers abroad may be overwhelmed by the dislocations generated throughout the economy.

The shortcomings of a tariff intended to reduce disruption costs suggest that another instrument is required. The most obvious option is a strategic petroleum reserve which, when released in a disruption, can reduce both wealth transfers and dislocation costs without the undesirable side effects that accompany a restriction on consumption. However, the benefits to be derived from a petroleum reserve are not costless either and, in addition, a reserve cannot address all disruption risks. There is, in other words, a potential role for an import policy that complements a petroleum reserve.

This chapter explores the relationship between a petroleum reserve and an import tariff as two instruments designed to fulfill the objectives implied by an oil import premium. It should be clear by now that this relationship also depends on private preparations for a disruption, including private oil inventories, and on the effect of government actions on private behavior. We begin by discussing the relationship between private and public inventories, then turn to the connection between total inventories and the components of the premium and, finally, to the role of import policy when there are petroleum reserves.

In view of the fact that the creation of a government-owned strategic petroleum reserve (SPR) has been public policy since 1974,[1] we take the existence of the public reserve as a starting place for our analysis and direct attention toward the optimal size of total reserves rather than the optimal mix of private and public holdings.[2] The private sector will adjust inventory holdings in relation to the size of the SPR, given expectations about the prospects for a disruption and the government's willingness to draw down the reserve in a disruption. The optimal mix of government and private stocks depends on factors that prevent private holdings from reaching the social optimum and on the feedback effect of government reserves on the size of private reserves. While we delve into these issues in the next section, rigorous analysis of their complexities is deferred to another study.[3] For present purposes, it is the size of total reserves, not the mix, that is of interest, for it is the total that is important to oil import policy.

Relation Between Private and Public Inventories

The importance of precautionary and speculative oil inventories was demonstrated dramatically when the Iran–Iraq war started in 1980. Oil shipments from the two countries suddenly declined by over 3 mmb/day, yet buyers did not have to scramble to secure replacement supplies and the price was not bid up. Private inventories were large enough to buffer the shock and no actions were required by governments to restrict consumption or to draw upon strategic reserves.

[1] Although the SPR was authorized in 1974, deliveries did not begin until 1977 and were subsequently interrupted during 1978–79. Filling resumed again in 1980 and the first phase, consisting of 250 million barrels, was completed in 1982. See Glatt (1982) for a history of the SPR.

[2] Teisberg (1981) and Chao and Manne (1982), among others, indicate that the SPR objective of one billion barrels is not excessive under even fairly conservative assumptions.

[3] Other topics in the energy and national security research program at Resources for the Future are optimal size, drawdown strategy, and public-private funding options for the SPR.

But, just as private inventories were comfortably large in 1979, they declined to uncomfortable levels over the next two years as slack demand for oil products reduced the prospect for higher future prices and high interest rates increased the cost of storage. What earlier seemed to be socially desirable inventory behavior soon appeared to be suboptimal, raising the question of whether national security can rely on the actions of the private sector. However, we will argue that the fact that private inventories fluctuate is not, by itself, evidence that they are suboptimal or will not contribute to national security. Fluctuations should be expected because of changes in market incentives.

The market incentive to hold inventories may be illustrated by analogy with the incentive to transport goods from one geographical location to another. Just as the difference in prices in two locations cannot exceed transportation costs between the two locations, it is also true that the expected price of a (storable) good at any point in the future cannot exceed the price today by more than the cost of storage. If the expected future price rises, or storage costs fall, more goods will be purchased today and stored for future sale. Adding to inventories will raise the current price, increase storage costs, and lower the expected future price. The consequence of storage is to narrow the difference between current and future prices, and to equate the price difference with the added cost of storage facilities.

The same process describes the transfer of oil from a normal to a disrupted market. Private agents have an incentive to build inventories as long as the expected value of price appreciation exceeds the marginal cost of storage. An increase in the probability of a disruption enhances the incentive for stockpiling, while a reduction in the probability or an increase in storage costs reduces this incentive. Thus, inventories will fluctuate with tensions in the oil market, or as interest rates and other cost factors change, because these changes alter expected benefits to be earned from reserve stocks.

The apparent instability in private holdings is often regarded as evidence that government-owned petroleum reserves are needed for national security. Private profit motives, it is sometimes alleged, are too unstable and myopic, while disruption risks are ongoing and long term. An additional argument is that the government can store oil cheaper than the private sector, because the government can take advantage of lower borrowing rates and can exploit economies of scale in storage facilities. Some care is required in interpreting these arguments, however.

Reasons why the private sector might be overly myopic have been discussed already in chapter 5. Briefly, because of externalities in the market, the private sector may underestimate the prospects for a disruption, or may act on estimated future prices that understate the marginal social value of oil. Private costs of acquiring oil for a stockpile are less than the social cost of imports, yet, as argued earlier, social costs of imports are likely to be larger in a disruption than in a normal period. As a result of these factors, expected private returns to stockpiling would be smaller than expected social returns, so that the optimal size of inventories determined from market criteria would be smaller than the size determined from social criteria. Thus, the same considerations involved in the determination of the oil import premium also apply to government storage.

The arguments based on a government cost advantage are weaker. The government's ability to borrow at lower interest rates than private individuals is not a relevant cost advantage. Since the interest rate advantage could be applied to any investment project, it is the nature of the project rather than the characteristics of government finance that justify government ownership. The question of the appropriate rate of discount affects design and funding decisions for projects already in the public domain, but not the choice of public or private ownership.

It is also true that large-scale storage facilities, particularly salt domes, enjoy significantly smaller average costs than conventional steel tanks used throughout the private sector. Furthermore, until the U.S. government began developing large-capacity salt domes, nothing on a comparable scale, with comparable technological and environmental problems, had ever been tried before. Thus, government involvement provided information that was not available before. Finally, salt domes cannot be continuously drained and refilled because of leaching, making salt dome storage more static than that compatible with changes in private incentives. Except for the last argument, these considerations tend to favor government-owned storage facilities rather than government-owned oil stocks. However, the physical constraint imposed by salt dome storage, coupled with the earlier arguments that social benefits from inventories are possibly larger and less volatile than private benefits, means that relatively static government reserves are required.

Although private storage may be smaller and more volatile than is socially desirable, there is nevertheless a symbiotic relationship between private and public reserves. For various reasons, public reserves are not expected to be used, except in more severe crises. The function of smoothing smaller and more frequent fluctuations in prices, whether they are the result of vagaries in the marketplace or minor interruptions in supply, is still left to the private sector. Consequently, even with a large strategic petroleum reserve, there remains an incentive for the private sector to hold precautionary and speculative inventories, and those inventories will play a beneficial role in society by buffering cyclical changes in prices and by moderating the need for adjustments elsewhere in the economy.[4]

While there is a place for both private and public holdings of precautionary and speculative reserves, establishing the optimal mix is a complex issue. Ideally, the optimal mix of reserves (and of other private and public investments in insurance against a disruption) would be jointly determined according to their relative cost in reducing the impact of a disruption. Each activity should be undertaken to the point where the last dollar spent in each direction achieves an equal value of expected social benefits during a disruption. However, in practice these decisions are not made jointly. In fact, the public stockpile decision has been made already and the private sector will adjust to that decision and how it is implemented.

It is of interest to trace the net benefits of the government reserve in view of the political decision that has been made, particularly since the full cost of the SPR is seldom recognized in official pronouncements. Both direct and indirect costs and benefits are involved. The direct costs and benefits of the SPR are illustrated in figures 6-1 and 6-2, respectively. It is assumed that a stockpile policy is pursued in conjunction with optimal tariffs in both normal and disrupted periods. The cost of filling the reserve in normal periods (figure 6-1) is related to the effect on the normal price. The fill rate is measured by the increase in normal imports from Q_N to Q_B which, with an upward-sloping import supply curve, increases the normal price from P_N to P_B. The direct cost of oil placed in reserve is not the market price P_B, but the marginal cost of imports. Purchases for the stockpile, moreover, increase the marginal cost of imports as measured by the demand

---

[4] This view implies that public oil reserves will be similar to buffer stocks in agricultural markets, defending a price ceiling and a price floor. Buffer stocks leave room for private inventory use in response to price fluctuations that remain between the ceiling and the floor but may not represent optimal stockpile management. When an import premium exists, private stocks may not even respond optimally to small market fluctuations. For an excellent economic characterization of buffer stocks, see Gardner (1979).

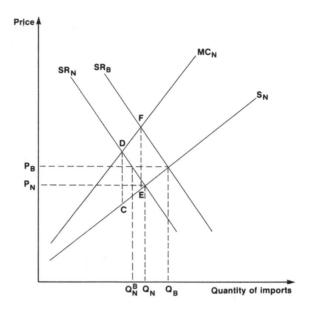

Figure 6-1.   Costs of filling a strategic oil
reserve in normal supply periods.

component of the premium. The premium is initially measured by the
distance from C to D, and it increases to the distance from E to F with
purchases for the stockpile. The marginal cost of imported oil added to
the reserve is therefore given by point F.

The direct benefit of using the reserve in a disruption (figure 6-2)
is the reverse of, but not equal to, the costs just described. The drawdown rate is indicated by the reduction in import demand from SR_D
to SR_B, which in turn lowers the disruption price from P_D to P_B. The
marginal cost of imports also declines, from point H to point J. The
marginal benefit of oil imports displaced by drawing down the reserve
is therefore given by point J. Although these benefits are the mirror
image of the costs described in figure 6-1, benefits will be larger in
absolute value because of the presumed lower elasticity of S_D relative
to S_N.

The short-run demand curves for imports, labeled SR_N and SR_D in
figures 6-1 and 6-2, represent the demand for imports for consumption. Stockpile purchases and releases make net import demand,
labeled SR_B, different from consumption demand. Stockpile purchases
and releases also change the world price and cause movements along
the consumption demand curves SR_D and SR_N, decreasing consump-

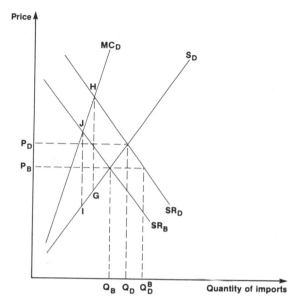

Figure 6-2. Benefits of drawing down a strategic
oil reserve in a disruption.

tion in a normal period to $Q_N{}^B$ and increasing consumption in a disruption to $Q_D{}^B$. Finally, stockpiling alters the expected price of oil and can shift the short-run demand curve.

The net effect of these changes on consumption during a disruption is unambiguous. Consumption will increase, but by less than the size of stockpile releases.[5] Thus, in a disruption, stockpiles tend to increase oil consumption but decrease imports. The effect of stockpiling on normal consumption is ambiguous. Because supply is less elastic in a disruption, removing a barrel of oil from the normal market and injecting it into the disrupted market will reduce the price more in the disrupted market than it will increase the price in a normal market. The result will be a fall in the expected price that may, if a disruption is sufficiently likely, discourage long-range conservation investments and increase normal consumption. The combined effect on normal consumption caused by the increase in the normal price and the reduction in the expected price depends on the relative magnitudes of the short-run and long-run demand elasticities and on the probability

[5] Stockpiles will displace imports one for one if supply is perfectly inelastic, so that the same quantity of oil is available to the United States no matter what price is paid.

of a disruption. Given the latter, the smaller the short-run elasticity relative to the long-run, the more likely it is that stockpiling will increase normal consumption. However, the smaller the probability of a disruption, the greater the importance of the higher normal price relative to the lower disruption price, and the more likely it is that normal consumption will fall because of stockpiling. In this case, the decrease in consumption will be less than the volume of purchases for the stockpile (unless oil supply is completely unresponsive to price), and net imports will rise.

Because stockpiling alters the volume of both imports and consumption, the marginal cost and benefit of one barrel added to the stockpile will equal the resulting change in imports multiplied by the marginal cost of imports plus the resulting change in consumption multiplied by the marginal value of consumption. When optimal tariffs are employed, the marginal value of consumption is set equal to the marginal cost of imports. In this case, the direct benefit of the reserve equals the reduction in the wealth transfer abroad during a disruption, while the direct cost of filling the reserve equals the increase in the wealth transfer during normal periods. If tariffs are not employed, the marginal value of oil during normal periods will be less than its social marginal cost. If normal consumption is reduced by the pressure of stockpile purchases, the result is an additional benefit of stockpiling. In contrast, the private valuation of oil in a disruption will be less than its social marginal cost. However, the presence of macroeconomic costs implies that the social marginal value of oil use during a disruption may be greater than its private value, and may indeed be greater than its social marginal cost. In a disruption, the increase in consumption stimulated by stockpile release therefore may be an additional cost or an additional benefit.

Larger macroeconomic costs increase the value of a reserve. Additions to the reserve lower normal consumption and indirectly make the economy less susceptible to a disruption, while releases from the reserve during a disruption permit higher consumption and reduce the dislocations caused by the disruption. These indirect benefits are measured by the higher level of national income that is maintained because the pressures for adjustments in prices and wages in nonoil markets are moderated. This additional benefit of course increases the optimal size of the stockpile.

The apparent benefit of government stocks is reduced, on the other hand, by any substitution for private inventories. Because the existence of government reserves reduces the incentive for private preparations, additions to government stocks will reduce the size of desired private stocks.[6] This feedback effect means that gross additions to government reserves are not net additions to total reserves in the country, and that the benefit of such additions is lower as a consequence. The aggregate social cost of precautionary inventories is not necessarily increased by substitutions, however, because the cost of storage is merely transferred from the private to the public sector. It is plausible, in fact, that social costs would decline with the transfer if the government can take advantage of economies of scale in storage facilities that the private sector cannot.[7]

We may conclude from our discussion that although an SPR may contain a billion barrels, it does not mean that a full billion barrels have been added to total precautionary reserves of the economy. On the other hand, government stocks may not completely replace private stocks if the government reserve is to be used only for large disruptions and private stocks can be used to arbitrage smaller price movements. Thus, total reserves are likely to be increased by government involvement, but their size is an open question. From an overall social point of view, the important issue is the total size of precautionary inventories, not the mix between private and public holdings. Furthermore, it is the size of total reserves that determines the oil import premium and the role of oil import policy. These latter topics are addressed in the rest of this chapter.

Total Reserves and the Components of the Import Premium

The optimal total stockpile size, comprised of both private and public holdings, is reached when the marginal cost of oil added to stocks plus the marginal cost of storage equals the marginal benefit of oil used in a disruption (all in present-value terms). To examine the relationship between optimal reserves and the components of the import premium, we extend the model introduced in chapter 5 to include reserves.

[6] Gilbert (1978) constructs an example in which public stockpiles reduce private investments equivalently so that the public reserve has no effect on the spread between normal and disrupted prices.

[7] Social costs would increase with the transfer, on the other hand, if there are surplus storage facilities in the private sector that could be used instead of enlarging government facilities.

Recall that the model includes three periods: in the first, decisions are made about capital stocks and import policy; in the second, normal supply conditions prevail with certainty; and in the third, there is some positive probability of a disruption. With the addition of inventories, the exposition is simplified and the distinction between stocks and flows is avoided if we also assume that a disruption is certain in the third period. Inventory decisions are made and announced in the first period, stocks are completely filled in the second, and all stocks are completely drawn down in the third period. This simplification enables us to abstract from the complex problem of optimal fill and drawdown rates and concentrate on the optimal size alone. It also avoids the artificial problem of unused stocks at the end of the third period that is found in a finite period model if a disruption fails to occur.[8]

The social planning problem, as before, is to maximize net national income over two periods, as given by[9]

$$F(K,Q_N) + F(K,Q_D) - P_N(Q_N + B) - P_D(Q_D - B)$$

$$- M(Q_N - Q_D) - rK - H(B)$$

where the first two terms measure potential gross output as a function of the capital stock and quantity of oil consumed in normal and disrupted periods, respectively; the next two terms measure payments for oil, where in a normal period a stockpile of size B is filled and in a disruption is drawn down, and the quantities in parenthesis indicate the volume of oil imports; M measures macroeconomic dislocations in a disruption, which are assumed to be a function of the difference between Q_N and Q_D [see the discussion of equation (5-3) in chapter 5]; and the last two terms measure the costs of capital and storage, respectively.

The first-order conditions for maximum net national income include[10]

---

[8] As in chapter 5, this simplified construction of the decision problem is designed to focus on the important branches of the decision tree in a dynamic programming problem. Our qualitative conclusions are unaffected by the simplification.

[9] Net national income, as in chapter 5, is defined as the difference between gross potential domestic production and payments for oil and capital plus reductions in potential output due to macroeconomic dislocation.

[10] See appendix B for additional discussion. The numbered subscripts, as before, refer to the partial derivative with respect to the ordered variable in parentheses and the prime denotes a derivative with respect to quantity.

$$F_2(K,Q_N) = P_N + P'_N(Q_N + B) + M' \tag{6-1}$$

$$F_2(K,Q_D) = P_D + P'_D(Q_D - B) - M' \tag{6-2}$$

$$P_D + P'_D(Q_D - B) - P_N - P'_N(Q_N + B) - H'(B) = 0 \tag{6-3}$$

Equations (6-1) and (6-2) define the optimum quantity of imports in normal and disrupted periods, respectively, while equation (6-3) defines the optimal stockpile size. The optimal stockpile size is determined by the familiar condition that the difference between the marginal cost of oil in a disruption and in a normal period should equal the marginal cost of storage. The macro cost term M does not show up directly in the stockpile equation, but indirectly through the optimal level of consumption, as indicated in equations (6-1) and (6-2).[11]

It was noted in chapter 4 that, in the absence of tariffs, private stockpiling will be carried out only to the point at which expected price appreciation equals the marginal cost of storage, or

$$P_N - P_D - H'(B) = 0$$

Compared to equation (6-3), we see that private storage will be insufficient if

$$P'_D(Q_D - B) - P'_N(Q_N + B) > 0$$

That is, if the demand component of the premium is larger in a disruption than in a normal period, as it will be if supply becomes smaller and less elastic in a disruption, then the capital gains available to private owners of oil reserves will be less than the capital gains accruing to society as a whole. Private investors will be unwilling to incur the costs of storage that are justified by the full social gains of stockpiling.[12]

[11] Notice that the larger the size of M', the smaller the size of Q_N and the larger the size of Q_D, and therefore the larger the optimal stockpile size in equation (6-3).

[12] Note that the mere existence of social costs for imports does not justify a government role in stockpiling. If the demand component remained unchanged across normal and disrupted periods, private stocks would be sufficient. If the demand component is smaller in a disruption than in a normal period, private stocks would be too large.

Because the private sector consumes and produces oil according to market prices P_N and P_D, the optimal tariffs are determined by

$$t_N = P'_N(Q_N + B) + M' \tag{6-4}$$

$$t_D = P'_D(Q_D - B) - M' \tag{6-5}$$

Compared to the optimal tariffs discussed earlier, the tariff in a normal period is increased by filling stockpiles while the tariff in a disruption is reduced by releases from stockpiles. These modifications of the pure demand component of the premium are in the same direction as the changes induced by macroeconomic dislocations. In both cases, the argument for a tariff in normal periods is reinforced, while the argument for a tariff in a disruption is diluted.

However, one thing these tariffs will not do is induce private agents to hold an optimal level of stockpiles. Stockpile size, as equation (6-3) indicates, should be based on the full difference between the value of the pure demand component in a disruption and that in a normal period. When tariffs are adjusted for macroeconomic costs of changes in oil consumption, private agents see a price difference that is smaller than the difference in the demand components.[13] Thus, private incentives additional to the tariff, or direct government oil stockpiling, are necessary to reach optimal reserve size.

Our results in this section, to summarize, suggest that the optimal policy mix must include both tariffs and additional actions to increase stockpiles. If there were no macroeconomic costs of the type we have described, tariffs alone could in principle be sufficient to encourage private stockpiling. But concerns about the workability and credibility of an announced tariff policy would remain, as would questions about whether private agents are fully cognizant of disruption risks.

The development of a petroleum reserve increases the optimal import tariff in normal supply conditions when the reserve is being filled, and reduces the optimal tariff in a disruption when oil is released from the reserve. The implications of a stockpile policy on tariff policy are therefore unambiguous. The converse relationship—the effect of a tariff policy on the optimal size of a petroleum reserve—is not as clear. When optimal tariffs [as defined in (6-4) and (6-5)] are in place, the optimal size of total reserves is that level which equates the

[13] Note that the change in landed prices, $P_D + t_D - P_N - t_N = P_D + P'_D(Q_D - B) - P_N - P'_N(Q_N + B) - 2M$.

marginal cost of storage to the difference between normal and disrupted demand components [as in equation (6-3)]. When optimal tariffs are not in place, there is a different marginal condition for optimal stockpiles which balances off all the costs of stockpiling discussed earlier.

There are two opposing factors that determine how tariffs affect optimal stockpile size.[14] Consider first the case where macroeconomic costs are small and the optimal tariffs are approximately equal to the demand components in normal and disrupted periods. The optimal disruption tariff may be expected to exceed the normal tariff and optimal tariffs may be expected to narrow the spread in prices between normal and disrupted periods.[15] The opportunity cost of oil put in the stockpile will be reduced, but if supply is less elastic in disrupted than in nondisrupted periods, the benefits of stockpile release will be reduced even more. Thus, tariffs can reduce the optimal stockpile size. On the other hand, when optimal tariffs are not in place, the marginal value of oil will not necessarily equal its marginal cost. The changes in oil consumption that result from a stockpile may impose net social costs by stimulating oil consumption when it is already excessive and reducing oil consumption when it is already too low. As a result, optimal stockpile size may be increased by tariffs.[16] These conflicting influences cannot be evaluated in a general model, because they depend on specific values of supply and demand elasticities and a measure of macroeconomic costs.[17]

[14] See appendix B for details.

[15] Assuming that supply is upward-sloping and that disrupted supply is steeper than normal supply.

[16] Appendix B shows that increasing the size of the stockpile increases consumption during a disruption when there are no tariffs. Whether this is a beneficial effect depends on whether the marginal value of oil is less than its marginal cost (which would be the case if a positive disruption tariff were justified) or greater than its price (which would be the case if a disruption subsidy were justified). In a normal period, increasing stockpiles may either increase or decrease consumption, depending on the relation between short-run energy use, which is discouraged, and long-run conservation investments, which are also discouraged because stockpiling reduces the expected price of oil. Since the marginal value of oil in a normal period is always less than its social marginal cost without tariffs, the net benefit of stockpiles depends on whether normal consumption is increased or reduced.

[17] Research is continuing on this topic at RFF in a project concerned with optimal stockpile size, drawdown strategy, and the financing of petroleum reserves.

The same indeterminacy arises even if macroeconomic costs are so important that the size of the disruption tariff is smaller than the normal tariff. In this case, tariffs could increase the spread in prices, making larger stockpiles desirable, but may at the same time eliminate benefits that arise from the effect that stockpiling has on demand. Indeed, if tariffs are not employed, it is possible that the optimal level of reserves could be less than that chosen in a competitive market. Increasing reserves above the level that private agents would choose on the basis of world prices would have two conflicting effects. On the one hand, larger reserves would convey social benefits based on the difference between the disrupted and normal demand components. On the other hand, larger reserves could impose net costs by stimulating oil consumption when its marginal value is less than its marginal social cost.[18] Adding optimal tariffs that recognize macroeconomic costs would remove the second (perverse) effect by restraining consumption directly. Consequently, adopting an optimal tariff policy would make the benefits of stockpiling more certain.

Policy Implications

It is useful to pull together a number of threads in our discussion of the relationship between import policy and stockpile policy. We have argued that the use of petroleum reserves simultaneously reduces the macroeconomic dislocations that are produced by an oil price shock and the economic cost of wealth transferred abroad when the price of imports rises. Strategic stockpiles therefore reduce the potential role of import policy as implied by the disruption component of the oil import premium.

It seems safe to conclude from our qualitative analysis that a large disruption tariff is not a defensible policy option. The potential dislocations caused by rapid changes in oil prices and oil consumption make it unwise to increase the tariff during a disruption. An adequate response to a disruption requires strategic stockpiles of crude oil and oil substitutes. Thus, a stockpile policy is required even in the presence of optimal tariffs while, conversely, an adequate stockpile reduces the importance of, and need for, a tariff policy aimed at disruption costs.

[18] As indicated in chapter 5, the marginal value of oil to U.S. society is equal to the price plus the increase in macroeconomic cost of a disruption that results from an increase in consumption.

In addition to the conceptual reasons associated with macroeconomic dislocations and petroleum reserves, earlier we encountered two major practical arguments against a larger tariff during a disruption than in normal periods. The first involves the impracticality of a variable tariff structure that can be finely tuned to changing events in the world oil market. The second argument involves the credibility of a disruption tariff as a policy the private sector will plan for. The full advantages of a disruption tariff are achieved only if the private sector can plan in advance for its eventuality, and thus depend on the credibility of a prior announcement. In view of the argument that a tariff can reduce employment and output in a disruption, that petroleum reserves make the tariff less defensible, and that the tariff serves to increase capital gains for speculators in a national crisis, it is unlikely that the private sector would make investments that are swayed in any measurable degree by such a pronouncement, or that politicians would be inclined to follow through when the time comes.

While these considerations recommend against a general policy of increasing the tariff in a disruption, it is important to recognize that specific circumstances can make a disruption tariff advantageous to the United States. For example, an embargo aimed at the United States that effectively reduces the quantity of available imports to a fixed amount, regardless of the price U.S. importers are willing to pay to attract additional supplies, means that the benefits of import controls will be very large and the tariff would not affect the domestic price of oil. In this case, increasing the tariff in a disruption would not impose additional macroeconomic costs. In addition, improved understanding of the relative importance of macroeconomic dislocations caused by an oil price shock, or improved capability of moderating these dislocations directly with other means, may alter the recommendation in favor of a disruption tariff. However, it is not possible at this time to be definite about the specific conditions that would warrant establishing a disruption tariff in advance of a crisis. In the absence of compelling reasons to the contrary, the normal tariff should remain constant during a disruption and stockpiles should be used to reduce import demand to avoid exacerbating macroeconomic costs.

There is still an important role to be played by import policy in normal supply periods. No matter how large the size of strategic reserves, the argument for a tariff based on the long-run demand component of the premium remains intact. The force of the argument is increased, in fact, by its additional advantage in reducing the opportunity cost of oil placed in a stockpile. The net benefits derived from stockpiled oil are increased as a consequence.

There is, in addition, a potential though diluted role for a tariff that reduces oil consumption in advance of a disruption. A tariff forces the economy to reduce dependence on oil through its induced effects on capital stocks. This result is achieved, as described in chapter 4, by encouraging private investment initiatives. A government-owned stockpile is complementary to a tariff because it works through the supply side by permitting more efficient utilization of existing capital stocks. The stockpile does not assist the economy in adjusting to the price change that takes place; rather, unlike the tariff, the stockpile discourages private investment incentives to prepare for a disruption. In further complement to a tariff, a stockpile reduces the significance of errors in expectations in the private sector by reducing the probability of a disruption and the expected price. A tariff cannot correct individual errors in expectations and may, as noted in chapter 4, distort expectations away from efficiency.

We conclude that a combined policy of a tariff and a strategic petroleum reserve effectively addresses the separate issues inherent in the oil import premium. The two are complementary because the tariff reduces the long-run demand for oil imports, making the economy more efficient in the use of energy, while the stockpile reduces the short-run demand for oil imports, enabling the economy to use its capital stock more efficiently.

One additional issue deserves comment because it relates to the benefits of a stockpile. There is concern that the benefits derived from releases from strategic reserves will be reduced because the stockpile will be shared with the rest of the world. This concern arises, not because of direct sales to foreigners, which are unlikely to be permitted, but because stockpile sales will indirectly substitute for imports. As a consequence, stockpile sales will not constitute a net addition to the amount of oil available to the United States during a disruption, but will instead serve to reduce the U.S. share of world imports. Much of this concern is misplaced because the primary benefits derived from a stockpile depend on the displacement of imports. The more stockpiled oil displaces imports, the more wealth transfers abroad are reduced and the more the world price is moderated.

It is possible to design a drawdown strategy that will moderate the price increase in the United States more than the world price, but at the cost of increasing wealth transfers abroad. For example, the U.S. oil market could be segmented from the world market by linking prior purchases from the stockpile to purchases of imports.[19]   The right to buy a barrel of oil from the stockpile would be linked with the purchase of a certain number of barrels of imported oil. The price of oil sold from the stockpile would be set below the world price in order to create a preference for stockpile purchases, and to maintain the incentive to purchase imports. The subsidy implied by selling oil from the stockpile below the market price would reduce the marginal cost of oil to U.S. importers, and would increase the amount of imports they would otherwise buy. The proportional relationship between the quantity of imports and stockpile sales could be adjusted to maintain the share of world imports flowing to the United States or, alternatively, set in a way that will increase or decrease the U.S. share.

This scheme lowers the price of oil to the private sector and thereby lowers the price shock imposed by a disruption on the U.S. economy. On the other hand, the scheme increases the quantity of imports and the cost of wealth transfers abroad. As discussed earlier in connection with tariff policy, the balance of the tradeoff depends on the relative importance of wealth transfers and dislocation costs. There is the additional consideration that schemes such as this will violate the spirit, if not the letter, of the International Energy Agency sharing agreements.

[19] This scheme would work like the Mandatory Oil Import Control Program during 1959–73, where domestic refiners were allowed to buy cheaper imports in proportion to the amount of domestic crude oil used. See Bohi and Russell (1978) for a discussion of this program.

7

Policy Conclusion

The uncertainties accompanying the arguments for an oil import premium preclude an unambiguous conclusion about the magnitude of the premium and the appropriate size of a tariff on imported oil. Policymakers must weigh the uncertainties in order to come to a reasoned judgment about the wisdom of a tariff and its expected net benefits. Our evaluation of the arguments leads us to the conclusion that a tariff is indeed warranted to reduce long-run imports and that it is an important complement to the strategic petroleum reserve. In our view, the uncertainties about supply and demand behavior do not negate the arguments for a tariff but do constrain the recommended size to a conservative magnitude. To be more specific, because of the uncertainties, we believe that the tariff should be less than the estimated size of the demand component (which, in our analysis, has an upper bound of $10 per barrel). Whether the tariff should be altered once a disruption occurs depends on conditions at the time, and we recommend against establishing a specific policy in advance.

Our conclusions are based on a number of threads that run through the preceding chapters. A plausible case can be made that market imperfections in the U.S. economy and in the world oil market drive a wedge between the value of oil to the economy and the price at which transactions are made. Because of these imperfections, the United States incurs avoidable costs in purchasing oil imports and faces avoidable damage from potential interruptions in world oil supply. A tariff on oil imports can serve to avoid some of these costs and damages, but a tariff is not a panacea. Other actions are necessary, especially strategic oil reserves, which can be used during a disruption. Also, some long-term measures should be explored which alter private investment incentives more efficiently than a tariff.

While we conclude that a tariff will be beneficial to the economic position of the United States, we also recognize the dangers of trying to do too much with a tariff. Because the volume of imports is not the only determinant of economic vulnerability, a tariff will not always improve security. In addition, because it is not possible to eliminate all the costs that an oil supply disruption will generate, the temptation to try should be resisted. When oil suddenly becomes scarcer, some costs cannot be avoided and no amount of advance planning will reverse this fact of life. On the contrary, excessive preparations and severe limitations on imports will lead to ongoing costs in normal supply periods that are greater than the benefits to be gained during a disruption, yet will not eliminate all disruption costs.

Of the various arguments for a tariff we have examined, two are most compelling: the effect on the current world price of oil and the adjustment of the economy to a lower level of oil consumption. Both arguments are valid if the social value of oil is higher than its market price, for a tariff will increase the market price to eliminate the discrepancy. However, as we have argued throughout this book, neither argument is without its drawbacks.

The effect of the tariff on the world price is uncertain because of the unpredictability of supplier reaction to a change in import demand and to an overt policy of import limitation. Additional uncertainties arise because of the potential effect of large price changes on the domestic economy. Because of these uncertainties, we advise policymakers to proceed cautiously in setting the tariff. We believe that it is better to err on the conservative side by setting the tariff too low (to equate marginal import costs and the price) than too high.

A tariff will aid in preparing for a disruption by encouraging capital investments that will reduce consumption and increase production of oil. The potential indirect macroeconomic costs of a disruption will be reduced with the decline in the contribution of oil to the production of all goods and services. However, as emphasized earlier, the intended adjustments in the capital stock produced by a tariff may sacrifice efficiency because investments are discouraged that would enhance the price responsiveness of import demand and because capital stocks will be underutilized. Most important, a tariff set at a level greater than the demand component alone will encourage oil production as well as conservation, although conservation is the primary means through which macroeconomic costs of a disruption can be reduced. Once a disruption occurs, a tariff is not always a feasible tool to reduce wealth transfer costs because of the added price shock. While a reduction in import demand is necessary to reduce the wealth transfer that occurs in a disruption, the reduction can be accomplished without adverse side effects only by displacing imports with domestic supplies, not by constraining consumption.

Maintaining, or even increasing, the tariff during a disruption is risky for the domestic economy, but can be justified in specific circumstances when the net benefits of import constraints appear to be large. This would occur, for example, when the disruption has the classical characteristic of an embargo with highly inelastic import supply, or, alternatively, if the macroeconomic impact of a jump in the domestic price of oil is judged to be small. Because the features of a disruption are not known in advance, and because the importance of potential macroeconomic dislocations is not yet well understood, we recommend against establishing in advance a specific tariff policy for a disruption. The tariff decision could be made in accordance with conditions at the time of a disruption, and in conjunction with decisions about releasing oil from the strategic petroleum reserve.

These considerations reinforce the importance of a strategic petroleum reserve in preparing the economy for a disruption, and discount the value of a tariff as an instrument to reduce disruption costs. In addition to an aggressive government stockpile policy, consideration should be given to enhanced incentives for private inventories of crude oil and substitute fuels.

While a strategic petroleum reserve is recommended over a tariff as the way to prepare for a disruption, we also conclude that the creation of a reserve on balance reinforces, rather than detracts from, the argument for a tariff in nondisrupted periods. This conclusion does not modify our recommendation for a conservative tariff policy. Our conservatism is strengthened by the fact that a petroleum reserve lowers the disruption component of the premium and, under reasonable assumptions, eliminates this argument for a tariff altogether. At the same time, a tariff in normal periods makes room for filling the reserve by reducing the marginal cost of oil in the reserve. Consequently, the consensus view that a strategic petroleum reserve is needed for security reasons also implies, as a corollary, that in normal periods a tariff is beneficial to the country.

Appendix A

OILSIM: A Simple Oil Market Model

This appendix describes a simple model of the oil market upon which the numerical examples in the text are based, and a computer program called OILSIM which performs the calculations.[1] The model uses linear supply and demand curves to solve five problems: (1) the optimal (demand component) tariff on imports where the importing country takes full advantage of its monopsony power; (2) the effect of expectations of supply disruptions on equilibrium conditions, during normal and disrupted periods; (3) the optimal (demand component) tariff given expectations of supply disruptions; (4) the tariff required to internalize in the normal price certain external macroeconomic costs of a disruption; and (5) the tariff that simultaneously accounts for the demand and disruption components given private anticipation of a disruption.

The Optimal Demand Tariff

The rationale behind a demand tariff and the derivation of a formula to calculate it are presented in chapter 2. Equations (2-4) and (2-5) are the normal long-run demand and supply curves for imported oil; equation (2-6) is an expression for the optimal quantity of imports, and equation (2-7) yields the optimal tariff. Given a set of values for

[1] A copy of the computer program will be provided upon request.

the parameters a, b, c, and d, the optimal tariff and import quantity are easily calculated.

OILSIM calculates the optimal tariff and import quantity directly from a set of values for a, b, c, and d. The program takes as its input values the pretariff price and quantity of imported oil when no supply disruptions are anticipated, and the elasticities of the supply and demand curves at that equilibrium point. From this information, the program calculates a, b, c, and d,[2] and solves for the optimal quantity and tariff. The program also calculates the difference between marginal social cost and market price at the pretariff equilibrium, and the prices paid by consumers and received by producers after the tariff.

The Effect of Disruption Expectations

As explained in chapter 4, when buyers of oil expect foreign supplies to be temporarily curtailed in the future, they will make adjustments in their capital stocks to prepare for periodic episodes of high prices. In doing so, they move to a new short-run oil demand curve. To determine the effect of this shift on equilibrium prices and quantities, it is necessary to find the slope and location of the new short-run curve. For the purpose of generating numerical examples, we assume that changes in the capital stock induce parallel shifts in the short-run demand curve. The inputs to OILSIM include the elasticity of SR_N at the point where it intersects the normal supply curve (S_N), and the long-run demand curve (D). From the elasticity at this equilibrium point we can calculate the slope of SR_N and, since changes in the capital stock induce parallel shifts in the demand curve, the slope of the family of short-run demand curves associated with various possible capital stocks. The problem, then, is to find the intercept of a new short-run demand curve that will maximize profits given a specified probability of a disruption.

The central assumption needed to locate the optimal short-run demand curve is that oil buyers, to maximize profits, will use the expected price as their planning price in making capital stock decisions. The expected price (P_E) is a weighted average of prices that will prevail during a disruption and during a normal period, where the weights

[2] The procedure of specifying supply and demand curves with elasticities at given points is used throughout OILSIM. This is possible because all such curves are assumed linear.

are the probabilities of disrupted and normal states, respectively. The planning price P_* is equal to P_E after the final adjustments in capital stocks have been made.

We can derive a solution for the intercept of the short-run demand curve which intersects the long-run demand curve at P_E. Given the following equations:

Normal supply: $\quad P = a + bQ$ $\hfill$ (A-1)

Disrupted supply: $\quad P = a' + b'Q$ $\hfill$ (A-2)

Long-run demand: $\quad P = c + dQ$ $\hfill$ (A-3)

Short-run demand: $\quad P = c' + d'Q$ $\hfill$ (A-4)

where all parameters but the intercept c' are known, we seek an expression for c' in terms of the known parameters such that the expected price will equal the planning price. Equations (A-1) and (A-4) give the normal price:

$$P_N = \frac{bc' - d'a}{b - d'} \tag{A-5}$$

Equations (A-2) and (A-4) give the disrupted price:

$$P_D = \frac{b'c' - d'a'}{b' - d'} \tag{A-6}$$

The expected price P_E is:

$$P_E = \frac{\pi(b'c' - d'a')}{b' - d'} + \frac{(1 - \pi)(bc' - d'a)}{b - d'} \tag{A-7}$$

The planning price P_* is given by the intersection of the short-run and long-run demand curves, which can be found from equations (A-3) and (A-4) as:

$$P_* = \frac{d'd}{d - d'}(c'/d' - c/d) \tag{A-8}$$

From the condition for profit maximization ($P_E = P_*$), we combine equations (A-7) and (A-8) to get:

$$c' = \frac{\dfrac{cd'}{d-d'} - \dfrac{\pi a'd'}{b'-d'} - \dfrac{(1-\pi)ad'}{b-d'}}{\dfrac{d}{d-d'} - \dfrac{\pi b'}{b'-d'} - \dfrac{(1-\pi)b}{b-d'}} \tag{A-9}$$

OILSIM uses the value of c' to find the normal price and quantity with equations (A-5) and (A-1), the disrupted price and quantity with equations (A-6) and (A-2), and the expected price (and planning price) with equations (A-8) and (A-4). As explained earlier, OILSIM does not accept the slopes and intercepts of the supply and demand curves directly, but calculates them from elasticity values the user supplies.

The Optimal Demand Tariff
Given Disruption Expectations

This problem is a combination of the first two. As explained in chapter 4, private adjustments in capital stocks will alter the optimal demand tariff (of problem 1) and, simultaneously, a tariff will alter private investment in capital stocks. Algebraically, it is a simple matter to solve this combined problem. Instead of using the normal supply cure (A-1) to find the normal price, we use instead the equation for the marginal cost curve, which (from chapter 2) is:

$$MC = a + 2bQ$$

Repeating the procedure above, we find that the intercept of the optimal short-run demand curve is:

$$c' = \frac{\dfrac{cd'}{d-d'} - \dfrac{\pi a'd'}{b'-d'} - \dfrac{(1-\pi)ad'}{2b-d'}}{\dfrac{d}{d-d'} - \dfrac{\pi b'}{b'-d'} - \dfrac{(1-\pi)2b}{2b-d'}} \tag{A-10}$$

Equations (A-6) and (A-2) are used to find the disrupted price and quantity, while equations (A-8) and (A-4) are used to find the planning price and quantity. To find the normal price (including the tariff) and quantity, we solve for the intersection of the short-run demand curve and the marginal cost curve. The optimal tariff given the capital stock implied by c' is equal to the normal price including the tariff minus the price to producers at the normal quantity. The price to producers is given by substituting the normal quantity into equation (A-1). This procedure assumes that the tariff is imposed only in normal periods, and is removed when a disruption occurs.

The Optimal Macro Externality Tariff Given Disruption Expectations

Chapter 5 describes a variety of external macroeconomic costs associated with oil import disruptions. One way of internalizing these costs is to impose a tariff during normal periods. This will stimulate a shift to a more oil-efficient capital stock, and thereby reduce the external costs when a disruption takes place. OILSIM calculates the optimal tariff for this purpose using a simple characterization of the external macroeconomic costs of disruptions. The marginal social value (MSV) of imported oil is assumed to be proportional to the marginal private valuation, as given by the short-run demand curve, for all units of imports less than the equilibrium level during normal supply conditions.

To relate this specification of macroeconomic costs to those described in chapter 5, we interpret the short-run demand curve for oil as the equation for the marginal product of oil. Then macroeconomic costs are a linear function of the difference between the marginal product of oil in a normal period, F_Q^N, and the marginal product in a disruption F_Q^D; that is,

$$M(Q_D, Q_N) = M (F_Q^D - F_Q^N)$$

By assuming a linear demand curve, we require the specification of the marginal product function to be $F_Q = c' + d'Q$. Substituting for F_Q^D and F_Q^N gives

$$M(Q_D, Q_N) = m (c' + d'Q_D - c' - d'Q_N) = md' (Q_D - Q_N)$$

Thus the specification of macroeconomic costs used in OILSIM is equivalent to the assumption that macro costs are proportional to the change in imports.

Social cost equals private cost (i.e., $MSV = SR$) at the normal domestic price of oil because the economy is assumed to be in equilibrium at that price. The domestic price equals the world price when there is no tariff and equals the landed cost when there is a tariff. The left-hand panel of figure A-1 shows the pretariff situation during normal supply conditions where P_N equals the existing market price of oil given by the intersection of short-run demand SR_1 and normal supply S_N. MSV_1 lies above SR_1 for all units of imports less than Q_N by a constant factor of proportionality. This characterization assumes that the social cost of a disruption will exceed private costs by the constant of proportionality.

Disrupted supply is given by S_D, which implies that the import price will rise to P_D and quantity of imports will fall to Q_D during a disruption. Compared to the private valuation of the last barrel of imports (P_D), the social valuation is V_D. The difference between V_D and P_D is determined by the externalities described in chapter 5. Because the required adjustments are a function of P_D, it follows that V_D is also a function of P_D. The relationship may be quite complex, but we assume for simplicity that it is linear.

The private planning price P_* does not include the additional social costs given by the difference between V_D and P_D. To internalize the additional social costs, the planning price should be

$$P_* = \pi V_D + (1 - \pi)P_N$$

which exceeds the private planning price by $\pi(V_D - P_D)$.

A tariff may be used to raise the private planning price by increasing the normal landed price. The required tariff will satisfy the condition:

$$P_* = \pi P_D + (1 - \pi)\,(P_N + t) \qquad\qquad (A\text{-}11)$$

which gives

$$t = \frac{\pi}{1 - \pi}\,(V_D - P_D) \qquad\qquad (A\text{-}12)$$

The effect of the tariff is illustrated in the right-hand panel in figure A-1. The tariff shifts short-run demand to SR_2 and the corresponding marginal social cost curve to MSV_2. Notice that MSV_2 intersects SR_2 at the new landed cost of oil (P'_N) equal to the world

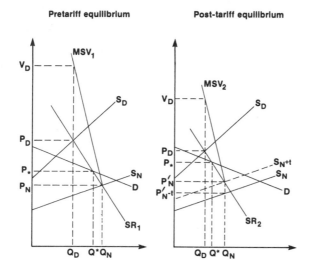

Figure A-1. The optimal macro externality tariff.

price plus the tariff, and that the new world price is below the original world price (P_N) because of the reduction in imports. The shift to SR_2 raises the planning price, lowers the disruption price, and lowers MSV, relative to their initial values, as shown in the left-hand panel.

OILSIM solves for the optimal tariff in this problem using a procedure similar to the one described above, although the procedure is slightly complicated by the addition of MSV. As before, we start with equations (A-1) through (A-4) to specify the normal and disrupted curves. To specify the MSV curve, the user provides a value for the ratio of the slope of the MSV curve to the slope of the short-run demand curve. The equation for the MSV curve is

$$V_D = c'' + d'RQ \tag{A-13}$$

where c'' is the intercept, d' is the slope of SR, and R is the ratio of the slopes of the MSV and SR curves.

Before the tariff is imposed, V_D equals P_N when $Q = Q_N$. Hence solving equations (A-4) and (A-13) for Q_N in terms of P_N gives

$$P_N = \frac{Rc' - c''}{R - 1} \tag{A-14}$$

With a tariff, MSV and SR intersect at the landed cost. Denoting the landed cost by P'_N,

$$P' = \frac{Rc' - c''}{R - 1}$$

and the world price is

$$P_N = P'_N - t = \frac{Rc' - c''}{R - 1} - \frac{\pi(V_D - P_D)}{1 - \pi} \tag{A-15}$$

using equation (A-12).

The solution to (A-15) requires values for c', c'', V_D, and P_D (the values for R and π are supplied by the user). Inspection of equation (A-13) for V_D and equation (A-6) for P_D indicates that c' and c'' are required for solutions. Hence, solving (A-15) is primarily a problem of solving for c' and c''. A solution for the optimal c' and c'' is found by identifying two equations in the two unknowns.

The first equation in c' and c'' is derived from

$$P_* = \pi V_D + (1 - \pi)(P'_N - t) \tag{A-16}$$

Each of the terms in this equation can be expressed in known parameters (a, b, a', b', c, d, π, and R), and our unknowns, c' and c''. P_* is given by equation (A-8). V_D is found by substituting the disrupted quantity for Q in equation (A-13):

$$V_D = c'' + \frac{d'R(c' - a')}{b' - d'} \tag{A-17}$$

P'_N is determined by equations (A-4) and (A-13):

$$P'_N = \frac{Rc' - c''}{R - 1} \tag{A-18}$$

t is found by substituting equations (A-6) and (A-17) into equation (A-12):

$$t = \frac{\pi}{1 - \pi}\left[c'' + \frac{d'R(c' - a')}{b' - d'} - \frac{b'c' - d'a'}{b' - d'} \right] \tag{A-19}$$

From (A-8) and (A-17) through (A-19), we obtain:

$$c'' = B1(c'B2 + B3) \tag{A-20}$$

where

$$B1 = \frac{R-1}{1-\pi}$$

$$B2 = \frac{-d}{d-d'} + (1-\pi) + \frac{1-\pi}{R-1} + \frac{\pi b'}{b'-d'}$$

$$B3 = \frac{cd'}{d-d'} - \frac{\pi d'a'}{b'-d'}$$

The second equation in c' and c'' is derived from another expression for $P'_N - t$. From the right-hand panel of figure A-1, note that at price $P'_N - t$ the quantity supplied (as determined S_N) is Q_N. Equations (A-4) and (A-13) give:

$$Q_N = \frac{c' - c''}{(R-1)d'} \tag{A-21}$$

Substituting equation (A-21) into equation (A-1) gives the expression:

$$P'_N - t = a + b\left[\frac{c' - c''}{(R-1)d'} \right] \tag{A-22}$$

Combining equations (A-18) and (A-19) also gives:

$$P'_N - t = \frac{Rc' - c''}{R-1} - \frac{\pi}{1-\pi}\left[c'' + d'R\frac{c'-a'}{b'-d'} - \frac{b'c'-a'd'}{b'-d'} \right] \tag{A-23}$$

Finally, equations (A-22) and (A-23) are solved for c'':

$$c'' = B4\left[(c' + B5) + B6\right] \tag{A-24}$$

where

$$B4 = \cfrac{1}{\cfrac{d'-b}{(R-1)d'} + \cfrac{\pi}{1-\pi}}$$

$$B5 = \frac{-b}{(R-1)d'} - \frac{\pi Rd'}{(1-\pi)(b'-d')} + \frac{\pi b'}{(1-\pi)(b'-d')} + \frac{R}{R+1}$$

$$B6 = \frac{(R-1)\pi d'a'}{(1-\pi)(b'-d')} - a$$

Using (A-20) and (A-24) we find

$$c'' = \cfrac{1}{1 - \cfrac{B4 \cdot B5}{B1 \cdot B2}} \left[B4 \cdot B6 - \left(\frac{B4 \cdot B5 \cdot B3}{B2} \right) \right] \qquad \text{(A-25)}$$

$$c' = \frac{c'' - (B4 \cdot B6)}{B4 \cdot B5} \qquad \text{(A-26)}$$

OILSIM reports two values for the difference between the social and market prices during disruptions. The first is the value when no tariff is imposed (the left panel of figure A-1), and the second is the value when the optimal tariff is imposed during normal periods (the right panel of figure A-1).

The Tariff Determined by Both Demand and Disruption Components

This problem brings together all the parts addressed in OILSIM for a joint tariff solution. The solution is derived using the procedure just discussed, with only minor adjustments in the equations for c' and c''. Specifically, wherever equation (A-1) for the normal supply curve appears above, the marginal cost curve ($MC = a + 2bQ$) is now substituted. Since the only difference between the two curves is that the slope of the marginal cost curve is multiplied by 2, only those terms containing b are affected. Of the elements $B1$ through $B6$ used in the previous section, only $B4$ and $B5$ change as a result:

$$B4 = \cfrac{1}{\cfrac{d' - 2b}{(R - 1)d'} + \cfrac{\pi}{1 - \pi}}$$

$$B5 = \frac{-2b}{(R - 1)d'} - \frac{\pi R d'}{(1 - \pi)(b' - d')} + \frac{\pi b'}{(1 - \pi)(b' - d')} + \frac{R}{R + 1}$$

All other calculations are the same as above except that the optimal tariff is no longer determined only by the difference between the social valuation and the market valuation of oil. This difference accounts for the disruption component only. The tariff is now equal to the landed price (P'_N) minus the price on the supply curve (S_N) at the normal quantity. As in the previous problem, OILSIM reports two values for the difference between the social value and market price of oil during a disruption. The first is the value when the tariff equals the demand component only, and the second is the value when the tariff equals both the demand and disruption components.

Numerical Results

Tables A-1 through A-4 summarize the output of OILSIM for problems (1) through (3), using a variety of market conditions, and table A-5 gives the results for problems (4) and (5).

Table A-1: Variations in Short-Run and Long-Run Demand

Table A-1 shows the effect of variations in the assumed short- and long-run demand elasticities as well as the effect of variations in the disruption probability. The elasticities refer to points on the demand curves at the price and quantity that would be demanded when the probability of disruption is zero. We also assume that 7 mmb/day imports at a $35 price is consistent with long-run equilibrium when disruption risk is zero.

Problem (1) assumes that the probability of a disruption is zero while problems (2) and (3) give results under two alternative probabilities (0.1 and 0.3). In problem (1), the tariff increases with long-

Table A-1. Variations in Input Values for Short-run and Long-run Demand Elasticities

	$\pi = 0.0$			$\pi = 0.1$			$\pi = 0.3$		
	L.R. Dem. Elast.:			L.R. Dem. Elast.:			L.R. Dem. Elast.:		
	-0.5	-0.4	-0.2	-0.5	-0.4	-0.2	-0.5	-0.4	-0.2

Problem 1: Optimal demand tariff

A. Optimal tariff ($/bbl)

1. SRDE $= -0.1$	7.88	8.02	8.35						
2. $\quad\quad\quad -0.05$	7.88	8.02	8.35						
3. $\quad\quad\quad -0.01$	7.88	8.02	8.35						

B. Price excluding tariff ($/bbl)

1. SRDE $= -0.1$	34.12	34.28	34.65						
2. $\quad\quad\quad -0.05$	34.12	34.28	34.65						
3. $\quad\quad\quad -0.01$	34.12	34.28	34.65						

C. Quantity (mmb/day)

1. SRDE $= -0.1$	6.30	6.42	6.68						
2. $\quad\quad\quad -0.05$	6.30	6.42	6.68						
3. $\quad\quad\quad -0.01$	6.30	6.42	6.68						

Problem 2: Disruption expectations

A. Normal quantity (mmb/day)

1. SRDE $= -0.1$	7.00	7.00	7.00	6.70	6.76	6.91	6.30	6.42	6.75
2. $\quad\quad\quad -0.05$	7.00	7.00	7.00	6.58	6.65	6.83	6.10	6.21	6.55
3. $\quad\quad\quad -0.01$	7.00	7.00	7.00	6.43	6.51	6.72	5.90	6.00	6.33

B. Normal price ($/bbl)

1. SRDE $= -0.1$	35.00	35.00	35.00	34.62	34.70	34.89	34.12	34.27	34.69
2. $\quad\quad\quad -0.05$	35.00	35.00	35.00	34.47	34.56	34.78	33.88	34.02	34.44
3. $\quad\quad\quad -0.01$	35.00	35.00	35.00	34.29	34.39	34.65	33.62	33.76	34.17

C. Expected quantity (mmb/day)

1. SRDE $= -0.1$	7.00	7.00	7.00	6.61	6.67	6.81	6.10	6.20	6.49
2. $\quad\quad\quad -0.05$	7.00	7.00	7.00	6.52	6.59	6.76	5.99	6.09	6.40
3. $\quad\quad\quad -0.01$	7.00	7.00	7.00	6.42	6.50	6.70	5.87	5.98	6.30

D. Expected price ($/bbl)

1. SRDE $= -0.1$	35.00	35.00	35.00	38.88	39.11	39.66	43.99	44.99	47.85
2. $\quad\quad\quad -0.05$	35.00	35.00	35.00	39.76	40.08	40.88	45.11	46.36	50.08
3. $\quad\quad\quad -0.01$	35.00	35.00	35.00	40.84	41.30	42.48	46.26	47.79	52.58

E. Disrupted quantity (mmb/day)

1. SRDE $= -0.1$	6.00	6.00	6.00	5.84	5.88	5.95	5.64	5.70	5.87
2. $\quad\quad\quad -0.05$	6.33	6.33	6.33	6.05	6.10	6.22	5.73	5.80	6.03
3. $\quad\quad\quad -0.01$	6.82	6.82	6.82	6.30	6.37	6.56	5.81	5.91	6.21

Table A-1. Variations in Input Values for Short-run and Long-run Demand Elasticities (*continued*)

| | π = 0.0 | | | π = 0.1 | | | π = 0.3 | | |
| | L.R. Dem. Elast.: | | | L.R. Dem. Elast.: | | | L.R. Dem. Elast.: | | |
	−0.5	−0.4	−0.2	−0.5	−0.4	−0.2	−0.5	−0.4	−0.2
F. Disrupted price ($/bbl)									
1. SRDE = −0.1	85.00	85.00	85.00	77.23	78.83	82.67	67.02	70.01	78.57
2. −0.05	101.67	101.67	101.67	87.38	89.80	95.78	71.33	75.16	86.58
3. −0.01	125.91	125.91	125.91	99.87	103.56	112.99	75.75	80.55	95.54

Problem 3: Optimal demand tariff given disruption expectations

| | π = 0.0 | | | π = 0.1 | | | π = 0.3 | | |
	−0.5	−0.4	−0.2	−0.5	−0.4	−0.2	−0.5	−0.4	−0.2
A. Optimal tariff ($/bbl)									
1. SRDE = −0.1	7.88	8.02	8.35	7.67	7.84	8.27	7.40	7.58	8.12
2. −0.05	7.88	8.02	8.35	7.59	7.76	8.19	7.26	7.42	7.94
3. −0.01	7.88	8.02	8.35	7.49	7.65	8.09	7.11	7.26	7.73
B. Normal quantity (mmb/day)									
1. SRDE = −0.1	6.30	6.42	6.68	6.14	6.27	6.62	5.92	6.07	6.50
2. −0.05	6.30	6.42	6.68	6.07	6.21	6.55	5.80	5.94	6.35
3. −0.01	6.30	6.42	6.68	5.99	6.12	6.47	5.68	5.81	6.19
C. Normal price excluding tariff ($/bbl)									
1. SRDE = −0.1	34.12	34.28	34.65	33.93	34.10	34.52	33.64	33.83	34.38
2. −0.05	34.12	34.28	34.65	33.84	34.01	34.45	33.50	33.68	34.19
3. −0.01	34.12	34.28	34.65	33.74	33.91	34.34	33.35	33.50	33.99
D. Expected quantity (mmb/day)									
1. SRDE = −0.1	6.30	6.42	6.68	6.09	6.22	6.54	5.80	5.92	6.30
2. −0.05	6.30	6.42	6.68	6.04	6.17	6.51	5.74	5.86	6.23
3. −0.01	6.30	6.42	6.68	5.98	6.11	6.46	5.67	5.79	6.16
E. Expected price ($/bbl)									
1. SRDE = −0.1	42.00	42.29	42.95	44.11	44.78	46.44	47.02	48.44	52.61
2. −0.05	42.00	42.29	42.95	44.58	45.35	47.31	47.65	49.28	54.22
3. −0.01	42.00	42.29	42.95	45.17	46.07	48.46	48.31	50.17	56.06
F. Disrupted quantity (mmb/day)									
1. SRDE = −0.1	5.72	5.78	5.92	5.64	5.71	5.89	5.52	5.60	5.82
2. −0.05	5.91	5.99	6.17	5.76	5.85	6.09	5.57	5.67	5.95
3. −0.01	6.19	6.30	6.54	5.91	6.03	6.35	5.63	5.74	6.09
G. Disrupted price ($/bbl)									
1. SRDE = −0.1	71.00	74.06	81.02	66.77	70.34	79.28	60.96	64.84	76.20
2. −0.05	80.67	84.65	93.71	72.92	77.53	89.36	63.72	68.36	82.44
3. −0.01	94.73	100.06	112.17	80.62	86.66	102.67	66.62	72.12	89.53

Note: Inputs held constant:

Normal price = $35.00/bbl
Normal quantity = 7.00 mmb/day
Disrupted quantity = 5.00 mmb/day

Normal supply elasticity = 4.0
mmb/day disrupted supply
elasticity = 0.14

149

run elasticity of demand, while the short-run elasticity is irrelevant. The results for problem (2) demonstrate that the expected price will increase with the probability of a disruption, while the normal quantity, normal price, disrupted quantity, and disrupted price will all decrease. When the probability of a disruption is zero, the expected price, normal price, and normal quantity are of course independent of the short-run and long-run demand elasticities. When the probability of a disruption is greater than zero, a decrease in the absolute value of the long-run demand elasticity will increase the normal and disrupted prices and quantities; while a decrease in the short-run demand elasticity will cause the normal price and quantity to go down and the expected price, disrupted quantity, and disrupted price to go up.

The results for problem (3) illustrate the effect of imposing a tariff when the private market adjusts to disruption risks. Compared with the results for problem (2), we see that imposing a tariff will, *ceteris paribus*, raise the expected price and lower the expected quantity, lower the normal price and quantity, and lower the disrupted price and quantity.

Table A-2: Variations in Disruption Size

Table A-2 illustrates the effect of changing the input value for the disrupted quantity. The disrupted quantity is measured at the normal price before a disruption and, along with the input value for the elasticity of disrupted supply, defines the disrupted supply curve. A change in the disrupted quantity will induce a change in both the slope and location of the disrupted supply curve.

The results for problem (1) in table A-2 are unaltered by changes in the input value for disrupted quantity. In problem (2), where the probability of a disruption is larger than zero, a smaller input value for the disrupted quantity will reduce the normal quantity and price, lower the expected quantity and the disrupted quantity, and increase the expected price and disrupted price. In problem (3), the addition of a tariff does not alter the directional impact of a change in the input value.

Table A-3: Variations in Normal Supply Elasticity

Table A-3 shows the effect of changes in the input value for the normal supply elasticity. This change alters the slope of the normal

Table A-2. Variations in Input Value for Disruption Size

	$\pi = 0.0$		$\pi = 0.3$		$\pi = 0.5$	
	$\pi = 0.0$ Dis. Quan. = 6.0 5.0 mmb/day		$\pi = 0.3$ Dis. Quan. = 6.0 5.0 mmb/day		$\pi = 0.5$ Dis. Quan. = 6.0 5.0 mmb/day	

Problem 1: Optimal demand tariff						
A. Optimal tariff ($/bbl)	7.88	7.88				
B. Price excluding tariff						
($/bbl)	34.12	34.12				
C. Quantity (mmb/day)	6.30	6.30				
Problem 2: Disruption expectations						
A. Normal quantity (mmb/day)	7.00	7.00	6.67	6.30	6.55	6.05
B. Normal price ($/bbl)	35.00	35.00	34.59	34.12	34.43	33.81
C. Expected quantity (mmb/day)	7.00	7.00	6.58	6.10	6.42	5.78
D. Expected price ($/bbl)	35.00	35.00	39.23	43.99	40.80	47.20
E. Disrupted quantity (mmb/day)	6.55	6.00	6.36	5.64	6.29	5.51
F. Disrupted price ($/bbl)	57.73	85.00	50.05	67.02	47.17	60.60
Problem 3: Optimal demand tariff given disruption expectations						
A. Optimal tariff ($/bbl)	7.88	7.88	7.82	7.40	7.80	7.22
B. Normal quantity (mmb/day)	6.30	6.30	6.26	5.92	6.24	5.77
C. Normal price excluding						
tariff ($/bbl)	34.12	34.12	34.08	33.64	34.06	33.46
D. Expected quantity (mmb/day)	6.30	6.30	6.25	5.80	6.23	5.61
E. Expected price ($/bbl)	42.00	42.00	42.54	47.02	42.75	48.92
F. Disrupted quantity (mmb/day)	6.24	5.72	6.22	5.52	6.21	5.44
G. Disrupted price ($/bbl)	45.00	71.00	44.03	60.96	43.64	57.16

Note: Inputs held constant:

Normal price = $35.00/bbl	Disrupted supply elasticity = 0.14
Normal quantity = 7.00 mmb/day	Short-run demand elasticity = −0.1
Normal supply elasticity = 4.0	Long-run demand elasticity = −0.5

period supply curve by rotating it around the position specified at zero disruption probability.

Table A-4: Variations in Disrupted Supply Elasticity

Table A-4 shows the effect of changes in the input value for the disrupted supply elasticity. When this input value is decreased, the effect is to rotate the disrupted supply curve so that its slope becomes steeper. Thus, the rotated supply curve will always be above the original supply curve. For problem (1) this rotation is of no consequence: the disrupted supply curve has no bearing on the calcula-

Table A-3. Variations in Input Value for Normal Supply Elasticity

	$\pi = 0.0$			$\pi = 0.1$			$\pi = 0.3$		
	Norm. Supply Elast. =			Norm. Supply Elast. =			Norm. Supply Elast. =		
	2.0	4.0	8.0	2.0	4.0	8.0	2.0	4.0	8.0
Problem 1: Optimal demand tariff									
A. Optimal tariff ($/bbl)	14.58	7.88	4.13						
B. Price excluding tariff ($/bbl)	32.10	34.12	34.77						
C. Quantity (mmb/day)	5.83	6.30	6.61						
Problem 2: Disruption expectations									
A. Normal quantity (mmb/day)	7.00	7.00	7.00	6.72	6.70	6.68	6.34	6.30	6.27
B. Normal price ($/bbl)	35.00	35.00	35.00	34.31	34.62	34.80	33.35	34.12	34.55
C. Expected quantity (mmb/day)	7.00	7.00	7.00	6.64	6.61	6.60	6.13	6.10	6.08
D. Expected price ($/bbl)	35.00	35.00	35.00	38.65	38.88	39.02	43.65	43.99	44.18
E. Disrupted quantity (mmb/day)	6.00	6.00	6.00	5.85	5.84	5.84	5.65	5.64	5.63
F. Disrupted price ($/bbl)	85.00	85.00	85.00	77.71	77.23	76.96	67.69	67.02	66.65
Problem 3: Optimal demand tariff given disruption expectations									
A. Optimal tariff ($/bbl)	14.58	7.88	4.13	14.40	7.67	3.99	14.14	7.40	3.80
B. Normal quantity (mmb/day)	5.83	6.30	6.61	5.76	6.14	6.38	5.66	5.92	6.07
C. Normal price excluding tariff ($/bbl)	32.10	34.12	34.77	31.91	33.93	34.61	31.64	33.64	34.42
D. Expected quantity (mmb/day)	5.83	6.30	6.61	5.74	6.09	6.31	5.59	5.80	5.92
E. Expected price ($/bbl)	46.68	42.00	38.89	47.65	44.11	41.87	49.09	47.02	45.78
F. Disrupted quantity (mmb/day)	5.53	5.72	5.84	5.49	5.64	5.73	5.44	5.52	5.57
G. Disrupted price ($/bbl)	61.67	71.00	77.22	59.70	66.77	71.27	56.81	60.96	63.44

Note: Inputs held constant:

Normal price = $35.00/bbl	Disrupted supply elasticity = 0.14
Normal quantity = 7.00 mmb/day	Short-run demand elasticity = −0.1
Disrupted quantity = 5.00 mmb/day	Long-run demand elasticity = −0.5

Table A-4. Variations in Input Value for Disrupted Supply Elasticity

	$\pi = 0.0$		$\pi = 0.1$		$\pi = 0.3$	
	Dis. S. El. =		Dis. S. El. =		Dis. S. El. =	
	0.14	0.01	0.14	0.01	0.14	0.01
Problem 1: Optimal demand tariff						
A. Optimal tariff ($/bbl)	7.88	7.88				
B. Price excluding tariff						
($/bbl)	34.12	34.12				
C. Quantity (mmb/day)	6.30	6.30				
Problem 2: Disruption expectations						
A. Normal quantity (mmb/day)	7.00	7.00	6.70	6.50	6.30	6.00
B. Normal price ($/bbl)	35.00	35.00	34.62	34.38	34.12	33.75
C. Expected quantity (mmb/day)	7.00	7.00	6.61	6.36	6.10	5.72
D. Expected price ($/bbl)	35.00	35.00	38.88	41.39	43.99	47.80
E. Disrupted quantity (mmb/day)	6.00	5.13	5.84	5.10	5.64	5.07
F. Disrupted price ($/bbl)	85.00	128.33	77.23	104.49	67.02	80.56
Problem 3: Optimal demand tariff given disruption expectations						
A. Optimal tariff ($/bbl)	7.88	7.88	7.67	7.50	7.40	7.11
B. Normal quantity (mmb/day)	6.30	6.30	6.14	6.00	5.92	5.69
C. Normal price excluding						
tariff ($/bbl)	34.12	34.12	33.93	33.76	33.64	33.36
D. Expected quantity (mmb/day)	6.30	6.30	6.09	5.91	5.80	5.50
E. Expected price ($/bbl)	42.00	42.00	44.11	45.90	47.02	50.01
F. Disrupted quantity (mmb/day)	5.72	5.10	5.64	5.08	5.52	5.05
G. Disrupted price ($/bbl)	71.00	102.20	66.77	87.65	60.96	72.28

Note: Inputs held constant:

Normal price = $35.00/bbl Normal supply elasticity = 4.0
Normal quantity = 7.00 mmb/day Short-run demand elasticity = −0.1
Disrupted quantity = 5.00 mmb/day Long-run demand elasticity = −0.5

tions. For problem (2), where the probability of a disruption is greater than zero, the steeper supply curve will increase the disruption price and reduce the disrupted quantity. Problem (3) shows no change from problem (2) in the directional effect of a decrease in the disrupted supply elasticity.

Table A-5: Variations in External Disruption Costs

Table A-5 shows the effect of changes in the input value for the ratio of the slope of the *MSV* curve to the slope of the short-run demand curve. When the ratio is increased, the *MSV* curve becomes steeper relative to the short-run demand curve. The gap between the social disruption price and the market disruption price becomes larger and raises the equilibrium tariff. The effect of an increase in the MSV/SR_D ratio is to decrease the normal quantity and price (exclusive of the

Table A-5. Variations in Input Value for Slope Ratio, MSV2/SRD

	Ratio MSV2/SRD 1.1			Ratio MSV2/SRD 1.5			Ratio MSV2/SRD 2.0		
	$\pi =$			$\pi =$			$\pi =$		
	0.0	0.1	0.3	0.0	0.1	0.3	0.0	0.1	0.3

Problem 4: The optimal macro externality tariff given disruption expectations

A. Optimal tariff ($/bbl)	0.00	0.47	1.31	0.00	2.10	5.12	0.00	3.78	8.05
B. Normal quantity (mmb/day)	7.00	6.66	6.23	7.00	6.54	6.03	7.00	6.42	5.88
C. Normal price excluding tariff ($/bbl)	35.00	34.57	34.04	35.00	34.43	33.80	35.00	34.28	33.60
D. Expected quantity (mmb/day)	7.00	6.58	6.05	7.00	6.47	5.89	7.00	6.35	5.77
E. Expected price ($/bbl)	35.00	39.20	44.53	35.00	40.32	46.09	35.00	41.46	47.29
F. Disrupted quantity (mmb/day)	6.00	5.83	5.62	6.00	5.79	5.56	6.00	5.74	5.51
G. Disrupted price ($/bbl)	84.99	76.60	65.94	85.00	74.37	62.82	85.00	72.08	60.43
H. MSV—disrupted price ($/bbl): with no tariff	5.00	4.26	3.29	25.00	21.31	16.45	50.00	42.61	32.89
I. MSV—disrupted price ($/bbl): with optimal macro externality tariff	5.00	4.16	3.06	25.00	18.92	11.95	50.00	34.02	18.78

Problem 5: The optimal demand/macro externality tariff given disruption expectations

A. Optimal tariff ($/bbl)	7.88	7.92	8.15	7.88	8.82	10.36	7.88	9.76	12.10
B. Normal quantity (mmb/day)	6.30	6.12	5.88	6.30	6.06	5.77	6.30	5.99	5.68
C. Normal price excluding tariff ($/bbl)	34.12	33.90	33.60	34.12	33.82	33.46	34.12	33.73	33.34
D. Expected quantity (mmb/day)	6.30	6.07	5.77	6.30	6.01	5.68	6.30	5.95	5.61
E. Expected price ($/bbl)	42.00	44.29	47.33	42.00	44.90	48.23	42.00	45.53	48.94
F. Disrupted quantity (mmb/day)	5.72	5.63	5.51	5.72	5.60	5.47	5.72	5.58	5.44
G. Disrupted price ($/bbl)	71.00	66.43	60.35	71.00	65.20	58.53	71.00	63.93	57.11

Table A-5. Variations in Input Value for Slope Ratio, MSV2/SRD
(*continued*)

	Ratio MSV2/SRD 1.1			Ratio MSV2/SRD 1.5			Ratio MSV2/SRD 2.0		
	$\pi =$			$\pi =$			$\pi =$		
	0.0	0.1	0.3	0.0	0.1	0.3	0.0	0.1	0.3
H. MSV—disrupted price ($/bbl): with optimal demand tariff (problem 3)	2.90	2.52	1.99	14.50	12.59	9.96	29.00	25.17	19.92
I. MSV—disrupted price ($/bbl): with optimal demand/macro externality tariff	2.90	2.46	1.86	14.50	11.28	7.36	29.00	20.44	11.67

Note: Inputs held constant:

Normal price = $35.00/bbl	Disrupted supply elasticity = 0.14
Normal quantity = 7.00 mmb/day	Short-run demand elasticity = −0.1
Disrupted quantity = 5.00 mmb/day	Long-run demand elasticity = −0.5
Normal supply elasticity = 1.0	

tariff), increase the expected price, and decrease both the disrupted quantity and price.

Table A-5 also shows the effect of changes in the probability of a disruption on the results. As expected, an increase in the probability increases the tariff based on macro dislocation costs. The effects are very similar to those of an increase in the slope of the *MSV* curve: the normal quantity and price and the disrupted quantity and price are all decreased, while the expected price is increased.

Lines *H* and *I* of problems (4) and (5) report values for the difference between *MSV* and the market price during a disruption when the tariff is set according to different criteria. In line *H*, an increase in the slope ratio sharply increases the difference between the marginal social valuation and the disrupted price, while an increase in the probability of disruption reduces the difference. This latter result occurs because of the leftward shift in the short-run demand curve as oil consumers change their capital stock to account for the greater threat of disruption. In line *I*, increases in the slope ratio and the disruption probability have the same directional effects on the results described above for line *H*. Of interest is the comparison between lines *H* and *I*, where the effect of imposing a tariff because of macro dislocations decreases the difference between the marginal social valuation and the price during disruptions.

Appendix B

Mathematical Analysis of Disruption Costs

This appendix provides a more formal and rigorous development of topics discussed in chapters 4, 5, and 6. The first section reviews the theory of private choice under uncertainty. A simple dynamic model, consistent with the well-established observation that short-run demand elasticities are less than long-run, is developed. The section concentrates on two questions: (1) under what conditions will an "action-equivalent" price of oil exist, and (2) what factors determine the relationship between the action-equivalent price and the expected value of the price? The relationship between long-term capital investments and the short-run elasticity of demand turns out to be critical.

The second section examines the welfare economics of oil markets under uncertainty. It is demonstrated that when the world oil price depends on the U.S. level of imports, there exists an optimal dynamic tariff that will maximize welfare for the United States. It is further shown that the outcome under a dynamic tariff cannot be replicated with a tariff applied during a normal period in a uniform fashion to all agents. This conclusion is derived from the analysis of action equivalent prices and flexibility presented in the first section.

The third section analyzes the optimal dynamic tariff when macro-economic costs are assumed to put a penalty on changes in oil consumption and/or prices. As oil consumption and production are assumed to have different roles in determining macroeconomic costs, a single dynamic tariff cannot adjust both consumption and production optimally.

The final section presents a model that integrates the analysis of tariffs and stockpiling. First, the problem of joint determination of optimal tariff and stockpile policies is addressed. It is demonstrated that with macroeconomic costs, there is no dynamic tariff that will support optimal import and stockpile levels. Two policy instruments are required. Second, the conditions for an optimal stockpile-only policy are derived. It is shown that when no tariffs on imports are employed, the relation between competitive and optimal stockpile sizes is theoretically ambiguous.

Individual and Market Behavior with Uncertain Prices

Private agents who believe that oil prices are uncertain will make a number of preparations for a disruption. Assuming a quasi-fixed capital stock that cannot be altered quickly, the short-run elasticities of domestic oil demand and supply will be less than their corresponding long-run elasticities. As the probability of a disruption increases above zero, investors with foresight will alter their capital stock to maximize expected profits or, more generally, utility. This change in the capital stock serves to shift the short-run demand (supply) curve along the long-run demand (supply) curve. The capital stock that is optimal in the presence of disruption risk will be associated with a short-run demand curve that intersects the long-run demand curve at a price between the lowest normal price and the highest disrupted price of oil.

This section analyzes how the capital stock is chosen in the presence of oil price uncertainty. Since neither risk aversion nor time preference are essential to the topics addressed, we make two simplifying assumptions:

1. All decision makers are assumed to be neutral toward risk, so that their goal is to maximize the expected value of profits or utility

2. All future prices are assumed to be discounted back to the present, so that explicit introduction of a discount rate can be avoided

These assumptions necessarily narrow our examination of the reasons for government intervention: problems arising because of inadequate risk markets or differences between private and social rates of time preference are not analyzed.

Consumption and production decisions both play a role in import demand. We treat the consumption decision explicitly, and then indicate how an analogous treatment of production would be constructed and what conclusions it would yield.

A disruption can be anticipated on the demand side of the market in decisions regarding the acquisition of energy-using capital stocks. To identify the value of anticipating future price increases in energy consumption decisions, we will use a formal model which makes explicit the cost of fixed investment.[1] Assume for simplicity that a firm produces a single good using a production process that requires capital (K) and oil (Q). That production process is represented by the function

$$Y = F(K,Q)$$

To avoid unnecessary symbols, we assume that the firm's output can be sold at a fixed price of \$1 per unit of Y. The cost of oil is uncertain, and equal to P_s if state of the world s occurs; the cost of capital is r. Let $du(s)$ represent the probability that s occurs, and Q_s represent oil use in state s. Then the expected price of oil is $\int_s P_s du(s)$, and expected profits are $\int_s [F(K,Q_s) - P_s Q_s] du(s) - rK$.

To formalize the notion of expectations, we assume that the firm must choose K before the state of the world s is known. In some examples we will assume two specific states, a disrupted state D and a nondisrupted state N, with probabilities of occurrence π and $1 - \pi$, respectively. Given a fixed capital stock K, and knowing that the price of oil is P_s, the firm chooses quantity Q_s of oil to maximize profits.

Since the cost of capital rK is fixed, it is irrelevant to decision making in the short run and maximizing profits is equivalent to

---

[1] This discussion is couched in terms of the derived demand for oil as an input in production for convenience in identifying the cost of fixed capital. It does not imply that final consumption is ignored. The derived demand for oil for final consumption is analogous to that for intermediate use, with, say, an automobile (fixed capital) and gasoline used to provide the transportation services the consumer desires. The distinction between short-run and long-run demand is similarly based on the fixity of the energy-using capital stock, but the concept of a utility function replaces the concept of a profit function.

maximizing short-run operating income, given by $F(K,Q_s) - P_sQ_s$.[2] The firm will choose Q to satisfy

$$\frac{\partial F(K,Q_s)}{\partial Q_s} = P_s \qquad \text{(B-1)}$$

so that the marginal productivity of oil, which depends on the capital stock, is equated to the price of oil in that state. Depending on the need for compactness, $\partial F(K,Q_s)/\partial Q_s$ will be denoted $F_Q(K,Q_s)$, or F_Q^s, and other partial derivatives similarly.

In general, we can use the rule that firms will purchase oil up to the point where the marginal product of oil is equal to the price in order to derive an equation which gives oil demand Q_s at price P_s with an installed capital of K. That is,

$$Q_s = Q(P_s,K) \qquad \text{(B-2)}$$

This is the equation of the short-run demand curve for oil.

When a firm is in a position to make a new capital investment decision, it will consider the effect of that decision on future oil requirements, and on profits at various prices. Since future oil use depends, in a known way, on the chosen capital stock and on the future price, equation (B-2) can be used to eliminate Q_s from the objective function for investment planning. To decide on a level for K, the firms will maximize the long-run expected profit function given by

$$\int_s \{ F[K,Q(P_s,K)] - P_sQ(P_s,K) \} \, du(s) - rK$$

The first-order condition for maximizing expected profits is

$$\int_s \left[F_K^s - (F_Q^s - P_s)\frac{\partial Q_s}{\partial K} \right] du(s) - r = 0$$

Because of the envelope theorem, it is possible to simplify this expression. Since $F_Q^s = P_s$, the term involving $\partial Q_s/\partial K$ vanishes, giving

$$\int_s F_K [K,Q(P_s,K)] \, du_s - r = 0 \qquad \text{(B-3)}$$

---

[2] We assume that costs do not become so high, for such a long time, that the firm decides to go out of business and thus avoid "fixed" costs.

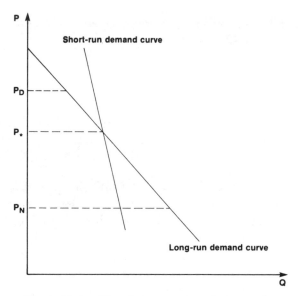

Figure B-1. The planning price relative to the normal and the disrupted price.

Choosing K on the basis of this condition serves to fix the location of the short-run demand curve. Changing the capital stock can be thought of as shifting the short-run demand along a long-run demand curve until expected profits are maximized.[3]

The implications of equation (B-3) can be illustrated for a case in which the probability of a disruption with a price P_D is π and the probability of normal supplies with a price P_N is $(1 - \pi)$ (see figure B-1). When oil prices are uncertain, choosing the capital stock that satisfies (B-3) will produce a short-run demand curve that intersects the long-run demand curve at a price P_*. We call the price at which these curves intersect the "planning price" because the firm can be thought of as making long-run investment decisions as if it faced this price with certainty.

The short-run demand curve will intersect the long-run demand curve at P_N when the capital stock is chosen under the assumption of a *certain* future price of oil P_N or, equivalently, a disruption probability equal to 0. The two curves will intersect at P_D when the capital

---

[3] In the long run, in the presence of fixed prices, it is possible to choose a capital stock and a level of oil inputs simultaneously. First-order conditions for maximizing profits are $F_K - r = 0$ and $F_Q - p = 0$.

stock is chosen under the assumption of a certain future price P_D or, equivalently, a disruption probability equal to 1. The planning price will necessarily be greater than P_N and less than P_D if $0 < \pi < 1$.

In the terminology of Newbery and Stiglitz (1981), P_* is an "action-equivalent" price. It leads an agent to take the same action that would be taken in response to full price uncertainty. Several authors, notably Turnovsky (1973) and Newbery and Stiglitz (1981), have demonstrated that the relation between the planning (action-equivalent) price and the expected price depends on characteristics of the underlying production function. Other authors (Fuss and McFadden, 1978b) have demonstrated that there are conditions under which no action-equivalent price can be found—that the action taken in response to uncertain prices is not an action that would be taken in response to *any* certain price. In the text we gave three examples of such actions: building fuel-switching capability, holding additional inventories, and choosing a flexible production process over one with rigid oil requirements.

Flexibility versus Static Efficiency

Problems with the existence of a planning price arise from a tradeoff between static efficiency and flexibility. When prices are certain, efficiency is a necessary condition for profit (or utility) maximization. Let $Y = (Y_1, \ldots, Y_n)$ denote a vector of outputs, $K = (K_1, \ldots, K_m)$ a vector of quasi-fixed factors (factors whose quantity is not variable in the short run), and $Q = (Q_1, \ldots, Q_r)$ a vector of variable factors. The vector of outputs and inputs $(Y, -K, -Q)$ is said to be in the production set if it is possible to produce the stated output with the given inputs. An input-output combination $(Y, -K, -Q)$ is efficient if there is no other vector $(Y' - K' - Q')$ in the production set such that $(Y', -K', -Q') > (Y, -K, -Q)$. Under certainty, profits can always be increased by moving from an inefficient input-output combination to an efficient one.

When input prices are uncertain, this is not necessarily the case. In figure B-2 we examine substitution between oil and other variable inputs using the three isoquants labelled I, I_E, and I_F to represent combinations of oil and other variable factors—say labor—with which it is possible to produce a given level of output. Isoquants I and I_F are each associated with a different stock of fixed capital. Ex post substitution possibilities are greater with I_F than with I. The envelope curve I_E traces out the efficient combinations of oil and labor inputs

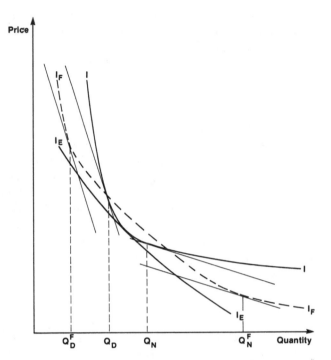

Figure B-2.   Tradeoffs between static efficiency and
flexibility.

with which it is possible to produce a given level of output if the
capital stock can also be varied. If the capital stock is continuously
variable, there will be a short-run isoquant like I tangent to this
envelope at each point.

The dashed curve I_F lies uniformly above the envelope curve I_E. It
is possible to find one of the family of short-run isoquants tangent
to I_E that requires less of both factor inputs to produce the same
level of output. Thus, with a fixed price at P_D or P_N (or any intermediate value), a capital stock associated with some isoquant tangent
to I_E will be chosen.

Equal cost lines are drawn into figure B-2 to locate the optimal
choice. The steeper set of parallel lines represents input costs during
a disruption, while the flatter set represents costs during a normal
period. Every point on a given line represents an input combination
with a cost equal to that of any other point on the line. The higher
the line, the greater the cost of input combinations on the line.

To choose an optimal point under uncertainty, let us first confine our attention to techniques that are efficient in a static sense—that is, to an isoquant tangent to the envelope curve at some point. Some isoquant, such as I, will offer maximum expected profits, and demand for oil will vary between Q_D and Q_N. The capital stock generating this isoquant would be chosen if the price of energy were fixed at the appropriate planning price.

If oil prices are uncertain, costs could be reduced by choosing a more flexible technique represented by the isoquant I_F. In a disruption $Q_D{}^F$ is the optimal input of oil with the flexible technique, and a lower equal-cost line is attainable compared to isoquant I and the rigid technique. Similarly, in a normal period $Q_N{}^F$ of oil is used, and again costs with I_F are lower compared with isoquant I. Thus, expected costs will be lower with the flexible process compared with the rigid one, because costs are lower in each state of the world.

We can now attempt to reverse the argument and ask what price, known with certainty, would lead to adoption of the technology that generates I^F. With a certain price, an efficient technology must be chosen; only an isoquant tangent to I_E can be efficient and every point on I_E lies below I_F. Consequently I_F will not be chosen at any certain price, and it is impossible to speak of a planning price at all.

A similar construction, involving long-run and short-run marginal cost curves, could be used to demonstrate that a statically inefficient oil production technology could be chosen in the face of price uncertainty (see Fuss and McFadden, 1978b).

Flexibility and the Production Function

Even if we assume that there are no opportunities for increasing flexibility at the expense of static efficiency, the relation between the capital stock and short-run flexibility will still affect the calculation of an action equivalent, or planning price. Let us return to the simple model developed earlier, in which output is a function of a homogeneous capital stock and oil; and no flexibility-efficiency trade-offs exist. Flexibility in this case is measured by the slope of the short-run demand curve for oil, F_{QQ}. (Recall that the short-run demand curve coincides with the marginal productivity curve F_Q.) Whether flexibility is increased or decreased by a change in the capital stock depends on how the slope of the short-run demand curve changes.

Our definitions of constant, increasing, and decreasing flexibility are illustrated in figure B-3. In each diagram, a change in the capital

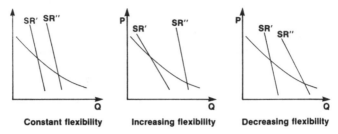

Figure B-3.   Constant, increasing, and decreasing flexibility in energy demand.

stock serves to shift the short-run demand curve from SR' to SR''. In the case of constant flexibility, the change in oil use that results from a change in the capital stock is the same at all prices. This implies that lines tangent to SR' and SR'' are parallel to one another along any horizontal line.

Increasing flexibility is defined as a case in which the short-run demand curve is moved in such a fashion that

$$Q'(P) < Q''(P) \text{ implies } \frac{dQ'}{dP} < \frac{dQ''}{dP}$$

Along any horizontal line, the demand curve becomes less steep as one moves from right to left. In other words, a change in the capital stock reduces demand more at higher than at lower oil prices. In this case, a change in the capital stock that reduces demand also makes demand more responsive to price.

Decreasing flexibility is the opposite case in which a change in the capital stock reduces demand less at higher than at lower prices. In this case a reduction in demand is accompanied by smaller responsiveness of demand to price.

These definitions can be restated algebraically in terms of the change in the slope of the short-run demand curve as the capital stock is changed. Definition: The production technology exhibits

(a) constant   flexibility if $(F_{KQ})\,(\partial^2 Q/\partial P \partial K) = 0$ for all P,K

(b) increasing flexibility if $(F_{KQ})\,(\partial^2 Q/\partial P \partial K) > 0$ for all P,K

(c) decreasing flexibility if $(F_{KQ})\,(\partial^2 Q/\partial P \partial K) < 0$ for all P,K

These definitions recognize that short-run demand is a function of the capital stock and the oil price. Holding price constant, and

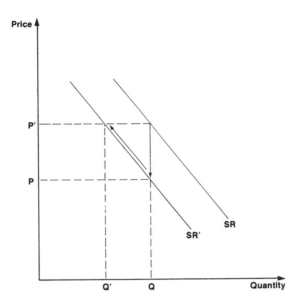

Figure B-4. Change in the marginal product of oil and in oil consumption.

changing the capital stock, induces a shift in and a movement along the demand curve. As figure B-4 illustrates, a change in the capital stock shifts the demand curve (marginal product) of oil vertically; then oil use moves along the new demand curve to a level consistent with the constant price. (The direction of the shift induced by an increase in K depends on the sign of F_{KQ}.) If the demand curve is not linear ($F_{QQQ} \neq 0$), the slope of SR at Q will differ from the slope of SR' at Q'; thus the curvature of the demand curve matters in determining how flexibility is affected by changes in the capital stock. In addition, changing the capital stock will rotate the demand curve, increasing or decreasing the slope algebraically at any given point greater or less than zero at that point.

We can derive an expression for $\partial^2 Q / \partial P \partial K$ by differentiating the slope of the inverse demand curve with respect to K, yielding

$$\frac{\partial^2 Q(P,K)}{\partial P \partial K} = \frac{-F_{QQ}F_{QQK} + F_{QK}F_{QQQ}}{F_{QQ}{}^3} \qquad \text{(B-4)}$$

If $F_{QQQ} = 0$, every short-run demand curve will be a straight line; if $F_{QQK} = 0$, a change in the capital stock serves to translate the short-run demand curve vertically. When both conditions hold, every member of the family of short-run demand curves generated by varying K will be parallel to every other; that is, flexibility is constant. An example of a production function satisfying these conditions is the quadratic function

$$F(K,Q) = a + bK + cQ + dK^2 + eQ^2 + fKQ$$

The Cobb-Douglas production function, of the form AK^aQ^b (with $0 < a + b < 1$), exhibits decreasing flexibility, since

$$\frac{\partial^2 Q(P,K)}{\partial P \partial K} = \frac{ab^2 A^2 K^{2a-1} Q^{2b-4}(b-1)(b-4)}{F_{QQ}^3} < 0$$

The expression (B-4) that determines whether or not flexibility is constant is analogous to one developed by Turnovsky (1973) in an analysis of the investment decision when output prices are uncertain. His results are directly relevant to the case of oil production, and can be easily adapted to the case of interest here, input price uncertainty. Turnovsky examines the relation between the capital stock chosen under uncertainty, K_u, and the capital stock chosen if prices are known to be fixed at their expected value, K_c.[4] For the case $F_{KQ} > 0$, his methods can be used to show that

$$\frac{\partial^2 Q}{\partial P \partial K} > 0 \text{ implies } K_u < K_c$$

$$\frac{\partial^2 Q}{\partial P \partial K} < 0 \text{ implies } K_u > K_c$$

$$\frac{\partial^2 Q}{\partial P \partial K} = 0 \text{ implies } K_u = K_c$$

Inequalities involving $\partial^2 Q/\partial P \partial K$ are reversed if $F_{KQ} < 0$.

If $\partial^2 Q/\partial P \partial K > 0$, the production function exhibits increasing flexibility. In this case, the capital stock chosen under uncertainty will be less than that chosen under certainty (of the expected price). If $F_{KQ} > 0$, this means that price uncertainty causes a downward shift in

----

[4] Uncertainty is introduced, following Rothschild and Stiglitz (1970 and 1971) by increasing the dispersion of prices around a constant mean.

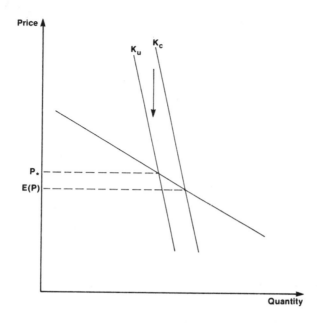

Figure B-5.   Increasing flexibility and the planning
price.

the short-run demand curve, compared to its location under certainty.
Other conditions can be interpreted analogously.

When price is certain and equal to $E(P)$, the short-run demand
curve, based on the capital stock K_c, will intersect the long-run demand curve at $E(P)$. If price uncertainty causes the short-run demand
curve to shift downward (as in the case of increasing flexibility), to a
location consistent with capital stock K_u, the short-run and long-run
demand curves will intersect at a price P_* greater than $E(P)$ (see
figure B-5). Note that if $F_{KQ} < 0$, increasing flexibility implies
$K_u > K_c$, but the increase in this case still shifts the short-run demand
curve downward. This train of reasoning can be repeated for other
cases to conclude that:

constant flexibility implies $P_* = E(P)$

increasing flexibility implies $P_* > E(P)$

decreasing flexibility implies $P_* < E(P)$

The same conclusions can be reached for oil production, as
demonstrated by Turnovsky (1973) and Hartman (1976). We will
simply sketch how a proof would be constructed.

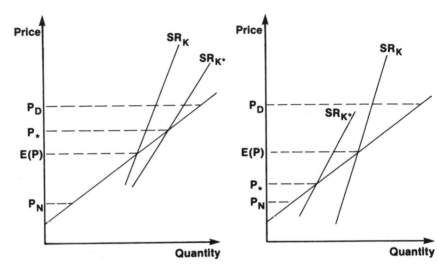

Figure B-6a.   Relation between marginal cost curves when the optimal capital stock K^* is greater than that chosen when the price is certain to be $E(P)$.

Figure B-6b.   Relation between marginal cost curves when the optimal capital stock K^* is less than that chosen when the price is certain to be $E(P)$.

Suppose that oil production technology is characterized by a production function $Q = F(K,L)$, where K represents inputs that are fixed in the short run (e.g., capital) and L represents inputs that are variable (e.g., labor). From the production function we can construct short-run and long-run marginal cost functions that determine oil output at different prices. Long-run marginal cost is defined as the cost of increasing output by one unit when both K and L are varied optimally. Short-run marginal cost is the cost of increasing output by one unit when K is fixed.

Figures B-6a and B-6b depict a typical relationship between long-run and short-run marginal cost curves. Increasing the use of some fixed factor of production shifts the short-run marginal cost curve to the right. Production will take place at a point along a given short-run marginal cost curve where price equals marginal cost. The position of the short-run curve is fixed by choosing inputs of fixed factors that will maximize expected profits.

Suppose, as in figure B-6a, that a small increase in capacity makes the short-run supply curve flatter, increasing output in a disruption at price P_D more than output at price P_N. In this case, the optimal level of fixed investment is greater than that which would be made if the expected price were certain to occur in the future. If the short-run supply curve became steeper (less elastic), as in figure B-6b, the opposite is true.

Optimal Preparations for a Disruption When Price Depends on Imports

Maximizing collective welfare in the presence of disruption risks requires recognition of the relation between total U.S. import demand and the world price of oil. That relation will differ, depending on the state of the world oil market. We will examine the conditions that determine optimal imports and investments for the economy as a whole, and contrast them with conditions that will be satisfied by private decisions in the absence of government intervention. An optimal tariff is represented as a rule for calculating an adjustment to the price of oil that makes private decisions satisfy the collective optimum.

Denote the world oil price in state s as a function of the quantity of U.S. imports $P_s(Q_s)$. We assume that there are $i = 1 \ldots n$ firms in the economy, and express the total value of output as $\Sigma_i F^i(K^i, Q_s^i)$. Total import demand $Q_s = \Sigma_i Q_s^i$ and the total capital stock is $\Sigma_i K^i$. In any state of the world, the objective for the economy as a whole is to maximize profits

$$\sum_i [F^i(K^i, Q_s^i) - P_s(Q_s) \cdot Q_s^i] \tag{B-5}$$

In advance of a disruption, K^i must be chosen to maximize expected profits

$$\int_s \sum_i \{ F^i[K, Q_s^i(K)] - P_s(Q_s) \cdot Q_s(K) \} \, du(s) - r \sum_i K^i \tag{B-6}$$

In order to maximize short-run profits after the state of the world is known, each firm should choose an oil demand to satisfy

$$F_Q^i - P_s - P_s Q_s = 0 \tag{B-7}$$

In the previous section, we saw that firms will instead choose Q_s^i according to the rule

$$F_Q^i - P_s = 0,$$

and market prices will adjust until total U.S. demand equals import supply to the United States. If equation (B-7) is solved for an optimal level of imports, Q^*_s, the government can impose a tariff equal to $P'_s(Q^*_s) \cdot Q^*_s$ on oil imports in state s. Faced with this tariff and the resulting equilibrium oil price, each firm will choose a level of oil use that satisfies (B-7).

We can express the chosen level of oil use, when an optimal tariff is in place in every state of the world, as a function of the quasi-fixed capital stock by solving equation (B-7) for Q. This yields a function $Q_s^i(K_i)$ which can then be substituted in the expected profit function. Expected profits are maximized when for all firms $i = 1, \ldots, n$,

$$\int_s \left[F_K^i + F_{Q^i_s}^i \frac{dQ_s^i}{dK_i} - P_s \frac{dQ_s^i}{dK_i} - P'_s Q_s^i \frac{dQ_s^i}{dK_i} \right] du(s) = r$$

If the optimal tariff is in place, each firm will adjust oil use in a disruption to satisfy (B-7,) and all terms involving dQ_s^i/dK_i will vanish. Therefore in addition to (B-7), the condition for maximizing expected profits becomes

$$\int_s F_K^i [K, Q_s^i (K^i)] \, du(s) = r \qquad \text{(B-8)}$$

This is exactly the condition a firm will satisfy when choosing a capital stock that is privately optimal, anticipating future prices that include the disruption tariff. Consequently, the variable disruption tariff equal to $P'_s(Q^*_s) \cdot Q^*_s$ will lead to short-run and long-run private behavior that is collectively optimal.

Our earlier results on flexibility and the planning price lead directly to the conclusion that there is no uniform tariff, whose value is independent of the state of the world, that will produce the same result. The proper tradeoff between flexibility and efficiency will be made only if agents face the full probability distribution of prices (which must include the variable tariff).

Even if this tradeoff is assumed away, it will remain true that the action equivalent of a variable tariff will be different for each agent in the economy. As we demonstrated above, the action equivalent price differs from the expected price by an amount that depends on technical features of the individual production process used by a firm or industry. Therefore the appropriate constant tariff will vary among individual consumers and producers of oil. Those who find that long-term reductions in oil use (or increases in production) decrease flexibility should face a constant tariff lower than the expected value of the variable tariff, while those who find that long-term reductions in oil use increase flexibility should face a constant tariff higher than the expected value of the variable tariff.

Optimal Import Policy with Macroeconomic Costs

When an oil supply disruption gives rise to external macroeconomic costs, a tariff set equal to the demand component of the premium is not optimal. A lower tariff in a disruption and a higher tariff in normal periods is necessary to achieve maximum benefits. The existence of macroeconomic costs introduces an additional dynamic complication because these costs depend on changes in import levels and prices between one state of the world and another. Moreover, the direction of change matters: an increase in price (or decrease in imports) is the direction that creates a macroeconomic cost. To use a simple model, we must adopt some artificial assumptions about sequencing. We assume two time periods of equal length: the first is characterized by normal markets and the second by a disruption. The capital stock is chosen before the first period begins, is acquired instantaneously, and cannot be subsequently changed. We do not need to introduce the probability of a disruption in the formulation, because it is known that a disruption will occur half the time. We ignore all events subsequent to the disruption, including any costs of adjusting to a lower price. To avoid cumbersome notation, we consider one representative firm to illustrate production of goods for the entire economy. We assume that no individual takes into account the effect of Q_s on macroeconomic costs or on the world price.

Macroeconomic costs are introduced by subtracting a function M from potential national income during a disruption.

One specification of macro costs is $M = M(Q_N - Q_D)$, i.e., that M is a function of the change in imports between normal and disrupted periods. This is the specification adopted in the oil market simulation model in appendix A. Alternative specifications are examined below, where we find that the qualitative conclusions remain unchanged under a surprisingly broad range of specifications. For the moment, we assume no domestic oil production in order to avoid the distinction between domestic consumption and oil imports. The macro costs function specified above captures the characteristics of "supply-side" costs discussed in chapter 5 if we assume:

$$M > 0 \text{ for } Q_N > Q_D$$

$$M' > 0 \text{ for } Q_N > Q_D$$

$$M = M' = 0 \text{ for } Q_N \leq Q_D$$

The first condition says that macroeconomic costs are positive when more is imported in normal than in disrupted periods. The second condition says that macroeconomic dislocations increase with the size of the decline in imports during a disruption, or, equivalently, that costs increase with change in the domestic shadow price of imports. The third condition says that there is no macroeconomic cost if a disruption does not result in lower imports.

Demand-side costs of a disruption, caused by an increase in the wealth transfer abroad, can be represented in the model by a term m. These costs are reduced by lowering the disrupted price and quantity of imports or by increasing the normal price and quantity of imports. The macroeconomic penalty from this leakage is a function of the *change* in oil producers' revenues.

Society's objective function, as modified by both kinds of macro costs, is given by

$$F(K,Q_N) - P_N Q_N + F(K,Q_D) - P_D Q_D$$
$$- m (P_D Q_D - P_N Q_N) - M(Q_N - Q_D) - rK$$

In period 2, the capital stock is fixed, and the optimum quantity of imports is a function of the capital stock as determined by the first-order condition

$$F_Q(K,Q_D) - (1 + m) (P_D + P'_D Q_D) + M' = 0 \qquad \text{(B-9)}$$

In period 1, the optimum quantity of imports is given by

$$F_Q(K,Q_N) - (1 - m) (P_N + P'_N Q_N) - M' = 0 \qquad \text{(B-10)}$$

In both the disrupted and normal period, short-run oil use decisions include the effect of oil consumption on disruption costs. To solve for the optimal capital stock, equations (B-9) and (B-10) are solved for optimal import levels Q_N and Q_D as functions of K, and used to eliminate Q_N and Q_D from the objective function. The first-order condition for an optimal capital stock then becomes

$$F_K(K,Q_D) + \frac{dQ_D}{dK} [F_Q - (1 + m) (P_D + P'_D Q_D) + M'] + F_K(K,Q_N)$$

$$+ \frac{dQ_N}{dK} [F_Q - (1 - m) (P_N + P'_N Q_N) - M'] - r = 0$$

(B-11)

Using (B-9) and (B-10) to eliminate terms containing dQ_D/dK and dQ_N/dK from (B-11) gives $F_K(K,Q_N) + F_K(K,Q_D) = r$.

Tariffs are necessary in normal and disrupted periods to make private decisions satisfy the optimality conditions. In a disrupted period, external costs include the direct effect of import demand on price and the two types of macroeconomic costs represented by m and M. The direct and macroeconomic costs associated with international wealth transfers require a specific tariff t that satisfies $P_D + t_D = (1 + m) (P_D + P'_D Q_D)$. Therefore t_D must equal $mP_D + (1 + m)P'_D Q_D$. However, this tariff causes a reduction in imports that increases supply-side macroeconomic costs. Hence the tariff is reduced by an amount equal to M'. For simplicity, we will assume that $m = 0$, since the effect of leakages that make $m > 0$ serves only to magnify the demand component of the disruption tariff. Moreover, leakages can also occur because of the collection of tariff revenues by the government; and in any event they can be corrected through conventional demand stabilization policies. With this simplification, the required tariff in a disruption is

$$T_D = P'_D Q_D - M'$$

This tariff may be positive or negative (a subsidy) depending on the relation between disrupted supply elasticities and the response of macroeconomic costs to changes in import levels.

In a normal period, import decisions must recognize their effect on normal prices and on the macroeconomic costs of a disruption. Thus a tariff

$$T_N = P'_N Q_N + M'$$

must be added to the normal price of oil. If $m > 0$, this tariff will be reduced by a term $mP + mP'_N Q_N$ because a higher normal world price reduces the change in producer revenues caused by a disruption and lowers macro costs.

With these tariffs, private decisions will satisfy conditions (B-9) and (B-10), and all terms in (B-11) involving dQ_D/dK and dQ_N/dK will vanish, leaving the familiar condition[5]

$$F_K(K,Q_N) + F_K(K,Q_D) = r \qquad \text{(B-12)}$$

This condition will be satisfied by private parties maximizing expected profits if they anticipate the optimal tariffs $t_D = P'_D Q_D - M'$ and $t_N = P'_N Q_N + M'$. Subtracting M' from the disruption tariff and adding it to the normal tariff reduces macroeconomic costs by dampening changes in oil consumption. Moreover, incentives for long-run conservation measures (through changes in K) are maintained because the lower domestic price in a disruption is balanced by a higher normal domestic price. No other incentives than the normal and disruption tariffs are required to bring about optimal investments in energy conservation.

However, this tariff policy discourages flexibility: if changes in the normal and disruption tariff to incorporate M' leave the expected domestic price of oil unchanged, their effect is to reduce price uncertainty. As proved above, the effect of reducing uncertainty is to reduce the incentive to invest in flexibility. If, as represented in this model, only the difference between Q_N and Q_D affects macroeconomic costs, reducing flexibility is clearly proper. Macroeconomic costs would indeed be eliminated if oil use were fixed in the short run so that Q_N and Q_D could not differ.

This conclusion is paradoxical, and may arise from the partial equilibrium nature of the model. Because the budget constraint is expressed in terms of resource endowments, it is impossible for the consumption of all goods to remain unchanged when the price of one good increases. Thus, if the use of oil is fixed, a disruption in oil prices will cause the consumption of other goods to fall. The resulting macroeconomic losses outside the oil market will be smaller if oil demand is more flexible. Partial equilibrium analysis of flexibility gives robust results only if the costs and benefits of flexibility are confined to the oil market, as they were in the analysis above. It may

[5] The cost of capital r should be thought of as the rental price for *two* periods.

be that a policy recognizing only macroeconomic costs of import changes, and narrowing the variability of domestic oil prices, serves to discourage choices that produce benefits by reducing the size of adjustments required elsewhere in the economy.

With this qualification, and assuming that changes in imports equal changes in consumption and that macroeconomic costs associated with international wealth transfers are zero, the conclusion emerges that if there are macroeconomic costs of a disruption that can be avoided only by dampening changes in oil consumption, the optimal tariff in a disruption equals the difference between a demand component and a macroeconomic cost component, and the optimal tariff in a normal period equals the sum of a demand component and a macroeconomic cost component. Moreover, no additional incentives are required to adjust the capital stock if these tariffs are anticipated.

A trivial but tedious extension of this model describes a case in which the price of oil in period 2 is uncertain, by assuming that the supply curve shifts to $P_D(Q_D)$ with probability π and remains at $P_N(Q_N)$ with probability $1 - \pi$. Assuming $m = 0$, the optimal disruption tariff remains $P'_D Q_D - M'$, but the tariff in period 1 becomes $P'_N Q_N + \pi M'$. Since the disruption occurs with probability π, the term $\pi M'$ in the normal tariff restores the incentive for long-run conservation removed by the term $-M'$ in the disruption tariff. All other conclusions of this section hold with this extended model.

To make this extension, it is necessary to consider three separate oil use decisions: oil use in a disrupted final period, oil use in a normal final period, and oil use during the normal first period. Working backward from optimal decisions in the final period, the first period objective function is $F(K,Q_N) - P_N \cdot Q_N + V(Q_N)$ where $V(Q_N)$ is the expected value of final period profits, maximized with respect to final period consumption in each state. Differentiating with respect to Q_N and applying the envelope theorem yields a first-order condition $F_Q - P_N - P'_N Q_N - \pi M' = 0$, from which the optimal tariff is derived.

Alternative Specifications of Macroeconomic Costs

The qualitative conclusion that macroeconomic costs reduce the optimal disruption tariff and increase the optimal normal tariff holds under a wide range of specifications of the macro cost function. This proposition is demonstrated in the rest of this section.

If macroeconomic costs are represented by a more general function $M(Q_N, Q_D)$, then the optimal tariffs are:

$$t_N = P'_N Q_N + \partial M/\partial Q_N \qquad\qquad\qquad (B\text{-}13)$$

$$t_D = P'_D Q_D + \partial M/\partial Q_D \qquad\qquad\qquad (B\text{-}14)$$

If reducing normal imports has a greater effect on macro costs than increasing disrupted imports, the increase in t_N will do more than just replace the price incentive subtracted from t_D. In this case, we can think of the normal tariff as serving three functions: the conventional demand component $P'_N Q_N$, the function of smoothing out oil demand, and the function of reducing long-run oil demand to reduce macro costs.

Another plausible specification of macroeconomic costs is a multiplicative function. If we assume that a rapid change in import levels causes a loss in output of the representative firm, we can express the production function in a disruption as [6]

$$M^i (Q_N, Q_D) F(K^i, Q_D^i)$$

where $M^i = 1$ if $Q_N \leq Q_D$: that is, output is unaffected by increases in oil consumption. If $Q_N \geq Q_D$, the disruption imposes macroeconomic costs and $\partial M/\partial Q_N < 0$ and $\partial M/\partial Q_D > 0$. Remembering that the individual firm does not take into account the effect of imports on the world price, the *firm* will choose K^i, $Q_D{}^i$, and $Q_N{}^i$ to satisfy

$$M^i F_Q (K^i, Q_D^i) + \frac{\partial M^i}{\partial Q_D^i} F(K^i, Q_D^i) = P_D \qquad\qquad (B\text{-}15)$$

$$F_Q(K^i, Q_N^i) + \frac{\partial M^i}{\partial Q_N^i} F(K^i, Q_D^i) = P_N \qquad\qquad (B\text{-}16)$$

$$F_K(K^i, Q_N^i) + M^i F_K(K^i, Q_D^i) = r \qquad\qquad\qquad (B\text{-}17)$$

The social planner will want each firm to satisfy

$$M^i F_Q(K^i, Q_D^i) + \sum_j \frac{\partial M^j}{\partial Q_D} F(K^j, Q_D^j) = P_D + P'_D Q_D \qquad (B\text{-}18)$$

[6] Let $Q_N = \Sigma_i Q_N{}^i$ and $Q_D = \Sigma_i Q_D{}^i$, and note that $\partial M/\partial Q_s{}^i = \partial M/\partial Q_s$.

$$F_Q(K^i,Q_N^i) + \sum_j \frac{\partial M^j}{\partial Q_N} F(K^j,Q_D^j) = P_N + P'_N Q_N \qquad \text{(B-19)}$$

$$F_K(K^i,Q_N^i) + M^i F_K(K^i,Q_D^i) = r \qquad \text{(B-20)}$$

(The indicated summation should be understood to be taken over all $j \neq i$.) Macroeconomic costs impose a true externality in this case. Each firm's decision to change oil use imposes macroeconomic costs on all firms [the term $\Sigma_j(\partial M^j/\partial Q_s^i)F(K^j,Q_D^j)$ in the social planner's problem], but each firm takes into account only the effect on its own output $(\partial M^i/\partial Q^i)F(K^i,Q_D^i)$, which is negligible if there are a large number of firms. Let us assume that the macro cost factor M is the same for all firms. In this case the optimal tariffs are:

$$t_D = P'_D Q_D - \sum_j \frac{\partial M}{\partial Q_D} F(K^j,Q_D^j) \qquad \text{(B-21)}$$

$$t_N = P'_N Q_N - \sum_j \frac{\partial M}{\partial Q_N} F(K^j,Q_D^j) \qquad \text{(B-22)}$$

The same qualitative conclusion emerges that a normal tariff should be increased and a disruption tariff decreased because of macroeconomic costs.

If each individual firm anticipates the size of total imports in normal and disrupted periods, each will apply the correct factor M in production decisions, according to the rational expectations hypothesis. Each firm will choose a capital stock that satisfies $F_K(K,Q_N) + MF_K(K,Q_D) = r$. If the macroeconomic cost of a disruption is not anticipated, they will instead choose a capital stock satisfying $F_K(K,Q_N) + F_K(K,Q_D) = r$. That is, firms will overestimate the marginal product of capital during a disruption. To compensate for this error in anticipations, the rental price of capital should be increased by the term $(1 - M)F_K(K,Q_D)$. Whether this adjustment will increase or decrease oil imports depends on whether reducing the capital stock increases or decreases the marginal product of energy.

The conclusion that a normal tariff should be larger and a disruption tariff smaller (and that with rational expectations the optimal investment decision will obtain), also holds if macroeconomic costs are specified as a function of the change in the domestic price of oil.

This is not surprising because of the fundamental duality of prices and quantities. To demonstrate, let the macroeconomic cost function be

$$M(P_D + t_D - P_N - t_N)Q_N$$

This function represents the argument that, with a given level of oil consumption Q_N, macroeconomic costs increase with the change in the domestic relative price; or, alternatively, with a given change in the price, macroeconomic costs increase with Q_N. The social planning problem is to choose tariffs in normal and disrupted periods, and the rental price of capital, that maximize expected net income less macroeconomic costs. The objective is to maximize

$$V_D = F(K,Q_D) - P_D(Q_D)Q_D - M(P_D + t_D - P_N - t_N)Q_N \qquad (B\text{-}23)$$

The first-order condition is

$$(F_Q^D - P_D - P'_D Q_D - M'P'_D Q_N)\frac{dQ_D}{dt_D} - M'Q_N = 0 \qquad (B\text{-}24)$$

Private agents will set $F_Q^D = P_D + t_D$, so t_D must satisfy:

$$(t_D - P'_D Q_D - M'P'_D Q_N)\frac{dQ_n}{dt_D} - M'Q_N = 0$$

where

$$\frac{dQ_D}{dt_D} = \frac{1}{F_{QQ}^D - P'_D}$$

We can express t_D as

$$t_D = P'_D Q_D + M'P'_D Q_N + M'Q_N(F_{QQ}^D - P'_D) = P'_D Q_D + M'Q_N F_{QQ}^D \qquad (B\text{-}25)$$

The second term in (B-25) is negative, reflecting the macroeconomic cost of raising the tariff to the full amount required to internalize direct costs.

In period 1, the government can choose t_N to maximize $V_N + V_D$ where $V_N = F(K,Q_N) - P_N(Q_N) \cdot Q_N$. The first-order condition is

$$\frac{\partial V_N}{\partial t_N} + \frac{\partial V_D}{\partial t_N} + \frac{\partial V_D}{\partial t d}\frac{dt_D}{dt_N} = 0$$

As t_D is chosen to make $\partial V_D/\partial t_D = 0$, only the direct effect of t_N on V_D need be considered. Thus, the first-order condition is

$$(F_Q^N - P_N - P'_N Q_N + M'P'_N Q_N)\frac{dQ_N}{dt_N} + M'Q_N - M\frac{dQ_N}{dt_N} = 0$$

and the normal tariff must satisfy

$$t_N = P'_N Q_N + M - M'Q_N (F_{QQ}^N - P'_N) \tag{B-26}$$

All terms in this expression are positive. The normal tariff includes the additional term M that is not subtracted from the disruption tariff. This follows from the specification of macro costs as proportional to the quantity of normal imports.

The government might also consider a tax (or subsidy) on capital investment. The optimal capital stock must maximize $V_N + V_D - rK$. The first-order condition is

$$\left[\frac{\partial V_N}{\partial K} + \frac{\partial V_N}{\partial Q_N}\frac{\partial Q_N}{\partial K} + \frac{\partial V_D}{\partial K} + \frac{\partial V_D}{\partial Q_D}\frac{\partial Q_D}{\partial K}\right.$$
$$\left. + \frac{\partial V_D}{\partial Q_D}\frac{\partial Q_D}{\partial Q_N}\frac{\partial Q_N}{\partial K} - r\right]\frac{dK}{dt_K} = 0 \tag{B-27}$$

But $\partial V_N/\partial Q_N = 0$ and $\partial V_D/\partial Q_D = 0$, so that the first-order condition reduces to

$$F_K(K,Q_N) + F_K(K,Q_D) = r \tag{B-28}$$

Hence, the optimal adjustment to the rental rate on capital is zero. Again, the qualitative conclusion follows that the disruption tariff decreases and the normal tariff increases because of macroeconomic costs, and that no change in the rental price of capital is required.

If the capital stock K enters directly into the macroeconomic penalty function, a change in the rental price of capital is required to obtain optimal investment decisions. This may be established in general by writing the planner's objective function as

$$V(K,Q_N,Q_D) = V_1(K,Q_N) + V_2(K,Q_N,Q_D) - rK \tag{B-29}$$

The term V_2 includes all terms that depend on Q_D; [e.g., $F(K,Q_D) - P_D(Q_D)Q_D - M(K,Q_N,Q_D)$]. These terms are controllable in period 2; thus, a necessary condition for maximizing V is $\partial V_2/\partial Q_D = 0$. Solving (B-29) for Q_D as a function of K and Q_N, and substituting for Q_D in V_2, will yield a new function $V_2[K,Q_N,Q_D(K,Q_N)]$. In period 1 all terms in V except K are controllable; thus, a necessary condition for maximizing V is

$$\frac{\partial V}{\partial Q_N} = \frac{\partial V_1}{\partial Q_N} + \frac{\partial V_2}{\partial Q_D}\frac{\partial Q_D}{\partial Q_N} + \frac{\partial V_2}{\partial Q_N} = 0 \tag{B-30}$$

Since $\partial V_2/\partial Q_D = 0$, this condition reduces to

$$\frac{\partial V}{\partial Q_N} = \frac{\partial V_1}{\partial Q_N} + \frac{\partial V_2}{\partial Q_N} = 0$$

where $\partial V_2/\partial Q_N$ is the partial derivative of the original function $V_2(K,Q_N,Q_D)$ with respect to Q_N, holding Q_D fixed. For example, $\partial V_2/\partial Q_N$ may equal $\partial M(K,Q_N,Q_D)/\partial Q_N$.

The equation $\partial V/\partial Q_N = 0$ can now be solved to give Q_N as a function of K, generating a new function[7]

$$V(K) = V_1[K,Q_N(K)] + V_2\{K,Q_N(K),Q_D[K,Q_N(K)]\} - rK \tag{B-31}$$

The necessary condition for maximizing $V(K)$ is

$$\frac{dV}{dK} = \frac{\partial V_1}{\partial K} + \frac{\partial V_1}{\partial Q_N}\frac{\partial Q_N}{\partial K} + \frac{\partial V_2}{\partial K} + \frac{\partial V_2}{\partial Q_D}\frac{\partial Q_D}{\partial K}$$

$$+ \left[\frac{\partial V_2}{\partial Q_N} + \frac{\partial V_2}{\partial Q_D}\frac{\partial Q_D}{\partial Q_N}\right]\frac{dQ_N}{dK} - r = 0 \tag{B-32}$$

[7] We are grateful to Michael Toman for pointing out this proof using the envelope theorem.

Since $\partial V_1/\partial Q_N + \partial V_2/\partial Q_N = 0$ and $\partial V_2/\partial Q_D = 0$, equation (B-32) reduces to

$$\frac{dV}{dK} = \frac{\partial V_1}{\partial K} + \frac{\partial V_2}{\partial K} - r = 0 \tag{B-33}$$

The first term is the marginal product of capital in a normal period, as K enters directly only in the production function. The second term will include more than the marginal product of capital in a disruption if K enters directly in the macroeconomic cost function. In this case

$$\frac{dV}{dK} = F_K^N + F_K^Q + M_K = r \tag{B-34}$$

An adjustment to the rental price of capital equal to the derivative of M with respect to the capital stock is required in addition to tariffs in each period.

Tariff Policy in an Economy with Oil Production

Suppose the economy also produces oil, so that imports and consumption are not identical. We assume that consumption, not imports, determines macroeconomic costs. Let Q_N and Q_D represent consumption in the normal and disrupted period; let S_N be domestic supply in the normal period and S_D be domestic supply in a disruption; and let $C(S_N,S_D)$ be the cost of producing S_N and S_D. This formulation allows for consideration of simple rigid production processes (i.e., $C = \infty$ if $S_N \neq S_D$) and processes that have some short-run flexibility, without explicitly introducing a fixed factor in oil production. The objective function is

$$F(K,Q_N) - P_N(Q_N - S_N) \cdot (Q_N - S_N) + F(K,Q_D)$$
$$- P_D(Q_D - S_D) \cdot (Q_D - S_D) - M(Q_N - Q_D)$$
$$- C(S_N,S_D) - rK \tag{B-35}$$

During a disruption, Q_D and S_D must satisfy

$$F_Q^D - P_D - P_D' \cdot (Q_D - S_D) + M' = 0 \tag{B-36}$$

$$C_2 = P_D - P_D' \cdot (Q_D - S_D) \tag{B-37}$$

Private individuals will set $F_Q{}^D = P_D$ and $C_2 = P_D$. To encourage collectively optimal oil consumption and production in a disruption, the price to consumers should be increased by $P'_D \cdot (Q_D - S_D) - M'$ (the demand component less the macroeconomic cost component), while the price facing producers should be increased by the larger amount $P'_D \cdot (Q_D - S_D)$. In a normal period an analogous result holds. Consumers should pay an amount equal to the price plus the term $P'_N \cdot (Q_N - S_N) + M'$, while producers should receive an amount equal to the price plus $P'_N(Q_N - S_N)$.

If there is no short-run flexibility in oil use, we can write $C(S_D, S_N) = C(S)$ with $S \equiv S_D \equiv S_N$. The first-order conditions are then

$$F_Q^D - P_D - P'_D \cdot (Q_D - S) + M' = 0 \tag{B-38}$$

$$F_Q^N - P_N - P'_N \cdot (Q_N - S) - M' = 0 \tag{B-39}$$

for consumers. Producers choose S initially, and it remains fixed. They must set the marginal cost of producing oil for two periods equal to the sum of marginal values of oil supply across both periods. That is,

$$C'(S) = P_N + P'_N \cdot (Q_N - S) + P_D + P'_D \cdot (Q_D - S) \tag{B-40}$$

It does not matter whether tariffs t_N and t_D include a macroeconomic cost component. As long as the term subtracted from the disruption tariff is added back to the normal tariff, the long-run incentive for oil production will be unaffected.

This is not true if S_N can be different from S_D. Then the flexibility issues described above apply. A tariff that increases the variance of prices without changing their mean value will encourage increased flexibility. Subtracting M' from t_D and adding M' to t_N does not alter the mean value of prices.

Stockpiling, the Premium, and Import Policy

This final section provides some mathematical background for the model discussed in chapter 6. The costs and benefits of stockpiling can be illustrated with a simple model that extends the analysis of previous sections to include a stockpiling decision.[8] In order to relate stockpiling and tariff policies as clearly as possible, it is useful to adopt some artificial assumptions about how decisions are sequenced. Suppose there are two time periods, where in the first period normal supply conditions prevail and in the second period a disruption occurs. In the first period an amount equal to B barrels of oil is purchased for the strategic reserve, and a fixed stock of energy-using capital is in place. Given the stockpile level and fixed capital stock, oil consumption is to equal Q_N.

During the second period, the supply curve of imported oil shifts to the left and the reserve of B barrels of oil is drawn down to zero. Given the stock of energy-using capital and the size of B determined in the first period, the only planning decision in the second period is the level of oil imports Q_D. Over both periods the optimal level of oil use depends on the stock of fixed capital K, and the size of the strategic reserve B. In order to choose values for K and B that maximize expected profits, private agents must recognize how oil consumption will vary as a function of K and B.

This hypothetical situation includes all the essential elements of decision-making under uncertainty. It is known that the price will be at a normal level in the first period and at a disrupted level in the second period. If both periods are of equal length, decisions will be made as if the probability of disruption is 0.5. As long as decision makers are neutral toward risk, there is no difference between the assumption of a 50 percent chance of a disruption and the assumption that a disruption is certain to occur in one of two periods of equal length.[9]

Optimal Stockpiles in the Presence of Optimal Tariffs

In this section we derive the joint solution for optimal stockpile size and optimal import tariffs. The solution indicates the effect of stockpile building on the optimal tariff policy. The following section is

---

[8] For a more elaborate treatment, see Teisberg (1981). The basic logic of Teisberg's approach is similar, but focuses on disruptions of varying size over many periods of time to arrive at an optimal strategy of stockpile purchase and sale rather than optimal size.

[9] We are also implicitly assuming that there is no discounting of future revenues, and that investors are neutral in their attitudes toward risk, that is, that they will maximize the expected value of profits.

concerned with the optimal stockpile size in the absence of tariffs to determine how an import tariff alters the optimal size.

The envelope theorem makes it possible to characterize optimal stockpiling policy compactly. The social planner's problem is to maximize

$$F(K,Q_N) - P_N(Q_N + B) \cdot (Q_N + B) - M(Q_N - Q_D) + F(K,Q_D)$$
$$- P_D(Q_D - B) \cdot (Q_D - B) - rK - H(B) \qquad \text{(B-41)}$$

where $H(B)$ is the cost of storing the stockpile for one period and r is the two-period rental price of capital. Necessary conditions for optimal oil consumption are

Period 1: $F_Q^N - P_N' \cdot (Q_N + B) - P_N - M' = 0 \qquad \text{(B-42)}$

Period 2: $F_Q^D - P_D' \cdot (Q_D - B) - P_D + M' = 0 \qquad \text{(B-43)}$

The capital stock must satisfy

$$F_K^N + F_K^D = r \qquad \text{(B-44)}$$

Equations (B-42) through (B-44) are derived by a method identical to that used in previous sections. Equations (B-42) and (B-43) can be solved for optimal levels of Q_D and Q_N as functions of K and B. These functions are then substituted for Q_D and Q_N in the objective function (B-41). Since P_N and P_D are already written as functions of Q_N, Q_D, and B, this substitution will render (B-41) a function of K and B alone. To generate a condition for optimality of the stockpile, the partial derivative of (B-41) with respect to B must be set equal to zero. All terms in the resulting equation involving $\partial Q_N / \partial B$ and $\partial Q_D / \partial B$ will vanish if (B-42) and (B-43) hold, giving

$$P_N + P_N' (Q_N + B) + H'(B) = P_D + P_D' (Q_D - B) \qquad \text{(B-45)}$$

That is, the optimal stockpile must satisfy the condition that the difference between the marginal cost of oil in a disruption and the marginal cost of oil in a normal period equals the marginal cost of storage.

Private decision makers who ignore macroeconomic costs and treat prices as parametric will choose K, B, Q_N, and Q_D to satisfy

$$F_Q^D = P_D \qquad\qquad\qquad \text{(B-46)}$$

$$F_Q^N = P_N \qquad\qquad\qquad \text{(B-47)}$$

$$F_K^N + F_K^D = r \qquad\qquad\qquad \text{(B-48)}$$

$$P_N + H'(B) = P_D \qquad\qquad\qquad \text{(B-49)}$$

These conditions are derived by methods parallel to those used above, assuming that P_N and P_D are constants.

Tariffs cannot be found that simultaneously support optimal consumption and stockpile levels in the presence of macroeconomic costs. If tariffs $t_D = P'_D \cdot (Q_D - B) - M'$ and $t_N = P'_N \cdot (Q_N + B) + M'$ are imposed, private agents will choose stockpiles according to the rule

$$P_N + t_N + H'(B) = P_D + t_D$$

or,

$$P_N + P'_N \cdot (Q_N + B) + H'(B) = P_D + P'_D \cdot (Q_D - B) - 2M'$$

The effect of adopting a tariff that is less variable than the marginal cost of imports is to decrease the price of oil in a disruption. This will reduce the incentive for stockpiling, compared to the optimal level given by equations (B-41) through (B-45).

Next, we wish to compare the optimal stockpile size when $M' = 0$ (i.e., when there are no macro dislocation costs) and $M' > 0$. Assume that the government purchases an amount of oil for a stockpile that satisfies equations (B-41) through (B-45), and imposes tariffs that are optimal given macroeconomic costs: $t_N = P'_N \cdot (Q_N + B) + M'$ and $t_D = P'_D \cdot (Q_D - B) - M'$. A lower disruption tariff leads to a higher level of disrupted imports and hence to a larger value of $P'_D(Q_D - B)$, whereas a higher normal tariff leads to a lower level of normal imports, and consequently a smaller value of $P'_N(Q_N + B)$. As a result, with macroeconomic costs, a larger stockpile is required to close the larger gap between the marginal cost of normal imports and the marginal cost of disrupted imports.

If the price at which oil can be sold from the reserve in the second period is uncertain, the optimal stockpile should satisfy the condition that the expected increase in the marginal cost of oil imports equals the marginal cost of storage. If there is uncertainty about a disruption in period 2, the mathematical condition is

$$(1 - \pi) \, [P_N + P'_N \cdot (Q_N^2 + B)] \; + \pi[P_D + P'_D \cdot (Q_D^2 - B)]$$
$$- \, [P_N + P'_N \cdot (Q_N^1 + B)] = H'\,(B)$$

The probability of disruption is assumed to be π. We denote oil consumption in a normal second period as $Q_N{}^2$, oil consumption in a disrupted second period as $Q_D{}^2$, and oil consumption in the normal first period as $Q_N{}^1$. In a strict two-period model, the stockpile must be sold off in period 2 whether or not there is a disruption. Thinking more realistically about the continuing likelihood of a disruption requires a model like Teisberg's (1981).

Optimal Stockpile Size Without Tariffs

It is of interest to inquire how the presence of optimal tariffs affects the optimal stockpile size. In the absence of any tariffs, finding the optimal stockpile size is a second-best problem and our simple model is unable to provide a definitive answer. Without tariffs, the social planner will not be able to use (B-42) and (B-43) to predict how oil consumption will vary as a function of stockpile size. Instead (B-46) to (B-48) must be solved for Q_N, Q_D, and K as functions of B, and the resulting functions substituted in the objective function (B-41). Differentiating the objective function with respect to B and letting $F_Q{}^D = P_D$ and $F_Q{}^N = P_N$ yields a condition for optimal stockpile size in which terms involving $\partial Q_D/\partial B$ and $\partial Q_N/\partial B$ no longer vanish:

$$P_D + P'_D\,(Q_D - B) - [P'_D\,(Q_D - B) - M']\,\frac{\partial Q_D}{\partial B}$$
$$- \, [P_N + P'_N\,(Q_N + B)]$$
$$- \, [P'_N\,(Q_N + B) + M']\,\frac{\partial Q_N}{\partial B} = H'\,(B) \qquad\qquad \text{(B-50)}$$

We can evaluate $\partial Q_D/\partial B$ and $\partial Q_N/\partial B$ by standard comparative statics analysis of the first-order conditions that predict market response. Taking changes in B to be perturbations of (B-46) through (B-48), differentiating totally and collecting terms yields the following matrix equation:

$$
\begin{bmatrix}
F_{QK}^{D} & F_{QQ}^{D} - P_{D}' & 0 \\
F_{QK}^{N} & 0 & F_{QQ}^{N} - P_{N}' \\
F_{KK}^{D} + F_{KK}^{D} & F_{KQ}^{D} & F_{KQ}^{N}
\end{bmatrix}
\begin{bmatrix}
dK \\
dQ_D \\
dQ_N
\end{bmatrix}
=
\begin{bmatrix}
-P_{D}'\,dB \\
P_{N}'\,dB \\
0
\end{bmatrix}
$$

Inverting the matrix and solving for $\partial Q_D/\partial B$ and $\partial Q_N/\partial B$ yields

$$
\frac{\partial Q_D}{\partial B} =
$$

$$
\frac{-[(F_{KQ}^{N})^2 - F_{KK}^{N}F_{QQ}^{N} - F_{KK}^{D}F_{QQ}^{N} + P_{N}'(F_{KK}^{N} + F_{KK}^{D})]P_{D}' - F_{KQ}^{D}F_{KQ}^{N}P_{N}'}{|D|} \tag{B-51}
$$

$$
\frac{\partial Q_N}{\partial B} =
$$

$$
\frac{[(F_{KQ}^{D})^2 - F_{QQ}^{D}F_{KK}^{D} - F_{KK}^{N}F_{QQ}^{D} + P_{D}'(F_{KK}^{N} + F_{KK}^{D})]P_{N}' + F_{KQ}^{D}F_{KQ}^{N}P_{D}'}{|D|} \tag{B-52}
$$

where

$$
\begin{aligned}
|D| = {}&(F_{QQ}^{N} - P_{N}')\,[(F_{KQ}^{D})^2 - F_{QQ}^{D}F_{KK}^{D}] \\
&+ (F_{QQ}^{D} - P_{D}')\,[(F_{KQ}^{N})^2 - F_{QQ}^{N}F_{KK}^{N}] \\
&+ P_{D}'F_{QQ}^{N}F_{KK}^{D} + P_{N}'F_{QQ}^{D}F_{KK}^{N} - P_{D}'P_{N}'(F_{KK}^{D} + F_{KK}^{N}) \tag{B-53}
\end{aligned}
$$

The determinant $|D|$ will always be positive (assuming demand is downward sloping and supply is upward sloping), because second-order conditions for profit maximization require that $F_{KK} < 0$, $F_{QQ} < 0$, and $(F_{KQ})^2 - F_{QQ}F_{KK} < 0$. These conditions are not sufficient to determine the sign of the numerator. It is possible, however, to develop some special cases to illustrate the factors that are involved in the relation between stockpile levels and privately optimal levels of consumption Q_D and Q_N.

No short-run flexibility. If consumption is fixed in the short run, so that $Q_N = Q_D = Q$, and $\partial Q_D/\partial B = \partial Q_N/\partial B$, the only effect of stockpiling is on long-run investment and conservation decisions. Since P'_D is greater than P'_N (by the definition of a disruption), increasing normal imports by dB and reducing disrupted imports by dB *reduces* the expected price. The normal price increases by $P'_N dB$ and the disrupted price falls by a larger amount $P'_D dB$. Therefore the average price falls by

$$dP = (P'_N - P'_D)dB$$

and $dP/dB = P'_N - P'_D < 0$. Since an increase in the expected price reduces long-run consumption, it follows that $\partial Q/\partial B > 0$. Increasing the stockpile increases consumption because it lowers the expected price. However, the effect of a change in the disrupted price on the expected price also depends on the probability of a disruption. The less likely a disruption is, the smaller will be the decrease in the expected price due to stockpiling.

No fixed factors. If there were no fixed factors of production, so that short-run and long-run demand elasticities were identical, increasing the stockpile would decrease normal consumption and increase consumption in a disruption. Analyzing this case involves the same comparative statics applied in the general case, but without need to consider capital stock adjustments. In this case

$$\frac{\partial Q_D}{\partial B} = -\frac{P'_D}{F_{22} - P'_D} > 0 \qquad\qquad (B\text{-}54)$$

and

$$\frac{\partial Q_N}{\partial B} = \frac{P'_N}{F_{22} - P'_N} < 0 \qquad\qquad (B\text{-}55)$$

General case. Putting these two results together gives a new perspective on the general case. Adding to stockpiles unambiguously increases consumption during a disruption. However, there are conflicting pressures on normal consumption. The short-run response to increased stockpile purchases is to reduce normal consumption, but the long-run response (to a lower expected price) is to increase consumption. The two polar cases indicate that if long-run and short-run elasticities are not substantially different, normal consumption will fall as stockpile purchases increase. If the short-run elasticity is very much smaller than the long run, normal consumption will rise.

Equation (B-50), which determines optimal stockpile size without tariffs, may be compared to (B-45), which gives the marginal condition for optimal stockpiles with optimal tariffs. The terms involving $\partial Q_D/\partial B$ and $\partial Q_N/\partial B$ do not appear in (B-45). They can be interpreted as additional marginal costs (benefits) of stockpiling that arise when there is no tariff. There are four cases to consider. In a disruption, the sign of $P'_D(Q_D - B) - M'$ is ambiguous, whereas in a normal period the sign of $\partial Q_N/\partial B$ is ambiguous.

(1) $P'_D(Q_D - B) > M'$: In this case, the macroeconomic penalty for changing consumption is less than the demand component in a disruption. This implies that the marginal product of oil in a disrup- the marginal product of oil is greater than its marginal social cost. by the positive amount $P'_D(Q_D - B) - M'$. Therefore, increasing stockpile size imposes an additional cost by stimulating consumption ($\partial Q_N/\partial B > 0$) when that consumption has a value less than the marginal social cost of oil.

(2) $P'_D(Q_D - B) < M'$: In this case, the macroeconomic penalty for changing consumption exceeds the demand component. Therefore, the marginal product of oil is greater than its marginal social cost. Increasing stocks increases disrupted consumption, which provides a net benefit on the margin.

(3) $\partial Q_N/\partial B < 0$: In a normal period, $P'_N(Q_N + B) + M' > 0$, so that the marginal product of oil is unambiguously less than its marginal social cost. If increasing the stockpile decreases normal consumption, it provides a net benefit on the margin.

(4) $\partial Q_N/\partial B > 0$: By the argument made above, if increasing stocks increases normal consumption, there is an additional net marginal cost of stockpiling.

If cases 2 and 3 hold, the benefits of stockpiling are unambiguously enhanced by the absence of an optimal tariff, whereas if cases 1 and 4 hold, the benefits are unambiguously reduced. If 1 and 3, or 2 and 4, hold, the result is ambiguous.

Equations (B-45) and (B-50) differ in another way. Let B^*, K^*, Q^*_N, and Q^*_D satisfy equations (B-42) to (B-45). Then subtracting (B-50) from (B-45) we have

$$[P^*_D + P^{*\prime}_D (Q^*_D - B^*) - P^*_N - P^{*\prime}_N (Q^*_N + B^*)]$$

$$- [P_D + P'_D(Q_D - B) - P_N - P'_N(Q_N + B)]$$

$$+ [P'_D(Q_D - B) - M'] \frac{\partial Q_D}{\partial B} + [P'_N(Q_N + B) + M'] \frac{\partial Q_N}{\partial B}$$

$$= H'(B^*) - H'(B) \qquad\qquad\qquad\qquad (B-56)$$

Note that the first term in square brackets is the difference between the normal demand component and the disrupted demand component, evaluated at the level of imports that are optimal when tariffs are in place. The second term in square brackets is the difference between the normal demand component and the disrupted demand component, evaluated at import levels that will be chosen in the absence of tariffs. If these differences are identical, comparing B^* and B depends only on the terms containing $\partial Q_D/\partial B$ and $\partial Q_N/\partial B$, discussed above. If $P'_D(Q_D - B) - M' \geq P'_N(Q_D + B) + M'$ [implying $M' < P'_D(Q_D - B)$, so that implicitly case 1 holds], the optimal tariff in a disruption will exceed that in a normal period and imposition of optimal tariffs will reduce the demand component in a disruption *more* than it reduces the normal demand component. Therefore we would expect the *gap* between disrupted and normal demand components to be smaller with optimal tariffs than without. This argues a general tendency for the optimal stockpile to be smaller with optimal tariffs in place than without. But if case 1 holds, the third bracketed term may be positive, suggesting that eliminating tariffs may make the optimal stockpile smaller. (This is the case in which additional consumption during a disruption has a marginal value less than its marginal cost.) Which will be the case depends on how specific numerical values for M' and for supply and demand elasticities balance out.

The indeterminacy also arises if the disruption tariff is less than the normal tariff; this is the case when $P'_D(Q_D - B) - M' < P'_N(Q_D + B) + M'$. In this case macroeconomic costs are so large as to imply an optimal disruption tariff less than that in a normal period. Imposing optimal tariffs may therefore increase the gap between disrupted and normal marginal costs and imports.

If $P'_D(Q_D - B) > M'$, so that the disruption tariff does not turn into a subsidy, case 1 will still hold. If case 4 ($\partial Q_N/\partial B > 0$) also holds, the effect of tariffs on optimal stockpile levels would be unambiguous: imposing tariffs would increase the optimal stockpile. If the disruption tariff does turn into a subsidy (case 2), or if $\partial Q_N/\partial B < 0$ (case 3), imposing optimal tariffs will eliminate one of the net benefits of stockpiling, its tendency to move consumption in a direction which brings the marginal value of oil closer to its cost. Thus again the optimal stockpile size may be increased or decreased by imposing optimal tariffs.

Optimal Stockpiles versus Market Stockpiles

Private individuals will hold stockpiles at a level that satisfies, according to (B-49),

$$\bar{P}_D - \bar{P}_N = H'(\bar{B})$$

Bars are used to denote values derived from the competitive equilibrium solution. If we subtract (B-50) from (B-49), we obtain

$$\bar{P}_D - \bar{P}_N - [P_D + P'_D(Q_D - B) - P_N - P'_N(Q_N + B)]$$
$$+ [P'_D(Q_D - B) - M']\frac{\partial Q_D}{\partial B} + [P'_N(Q_N + B) + M']\frac{\partial Q_N}{\partial B}$$
$$= H'(\bar{B}) - II'(B) \tag{B-57}$$

If the gap between normal and disrupted demand components is greater than the gap between prices, the difference between the first two terms in square brackets will be negative; thus if the presence of optimal tariffs justifies leaving aside terms involving $\partial Q_D/\partial B$ and $\partial Q_N/\partial B$, $H'(B) > H'(\bar{B})$ and the optimal stockpile size is larger than the one private markets would choose. This line of reasoning is used in chapter 6 to demonstrate that the optimal stockpile size with tariffs exceeds the size that would be accumulated privately without tariffs. But when there are no optimal tariffs, there can be net additional costs of increasing stocks, due to the effect of stockpiles on consumption. If cases 1 or 4 discussed above hold, the term involving $\partial Q_D/\partial B$ and $\partial Q_N/\partial B$ may be positive, and in the absence of tariffs the optimal stockpile might not be larger than that chosen privately.

References

Adelman, M. A. 1980. "The Clumsy Cartel," *The Energy Journal* vol. 1 (January) pp. 43–53.

Alterman, Jack. 1982. *Long-Term Changes in Energy Consumed per Dollar of Real Output in the United States* (Washington, D.C., Resources for the Future).

Arrow, Kenneth. 1964. "The Role of Securities in the Optimal Allocation of Risk Bearing," *Review of Economic Studies* vol. 31 (April).

Bergman, Lars, and Karl-Göran Mäler. 1981. "The Efficiency-Flexibility Trade-Off and the Cost of Unexpected Oil Price Increases," *Scandinavian Journal of Economics* vol. 83, no. 2, pp. 253–269.

Bhagwati, Jagdish, and V. K. Ramaswami. 1963. "Domestic Distortions, Tariffs, and the Theory of Optimum Subsidy," *Journal of Political Economy* vol. 71, no. 1, pp. 44–50.

Bickerdike, C. F. 1906. "The Theory of Incipient Taxes," *Economic Journal* vol. 16, p. 529.

Blanchard, Olivier, and Mark Watson. 1982. "Bubbles, Rational Expectations, and Financial Markets," Discussion Paper No. 877, Harvard Institute of Economic Research, Cambridge, Mass.

Blankenship, J., M. Barron, J. Eschbach, L. Bower, and W. Lane. 1980. *The Energy Problem: Costs and Policy Option*. Staff Working Paper (Washington, D.C., U.S. Department of Energy, Office of Oil Policy Analysis).

Bohi, Douglas R. 1981. *Analyzing Demand Behavior: A Study of Energy Elasticities* (Baltimore, Md., Johns Hopkins University Press for Resources for the Future).

———, and Milton Russell. 1975. *U.S. Energy Policy: Alternatives for Security* (Baltimore, Md., Johns Hopkins University Press for Resources for the Future).

———, ———. 1978. Limiting Oil Imports: *An Economic History and Analysis* (Baltimore, Md., Johns Hopkins University Press for Resources for the Future).

———, and Michael A. Toman. 1982. "Energy Supply Behavior: Theoretical and Empirical Problems in Nonrenewable Resources," Draft (Washington, D.C., Resources for the Future).

Branson, William H. 1972. *Macroeconomic Theory and Policy* (New York, Harper and Row).

Broadman, Harry G. 1981. "Review and Analysis of Oil Import Premium Estimates," Discussion Paper D-82C, Energy and National Security Series, Resources for the Future, Washington, D.C.

Burness, H. Stuart, Ronald Cummings, and James P. Quirk. Undated. "Speculative Behavior and the Operation of Competitive Markets Under Uncertainty: A Survey Article." Material based upon work supported by the National Science Foundation under Grant No. DAR 7909933 (Washington, D.C., National Science Foundation).

———, W. David Montgomery, and James P. Quirk. 1980. "Capital Contracting and the Regulated Firm," *American Economic Review* vol. 70, no. 3 (June) pp. 342–354.

Chao, Hung-Po, and Alan Manne. 1982. "An Integrated Analysis of U.S. Oil Stockpiling Policies," in James Plummer, ed., *Energy Vulnerability* (Cambridge, Mass., Ballinger).

Corden, W. M. 1975. "The Costs and Consequences of Protection: A Survey of Empirical Work," in Peter R. Kenen, ed., *International Trade and Finance: Frontiers for Research* (Cambridge, Cambridge University Press) pp. 51–92.

Denison, Edward F. 1962. "The Sources of Economic Growth in the U.S. and the Alternatives Before Us." Supplementary Paper 13, Committee for Economic Development (New York).

———. 1974. *Accounting for United States Economic Growth 1929–1969* (Washington, D.C., Brookings Institution).

———. 1979. *Accounting for Slower Economic Growth: The United States in the 1970s* (Washington, D.C., Brookings Institution).

Dorfman, Robert. 1981. "Two Taxes Are Sometimes Better Than One," Discussion Paper No. 867, Harvard Institute of Economic Research, Harvard University, Cambridge, Mass.

Friedman, Benjamin. 1979. "Optimal Expectations and the Extreme Information Assumptions of 'Rational Expectations' Macromodels." *Journal of Monetary Economics* vol. 5 (January), pp. 23–41.

Fry, Robert, Jr., and R. Glenn Hubbard. 1981. "Policy Responses to Oil Supply Interruptions—The Case of the 'Disruption Tariff'." Paper (Cambridge, Mass., Harvard University, Energy and Environmental Policy Center, John F. Kennedy School of Government).

Fuss, Melvyn, and Daniel McFadden, eds. 1978a. *Production Economics: A Dual Approach to Theory and Applications*, vol. 1 (Amsterdam, North-Holland).

———, and Daniel McFadden. 1978b. "Flexibility versus Efficiency in *Ex Ante* Plant Design," in Melvyn Fuss and Daniel McFadden, eds., *Production Economics: A Dual Approach to Theory and Applications*, vol. 1 (Amsterdam, North-Holland) pp. 311–363.

Gardner, Bruce. 1979. *Optimal Stockpiling of Grain* (Lexington, Mass., D.C. Heath).

Gilbert, Richard. 1978. "Factor Price Stabilization with Flexible Production," *Annals of Economic and Social Measurement* vol. 6, no. 5 (Winter/Spring).

———, and Knut Anton Mork. 1981. "Managing Oil Supply Disruptions." Working Paper no. MIT-EL-81-048WP (Cambridge, Mass., Massachusetts Institute of Technology Energy Laboratory).

Glatt, Sandra. 1982. "The Strategic Petroleum Reserve: Progress After Seven Years," Discussion Paper D-82E, Energy and National Security Series (Washington, D.C., Resources for the Future).

Grossman, Sanford L. 1980. "Rational Expectations and the Allocation of Resources Under Asymmetric Information: A Survey." Working Paper no. 22-79 (Philadelphia, Pa., University of Pennsylvania, Rodney L. White Center for Financial Research).

Hall, Robert E., and Robert S. Pindyck. 1981. "Energy and American Economic Policy." Working Paper no. MIT-EL-81-035WP (Cambridge, Mass., Massachusetts Institute of Technology Energy Laboratory).

Hartman, Richard. 1976. "Factor Demand with Output Price Uncertainty," *American Economic Review* vol. 66, no. 4 (September) pp. 675–681.

Hausman, Jerry A. 1981. "Exact Consumer's Surplus and Deadweight Loss," *American Economic Review* vol. 71, no. 4 (September) pp. 662–676.

Henderson, James, and Richard Quandt. 1971. *Microeconomic Theory: A Mathematical Approach.* 2nd ed. (New York, McGraw-Hill) p. 69.

Hogan, William W. 1981. "Import Management and Oil Emergencies," in David A. Deese and Joseph S. Nye, eds., *Energy and Security* (Cambridge, Mass., Ballinger) pp. 261–302.

———, and Alan S. Manne. 1977. "Energy-Economy Interactions: The Fable of the Elephant and the Rabbit?" in Charles Hitch, ed., *Modeling Energy-Economy Interactions: Five Approaches.* Research Paper R-5 (Washington, D.C., Resources for the Future).

Horwich, George. 1981. "Government Contingency Planning for Petroleum Supply Interruptions: A Macro Perspective." Presented at the Conference on Policies for Coping with Oil Supply Disruptions, American Enterprise Institute for Public Policy Research, Washington, D.C., September 8-9.

Jacobsen, Laurence, and Stephen Thurman. 1981. "Oil Price Indexing versus Large Price Shocks: Macroeconomic Impacts." International Finance Discussion Paper no. 180 (Washington, D. C., Board of Governors of the Federal Reserve System).

Johnson, H. G. 1966. "The Neo-Classical One-Sector Growth Model: A Geometrical Exposition and Extension to a Monetary Economy," *Economica* vol. 33, p. 265.

Jorgenson, Dale, Lawrence Lau, and Thomas Stoker. 1980. "Aggregate Consumer Behavior and Individual Welfare," Discussion Paper no. 778, Harvard Institute for Economic Research, Cambridge, Mass.

Kline, D. 1981. "Long-Run Import Reduction and the Import Premium," Working Paper EMF 6.7 (Energy Modeling Forum, Stanford, California, Stanford University).

Kreinen, Mordechai E. 1971. *International Economics: A Policy Approach.* 2nd ed. (New York, Harcourt Brace Jovanovich).

Krugman, Paul. 1981. "Real Exchange Rate Adjustment and the Welfare Effects of Oil Price Decontrol." Working Paper no. MIT-EL-81-025WP (Cambridge, Mass., Massachusetts Institute of Technology Energy Laboratory).

Lau, Lawrence J. 1976. "A Characterization of the Normalized Restricted Profit Function," *Journal of Economic Theory* vol. 12, no. 1, pp. 131–163.

———. 1978. "Applications of Profit Functions," in Melvyn Fuss and Daniel McFadden, eds., *Production Economics: A Dual Approach to Theory and Applications,* vol. 1 (Amsterdam, North-Holland) pp. 133–215.

Lucas, Robert E., Jr., and Thomas J. Sargent. 1981. *Rational Expectations and Econometric Practice* (Minneapolis, University of Minnesota Press).

McFadden, Daniel A. 1978. "Cost, Revenue and Profit Functions," in Melvyn Fuss and Daniel McFadden, eds., *Production Economics: A Dual Approach to Theory and Applications,* vol. 1 (Amsterdam, North-Holland) pp. 3–101.

Michaely, Michael. 1977. *Theory of Commercial Policy: Trade and Protection* (Chicago, University of Chicago Press).

Mork, Knut Anton. 1979. "Electricity Demand in Primary Aluminum Smelting." Working Paper no. MIT-EL-79-055WP (Cambridge, Mass., Massachusetts Institute of Technology Energy Laboratory).

———. 1981a. "A Case Against the Oil Import Premium." Working Paper (Cambridge, Mass., Massachusetts Institute of Technology Energy Laboratory).

———. 1981b. "External Effects of Investment in Ex-Post Flexibility of Energy Use and Energy Supply Under the Risk of Oil Supply Disruption," Discussion Paper no. 10, (MIT-EL-062WP) Studies in Energy and the American Economy, Massachusetts Institute of Technology, Cambridge, Mass.

———. 1982. "The Economic Cost of Oil Supply Disruptions," in James Plummer, ed., *Energy Vulnerability* (Cambridge, Mass., Ballinger).

———, and Robert E. Hall. 1981. "Macroeconomic Analysis of Energy Price Shocks and Offsetting Policies: An Integrated Approach," in Knut Mork, ed., *Energy Prices, Inflation, and Economic Activity* (Cambridge, Mass., Ballinger) pp. 43–62.

Muth, J. F. 1961. "Rational Expectations and the Theory of Price Movements," *Econometrica* vol. 24 (July) pp. 315–335.

Nagatani, K. 1975. "On a Theorem of Arrow," *Review of Economic Studies* vol. 42 (October).

National Petroleum Council. 1981. "Emergency Preparedness for Interruption of Petroleum Imports into the United States." Draft Report of the Committee on Energy Preparedness.

Neff, Thomas L. 1981. "The Changing World Oil Market," in David A. Deese and Joseph S. Nye, eds., *Energy and Security* (Cambridge, Mass., Ballinger) pp. 23–46.

Newbery, David M. G., and Joseph Stiglitz. 1981. *The Theory of Commodity Price Stabilization* (Oxford, Clarendon Press).

Nordhaus, William. 1980. "The Energy Crisis and Macroeconomic Policy," *The Energy Journal* vol. 1, no. 1, pp. 11–19.

———, and James Tobin. 1972. "Is Growth Obsolete?" in *National Bureau of Economic Research, The Fiftieth Anniversary Colloquia Series,* vol. V.

Okun, Arthur M. 1981. *Prices and Quantities: A Macroeconomic Analysis* (Washington, D.C., Brookings Institution).

Plummer, James L. 1981. "Methods for Measuring the Oil Import Reduction Premium and the Oil Stockpile Premium," *Energy Journal* vol. 2, no. 1.

———, and coauthors. 1981. *Energy Vulnerability* (Cambridge, Mass., Ballinger).

Radner, Roy. 1968. "Competitive Equilibrium Under Uncertainty," *Econometrica* vol. 36 (January) pp. 31–58.

———. 1970. "Problems in the Theory of Markets Under Uncertainty," *American Economic Review* vol. 60 (May) pp. 454–460.

Rothschild, M., and J. E. Stiglitz. 1970. "Increasing Risk I: A Definition," *Journal of Economic Theory* vol. 2 (September) pp. 225–243.

———, ———. 1971. "Increasing Risk II: Its Economic Consequences," *Journal of Economic Theory* vol. 3, pp. 66–84.

Samuelson, Paul A. 1966. "Intertemporal Price Equilibrium: A Prologue to the Theory of Speculation," no. 73 in Joseph Stiglitz, ed., *The Collected Scientific Papers of Paul Samuelson,* vol. 2 (Cambridge, Mass., MIT Press).

Solow, Robert. 1978. "Resources and Economic Growth," *The American Economist* vol. 22, no. 2 (Fall) pp. 5–11.

Stigler, George. 1939. "Production and Distribution in the Short Run," *Journal of Political Economy* vol. 47, pp. 305–357.

Stiglitz, J. E. 1972. "On the Optimality of the Stock Market Allocation of Investment," *Quarterly Journal of Economics* vol. 86 (February) pp. 25–60.

————. 1979. "A Neoclassical Analysis of the Economics of Natural Resources," in V. Kerry Smith, ed., *Scarcity and Growth Reconsidered* (Baltimore, Md., Johns Hopkins University Press for Resources for the Future) pp. 36–66.

Stigum, Bent. 1969. "Competitive Equilibrium Under Uncertainty," *Quarterly Journal of Economics* vol. 83 (November).

Stobaugh, Robert, and Daniel Yergin. 1979. *Energy Future: Report of the Energy Project at the Harvard Business School* (New York, Random House).

Svenson, L. 1976. "Sequences of Temporary Equilibria, Stationary Point Expectations, and Pareto Efficiency," *Journal of Economic Theory* vol. 13, no. 2 (October 1976) pp. 169–183.

Sweetnam, Glen. 1979. "An Analysis of Acquisition and Drawdown Strategies for the Strategic Petroleum Reserve." Draft Analysis from the Office of Oil Policy and Policy Evaluation.

Teisberg, Thomas J. 1981. "A Dynamic Programming Model of the U.S. Strategic Petroleum Reserve," *Bell Journal of Economics* vol. 12, pp. 526–546.

Tolley, George S., and John D. Wilman. 1977. "The Foreign Dependence Question," *Journal of Political Economy* vol. 85, no. 2, pp. 323–349.

Turnovsky, Stephen J. 1973. "Production Flexibility, Price Uncertainty and the Behavior of the Competitive Firm," *International Economic Review* vol. 14, no. 2 (June).

U.S. Department of Energy (DOE). 1980. *Draft Policy, Programming and Fiscal Guidance: FY 1982–1986.* Memorandum from Secretary of Energy, C. W. Duncan, Jr. (January 30).

Wan, Henry Y. 1971. *Economic Growth* (New York, Harcourt Brace Jovanovich).

Willig, Robert. 1976. "Consumers' Surplus Without Apology," *American Economic Review* vol. 66, no. 4 (September) pp. 589–597.

Index

Action equivalent price. *See* Planning
  price
Aggregate demand, and income
  redistribution, 45
Arab oil embargo, 1

Capital-intensive production, and
  disruption risks, 71
Capital markets, and world oil supply,
  32
Capital stock. *See also* Investment
  with disruption risk, 9, 157
  and energy demand, 61–62
  and oil prices, 16, 50–52
  and short-run demand, 62–63, 138
  tariff effect on, 104
Commodity markets, 98
Consumption reduction, 65–66

Demand component, 6–8. *See also*
  Disruption component; Oil import
  premium
  alternative view of, 29–37
  conventional view of, 13–29
  in disruption, 106
  with disruption component, 109–111
  with disruption costs, 101–105
  in normal period, 106
  and private adjustments, 81–86
  tariff determined by, 146
Demand curves, 78
Demand tariff. *See also* Tariff
  and disruption expectations, 140–141
  optimal, 137–138

Dislocation costs
  and oil imports, 102
  specification of, 105–108
  tradeoff with wealth transfer, 104
Disruption component, 8–10. *See also*
  Demand component; Disruption
  costs; Oil import premium; Supply
  disruption
  with demand component, 108–111
  tariff determined by, 146
Disruption costs
  alternative specifications of, 175–181
  with demand component, 101–105
  identification of, 114
  macroeconomic, 9–10, 96–100
  and optimal tariffs, 101–108,
    141–146, 171
  preparations for, 35, 169–171
  private anticipation of, 90
  and stockpile benefits, 124
  variations in, 153–155
Disruption risks
  consumer responses to, 61–67
  defined, 60–61
  effect of expectations, 138–140
  and expected oil price, 75
  and imports volume, 92–93
  effect on short-run demand, 77
  private adjustments to, 9, 60–72, 110
  private underestimation of, 91–93
  and rational expectations, 78–79
  tariff effect on, 84–85
Disruption size
  OILSIM input values for, 151
    (table)
  variations in, 150

Disruption tariff, 94–96, 117, 130–131, 136. *See also* Tariff
Domestic markets, and tariff adjustment, 39
Domestic oil producers
  and disruption risks, 68–72
  tariff response of, 22

Elasticities. *See* Supply elasticities
Energy
  demand flexibility, 164 (figure)
  for nonresidential business, 56
  price effects, 56, 57
  share in gross output, 54
  substitution elasticity, 53–57
  supply flexibility, 106
Excise tax, 108

Factor productivity, 53–57
Flexibility
  and consumption reduction tradeoff, 65–66
  partial equilibrium analysis of, 174–175
  and static efficiency tradeoff, 162 (figure)

Government intervention
  to correct private anticipations, 88
  and market behavior, 59
  rationales for, 91–101
  tariff income transfers, 46

Import demand. *See also* Oil import
  elasticity of, 16, 24–25, 28, 47, 148–149
  and employment effects, 48
  long-run derivation, 16–17
  long-run reductions in, 92
Import policy
  alternative reduction schemes, 46–47
  benefits/costs of, 2, 12
  to lower marginal cost, 19
  with macroeconomic costs, 171–182
  in normal supply periods, 131
  quotas, 1
  and stockpile policy, 130–133

Import supply. *See also* Oil import
  elasticity of, 16, 46
  long-run derivation, 16
  marginal social cost of, 18 (figure)
Income
  determination, 49–57
  distribution changes, 22, 35, 44–47, 99
  marginal value of, 44
  oil price effects on, 43
Information costs, 91
International Energy Agency, 133
Investment. *See also* Capital stock
  and disruption risks, 76
  to increase flexibility, 62, 67
  optimal strategy, 66–67
  options, 65
Iran-Iraq war, 118

Macroeconomic costs. *See* Disruption costs
Mandatory Oil Import Control Program, 1, 133 n19
Market prices, difference from planning prices, 83
Markets
  behavior in, 59, 157–171
  disequilibrium conditions, 96
  inefficiencies in, 2, 99
Monopoly power, 37
Monopsony power, 8
Multiple prices, 107

Oil
  consumption tax on, 106
  demand for, 62, 63 (figure), 65 (figure), 158 n1
  equilibrium prices, 77 (figure)
  as exhaustible resource, 14–15
  long-run demand for, 62
  marginal cost during disruption, 94–96
  marginal product of, 159, 165 (figure)
  marginal social value of, 111–112
  optimal consumption, 103
  as production factor, 43
  production technology, 168
  surge production capacity, 68

Oil import. *See also* Import demand;
    Import supply
  benefits from, 5
  demand for, 13–17, 73–75
  and dislocation costs, 102
  and disruptions likelihood, 92–93
  insecure sources of, 92
  marginal cost of, 17–20, 26
  and market adjustments, 72–81
  optimal, 103, 107
  and optimal tariff, 24
  price uncertainty adjustments, 74
    (figure)
  reduction benefits, 5
  supply of, 13–17, 75–76
  supply elasticities, 112
  and world price, 6
Oil import premium. *See also* Demand
    component; Disruption component
  ambiguities, 134
  as benefit measure, 3
  defined, 2
  disruption cost contribution to, 115
  with domestic production, 108
  empirical estimates of, 3
  implementation of, 37–41
  as marginal concept, 5
  and monopsony power, 13
  optimal policy mix, 128
  as optimal tariff, 2, 19–20
  private adjustments effect on, 89
  size of, 111
  and stockpiling, 182
  and total reserves, 125–130
Oil market
  equilibrium, 76–81
  excess capacity in, 92–93
  expected intervention in, 93–94
  game theory models of, 14
  price adjustments to, 11
  producer motivations in, 14
  structure of, 12
Oil prices
  and adjustment scenarios, 80
  and aggregate demand changes, 98
  and capital formation, 50–52
  and exchange rates, 47–48
  and factor productivity, 53–57
  and import demand, 39

  and income effect, 51
  and macroeconomic costs, 41, 131
  and market disequilibrium, 99
  and normal wage rates, 97
  reduction effects, 35
  response to tariff, 20
  uncertainty, 64, 87
Oil supply, 13
  backward-bending, 29, 30–32, 31
    (figure), 36 (figure), 114–115
  and capital markets, 32
  disruptions, 60, 69 (figure)
  function slope, 19
  indeterminance of, 14–15
  multiple-equilibrium points, 30
  and tariff policy, 42
  as world price function, 15
Optimal tariff, 12, 20–25, 174. *See
    also* Tariff
  under alternative assumptions, 109
    (figure), 113 (table)
  with backward-bending supply,
    33–37
  calculations of, 111
  defined, 23
  and disruption probability, 83–86
  and elasticities, 27
  and macroeconomic costs, 130, 175
  and optimal stockpile size, 183–186
Organization of Petroleum Exporting
    Countries (OPEC)
  non-monopoly behavior, 37
  returns from revenues, 32

Payroll tax adjustments, 100
Planning price, 64, 138, 156
  difference from market price, 83
  and externalities, 142
  and increasing flexibility, 167 (figure)
  and investment decisions, 67
  and market demand, 75 (figure)
  in oil market, 74
  relative to normal price, 160 (figure)
Premium. *See* Oil import premium
Prices
  deviation from social costs, 112
  discrepancy with marginal cost, 7
  as incentives, 106

Private adjustments
  effect on demand component, 82
    (figure), 86 (table)
  importance of, 80–81
  and optimal tariff, 81–86
Private expectations
  bias in, 88
  efficiency of, 86–89
Private sector
  equilibrium price forecasting, 79
  myopia of, 120
  risk adjustment of, 77–78, 80 (table)
Production function
  concept of, 53–54
  and flexibility, 163–169
Productivity, 56
Project Independence, 1

Rational expectations, 87
  and demand estimation, 78–79
  response to, 93–94
Regulations, and private adjustments,
    93
Resources, substitution elasticity,
    55–56

Saudi Arabia, 92
Social costs, 112
Speculative behavior, 87
SPR. See Strategic petroleum reserve
Static efficiency, 162 (figure)
Stockpiling. See also Strategic
    petroleum reserve
  aggregate social cost of, 125
  compared with tariffs, 94
  and consumption, 123, 129 n16
  effect on optimal tariff, 128
  government versus private, 127 n12,
    191
  and import policy, 130–133
  and oil import premium, 182
  optimal, 121, 125, 127, 183–191
  price spread narrowing, 72
  private inventories, 72, 118–125, 136
  private returns to, 120–121
  sales below price, 133
  sales to foreigners, 132

Strategic petroleum reserve (SPR), 96,
    117, 136. See also Stockpiling
  cost of filling, 122 (figure 6-1)
  drawdown strategies, 132–133
  full cost of, 121–123
  with optimal tariffs, 124
  and private inventories, 118–125
  use benefits, 122 (figure 6-2), 123
Supply disruption. See also
    Disruption component
  behavior during, 75
  economic costs of, 8–9, 91
  preparation costs of, 59–60
  supply side problems, 97
Supply elasticities, 81, 112
  OILSIM input values for, 152–153
    (table)
  and optimal tariff, 23–25, 27–28
  tariff sensitivity to, 27
  variations in, 150
Synthetic fuels
  and disruption risks, 69–70
  wealth transfer of, 71

Tariff, 4. See also Demand tariff;
    Disruption tariff; Import policy;
    Optimal tariff
  adjustment costs, 39–41
  ad valorem, 39
  adverse effect of, 58
  for alternative elasticities, 28 (table)
  benefits of, 22–23, 115
  calculating optimal, 25–29
  and capital investments, 135
  consumer costs, 21–22
  deadweight loss from, 22, 52
  and disruption costs, 101–108
  efficiency of, 20
  and exporters, 49
  fixed, 105
  and flexibility, 174
  gains/losses from, 21 (figure), 34, 38
    (figure)
  and imported oil costs, 81, 84 (figure)
  incidence of, 23–24
  income effect of, 46–47, 52
  and investment decisions, 101
  limitations of, 135

long-run optimal, 52
macroeconomic costs of, 41
magnitude factors of, 108–115
and oil consumption reduction, 132
optimal macro externality, 143
   (figure)
private adjustments effect on, 82
and private incentives distortions,
   88–89
to raise planning price, 142–143
recommendation for, 134
and retaliation, 12, 37–39
and stockpiling, 94, 129
surprise potential of, 34–35
and terms of trade, 49
variable structure, 131

in various supply states, 104
and world price, 12, 43, 135
Taxes
deadweight losses from, 22 $n7$
and income redistribution, 45
Technical change, 53–54, 56
Terms of trade, 47–49

Wages, 97
Wealth transfer
dislocation costs tradeoff, 101–102,
   104
during disruption, 9–10, 100
policy for, 96
Windfall gains, 68

The book was set in Linotype Palatino by the Hendricks-Miller Typo-graphic Company, Washington, D.C., and printed by the R. R. Don-nelley & Sons Company, Harrisonburg, Virginia.